MANAGING
POLITICAL RISK ASSESSMENT

STUDIES IN INTERNATIONAL POLITICAL ECONOMY

Edited by Stephen D. Krasner
Department of Political Science
Stanford University

MANAGING
POLITICAL RISK ASSESSMENT

Strategic Response to
Environmental Change

by
Stephen J. Kobrin

UNIVERSITY OF CALIFORNIA PRESS

Berkeley / Los Angeles / London

University of California Press
Berkeley and Los Angeles, California

University of California Press, Ltd.
London, England

Library of Congress Cataloging in Publication Data

Kobrin, Stephen Jay.
  Managing political risk assessment.

  (Studies in international political economy)
  Bibliography: p. 211
  Includes index.
  1. Investments, Foreign—Political aspects.
2. International business enterprises—Political
aspects.   I. Title.   II. Title: Political risk
assessment.   III. Series.
HG4538.K59   658.1'52   81-21979
ISBN 0-520-04540-8   AACR2

Printed in the United States of America

For Jeanne

Contents

Preface

My interest in political risk assessment was aroused by a discordance between research results and managerial perceptions. Earlier empirical work suggests that the relationship between political events and foreign direct investment is complex: it is specific changes in government policy rather than dramatic systemic events, such as revolution, which account for most impacts on firms. While there are exceptions, vulnerability to political risk appears to depend as much on project characteristics as it does on political events.

Yet much of the literature, and my own experience, indicate that it is dramatic systemic change—revolution, violent political conflict, and sharp shifts in ideology—which is the primary focus of managerial attention. Managers are asking the wrong questions of the wrong data. As a result, I believe that risks are overstated and that potentially profitable opportunities are avoided.

That is, I first saw the problem as one of improving corporate intelligence. More effective political assessment requires a more accurate understanding of the risks facing the firm, better information sources, and more sophisticated processing methods. My view changed markedly, however, as I studied the survey results and interviewed managers. Although concern with politics abroad may be new and somewhat exotic, the problems that managers face in its assessment certainly are not. Political risk assessment is an emerging managerial function, and as with any such function, more effective performance requires setting objectives and then developing strategies and organizational structures to facilitate their implementation. While information sources and processing methods are important, they are technique. The critical strategic issue is the management of resources.

As the title indicates, this book focuses on the management of political risk assessment. It explores, both theoretically and analytically, such topics as the relationship between a business firm and its environment, the development of organizational structures to facilitate effective assessment and their institutionalization, communication between staff groups and line managers, and the use of assessments in planning and decision making. It deals with the fundamental issue of organizational response, strategically and structurally, to environmental change.

I owe a great deal to a number of colleagues who made significant contributions. Dick Robinson, my area head at Sloan, suggested the idea to me. While he managed to do it in a way that provided absolutely no hint of what I was getting into, he more than made up for it over the next few years through substantial released time and, more important, friendship and intellectual support.

In one of those rare, but critically fortuitous, circumstances, I discovered shortly thereafter that the Conference Board was about to undertake a similar effort under the direction of Stephen Blank. We joined forces in what was to result in a very productive and stimulating collaboration. The survey and the fieldwork, which were conducted jointly, also involved Joseph La Palombara of Yale University and John Basek of the Conference Board. Stephen Blank and I have continued to collaborate, and some of the ideas in this book were developed together. The Conference Board, under the sponsorship of Walter Hamilton who was vice-president for public affairs research, underwrote the cost of the survey and the field research.

I think that the success of our collaboration is important at a time when traditional sources of foundation and government research funding are becoming scarce. Through planning we were able to meet the Conference Board's needs for information and for a publication for the general manager and my needs for sufficient methodological rigor to support this book for academics and specialists. We all believe that the cross-fertilization was valuable.

Many other individuals made major contributions. Jolene Larson and Jan Hack Katz provided very able research assistance. The results, however, are mixed. After working on this book Jolene gave up a promising academic career for banking while Jan has remained within the fold. Gene Skolnikoff and Amy Leiss at the Center for International Studies at M.I.T. provided substantial support including funding, office space, and a very stimulating intellectual environment in which to work. Virtually all the analysis and writing were done at the C.I.S. More often than she may care to remember, Amy took time from a very busy schedule to listen to my problems. The support of the C.I.S., at both the personal and the organizational level, was essential.

A number of colleagues reviewed the manuscript in its entirety. Ed Schein provided critical comments and also a good deal of encouragement at a time when it was sorely needed. David Blake, Lou Wells, Tom Gladwin, and Steve Krasner all made helpful comments on earlier drafts. I also am indebted to anonymous reviewers for their efforts.

Chuck Lockman at the C.I.S., a true virtuoso on the word processor, typed the entire manuscript and made innumerable changes cheerfully and rapidly. I am also indebted to the many managers who took the time to respond to the mailed survey and to be interviewed. I hope that they regard their efforts as worthwhile.

Last, it would be an unpardonable omission not to thank my wife Jeanne for having the good common sense never to agree with anything I ever said about this book.

S.J.K.

1
Introduction

Venturing abroad has always been accompanied by risk and uncertainty. The traveler leaves the comforts of home and enters an unfamiliar environment where events seem to take a different course and their meaning and significance are difficult to fathom. De Tocqueville (1956:225) caught the essence of the problem more than a century and a half ago. An American traveling to Europe, he wrote,

> . . . has been informed that the conditions of society are not equal in our part of the globe; and he observes that among the nations of Europe, the traces of rank are not wholly obliterated. . . . He is therefore profoundly ignorant of the place which he ought to occupy in this half-ruined scale of classes. . . . He is afraid of ranging himself too high, still more is he afraid of being ranged too low; this twofold peril keeps his mind constantly on the stretch, and embarrasses all he says and does.

Business firms are no exception. International business requires that plans be made and decisions taken in one culture based on stimuli arising in another. Going abroad to exploit new opportunities exposes a firm to new environments and new sources of risk. One source of risk receiving considerable attention in the past decade is the political environment, particularly in less developed countries. Although political risk is not a new phenomenon, concern over it has increased significantly in recent years. This new prominence has been reflected in an outpouring of articles on the subject in the business press, wider academic attention, commitment of resources to assess political risk by a significant number of international firms, and, finally, the most important indicator of legitimacy, the emergence of a large number of consulting firms offering services to help management come to grips with political problems abroad.

The high level of attention paid to political risk is an indication that external political environments have become directly relevant to the managerial strategy of the international firm. This relationship is not a short-run departure from the norm; rather, it is a result of fundamental secular changes in both organization and environment in the decades since the end of World War II.[1] The political environment has become a critical factor in the setting and achievement of corporate goals. Even the largest, most international corporation must function in a transnational reality of fragmented and independent nation-states. The need to keep corporate objectives in sight while operating in a large number of widely different external environments is the basic strategic problem facing the modern multinational firm.

Much of the work on political risk assessment to date—aside from that concerned with the basic nature of the problem—has focused on traditional concerns of intelligence analysis such as data sources and processing methods. Wilensky (1967:3) defines organizational intelligence as "the problem of gathering, processing, interpreting, and communicating the technical and political information needed in the decision-making process." His emphasis, however, is clearly placed on intelligence as a problem in the sociology of complex organizations.

In much the same vein, I am approaching political risk assessment as a problem of managerial process. It is seen as a specific manifestation of the more general problem of complex organizations existing as systems open to, and interacting with, their external environment. As with any managerial function, the effective assessment of political risk requires setting objectives, developing strategies to achieve them, and establishing organizational structures to implement the strategies.

The specific subject of this book is the assessment and evaluation of political environments abroad and the use of those assessments in strategic planning and decision making. The process is described as the political assessment function. It includes perception of external political environments by individuals and organizations, crossing or spanning the firm's boundaries in order to scan those environments, processing and transmitting information about political environments within the firm, and incorporating the information into managerial strategy.

My major theme encompasses the emergence and institutionalization of the political assessment function in international firms based in the

---

1. Significant changes in both intrastate and interstate social and political environments are discussed in depth in chapter 4. These include, inter alia, the increase in political conflict, the effects of widespread decolonialization, increased nationalism, increased pressure on policymakers to exert control over their economies, an increase in the number of states and in their diversity, and a decline in United States hegemony.

United States. Institutionalization entails differentiation of the function by explicit assignment of responsibililties for its performance and by development of specialized organizational positions and formalization or systematization of the analytical process. In particular, institutionalization of the political assessment function is an adaptive response by management to perceptions of potentially significant managerial contingencies arising from political environments abroad. The probability that such contingencies will arise is a function both of the nature of external political environments and of the strategy and structure of the corporation. Contingencies result from organization-environment interaction.

APPROACH

My approach to political risk assessment is interdisciplinary, applied, and exploratory. Although the literature dealing directly with political assessment by international firms is somewhat limited, a large body of work in related disciplines is directly material. I therefore draw upon the literature of organizational theory, international management, political economy, and international relations to develop a conceptual framework that will be of use in my specialized field.

The study is applied in that no attempt is made to contribute to the theoretical base in any of the relevant disciplines. The relationship between theory and practice is, however, not unidirectional. Whereas theory is used in an effort to understand reality, the application of theory should have feedback effects on its development.

The study is exploratory at the analytical level: it is designed to generate rather than to test hypotheses. The relationship between theory and data is considerably more interactive than is the norm, and in some instances I first became aware of potentially important relationships during data collection and analysis. Thus, theory drawn from the disciplines discussed above serves as a context in which to interpret research findings rather than as a basis for the a priori deduction of testable hypotheses.

RESEARCH OBJECTIVES

My first objective is to be able to make inferential statements about current practice by United States–based international firms. The study should serve as a benchmark, describing how firms in the target population assess foreign political environments, how those assessments are evaluated and processed within the firm, and, most important, how evaluations of political factors are utilized in strategic planning and investment decision making.

My second objective is analytical. As seen in chapter 2, this study is based on an open systems perspective which posits an interdependent relationship between organizations and the larger external environment. Thus an attempt is made to explain practice, relating the findings to an interdisciplinary conceptual framework by analyzing variables that characterize organizational strategy and structure and the causal texture of the external political environment. This framework facilitates a deductive analytical process. It serves to inform empirical results, allowing for the analysis of phenomena and relationships against a more general context. The structure serves to guide exploration and to increase confidence in the validity of the findings. As noted above, the framework is not intended to generate testable hypotheses. Rather, my intention is to explore the nature of the phenomenon and, in so doing, to suggest an appropriate explanatory theory that will guide further research.

METHOD

The choice of method follows directly from the research objectives. Making inferential statements about population parameters, that is, accurately describing current practice, requires a survey of the population or a probability sample. Understanding practice, that is, analyzing components of the complex phenomenon in question and relating it to an appropriate conceptual framework, requires in-depth and flexible personal interaction with a limited number of respondents.

The actual study combined survey and qualitative research techniques. A questionnaire mailed to the entire target population of large United States–based international firms was followed by in-depth personal interviews with managers in a subset of firms selected via a stratified quota sample of respondents to the survey. The survey and interviews were undertaken jointly by myself and the Conference Board in late 1978 and early 1979.[2] More technical details about the methods used are contained in Appendix A.

2. The mailed survey and the interviews were conducted by myself, by Dr. Stephen Blank and John Basek of the Conference Board, and by Dr. Joseph La Palombara of Yale

DESIGN

The target population was defined as relatively large, industrial, United States–based international firms. Firms in the financial sector, such as banks and insurance companies, were not included. A "relatively large" firm is one whose 1976 sales amounted to $100 million or more, a categorization approximating the Fortune 1000.[3] "International" is defined minimally in terms of at least one substantive productive operation abroad which was established through foreign direct investment or contract.[4]

Applying these criteria, a target population of 455 firms was selected from the 5,000 companies listed in the Conference Board's *Key Company Directory*.[5] To questionnaires mailed in August 1978, 193 usable replies (42.4 percent) were received by the cutoff date of November 1, 1978. Thus all replies were received before the 1978–79 Iranian crisis reached the boiling point and significantly increased the salience of the political assessment function for American managers.

The decision to draw the stratified quota sample for follow-up personal interviews from the respondents to the mailed questionnaire, rather than from the target population as a whole, was a practical one. Firms that refused to respond to the questionnaire would probably not agree to extensive personal interviews. In addition, using respondents as a sampling frame gives the researcher the advantage, in both selection and analysis, of being able to draw on the substantial information provided by the survey. In accordance with previous research, industrial sector and size (global sales) were selected as the primary and secondary bases for stratification.[6]

University. The research has generated two other publications: Blank et al. (1980) and Kobrin et al. (1980).

3. The thousandth firm in the 1976 Fortune industrial listing had sales of $100.6 million. The 1976 sales of the smallest firm in our target population were exactly $100 million.

4. Foreign direct investment (FDI) entails managerial control, by full or partial equity ownership, over an enterprise in another country. A number of firms in the sample, such as those in petroleum and construction, maintained substantive operations, abroad through contract rather than through FDI.

5. The *Key Company Directory* contains data on approximately 5,000 United States firms. It should be noted that, since usable data on internationalization were limited, comparison of respondents with the target population was made on the basis of variables such as sales, sector, the number of countries with manufacturing operations, and the existence of mining or extractive ventures abroad.

6. Research on international organization (e. g., Stopford and Wells, 1971) and on phenomena such as expropriation (Kobrin, 1980) suggests that industrial sector is an important determinant of factors such as organizational strategy and the potential impact of the

The request for multiple interviews within each firm was generously met: 113 managers in 37 firms were actually interviewed. Because three firms did not provide sufficient access, the base for analysis is 110 managers in 34 firms.

IMPLEMENTATION

As noted above, 193 usable questionnaires were returned in response to the mail survey. The relatively high response rate (42.4 percent) is a clear indication of management interest in the topic. Respondents to the survey are representative of the target population on the basis of firm size (global sales), industrial sector, and the existence of mining or extractive operations abroad.[7] Respondents were, however, significantly more likely to operate majority-owned manufacturing subsidiaries in a larger number of countries than was the population as a whole (8.1 versus 5.9).

Some bias is evident in the subsample of firms interviewed. Clearly those firms are larger: their mean sales are more than double those of the total population ($4,181 versus $2,028 million). Although differences in industrial sector are not statistically significant, considerably more variation (versus the distribution for the target population) is evident for subsample firms than for respondents to the survey. In particular, consumer products and high technology firms tend to be underrepresented. The subsample of firms interviewed also seems to be considerably more international than the target population as a whole.

In summary, the respondents to the mailed questionnaire are reasonably representative of the target population, and inferences are likely to contain little bias. The subsample firms interviewed, however, are

environment. Factors such as technological and advertising intensity directly affect foreign investment. Oil firms are clearly more vulnerable to political factors than are high technology industries. Organizational size is a major determinant of the propensity to differentiate managerial functions (see chap. 5).

7. As mentioned in note 5, comparison of the respondents with the target population was affected by the limited data in the *Key Company Directory* on internationalization of the firms. The percentage of sales generated abroad and the total number of countries in which the firm has substantial operations were not available. Nevertheless, given the data that are available and the relatively high response rate, I am confident that the respondents are representative of the population. Data on size and sector, which are important determinants of many of the factors of interest in this study, were available and complete.

larger and more international than the population as a whole. Thus, while it is reasonable to explore the development of the environmental assessment process through the interview data, the distribution of responses across firms may not be representative of the target population. Data from the mail survey and those from the follow-up interviews serve somewhat different purposes. Inferential statements about population parameters, that is, about the extent, scope, and determinants of the political assessment function, are based on the data derived from the mail survey, whereas the personal interviews are used to interpret the survey data and to generate hypotheses about the development of the function and causal relationships among organizational and environmental characteristics. Obviously the distinction is not absolute. The mail survey data serve analytical as well as descriptive purposes, and, in a few instances where interview data allow inferential statements, given the bias in the subsample, they serve as the basis for assessments of current practice.

CONSTRAINTS

Because of the recent emergence of the field as a focus of managerial and academic attention, and the paucity of experience with impacts imposed on firms as a result of political factors abroad, basic concepts such as political risk, the investment climate, and even political assessment remain vague and have been only subjectively defined. The lack of agreement on the definition of key concepts, much less on their actual operationalization, substantially increased the difficulty of designing research instruments and, more important, of conceptualizing the nature of the phenomenon and relationships among its components.

Furthermore, the exploratory character of the study meant that some hypotheses to be examined through analysis of the survey data were suggested well after the instrument had been designed, indeed, after the data had been collected. Constructs had to be made operational ex post facto, utilizing data not collected for that purpose. Put another way, it was necessary to explore relationships after the fact which were not obviously important when the design of research instruments was undertaken. While the results are often of interest, they are not based on data generated through the rigorous operationalization of concepts combined with specific and systematic collection procedures.

PLAN OF THE BOOK

Chapter 2 develops a basic conceptual framework from the literature on organization-environment interaction. The framework is an essential foundation for later analysis, but the reader interested primarily in the description of the political analysis function should skip to chapter 3, which deals directly with the nature of political risk and the role of uncertainty in political assessment. Chapter 4 draws on concepts from international business and international political economy to explain the recent emergence of political environments as a subject of concern to managers of international firms.

Chapter 5 suggests theory explaining the propensity to institutionalize the political assessment function and analyzes the empirical evidence derived from the mail survey and the interviews. Chapter 6 describes the organization of the political assessment function in the firms surveyed. It describes current practice on the basis of short case studies in the context of a typology developed from the interview data.

Chapter 7 draws on both survey data and personal interviews to discover how managers perceive the political environment. Chapter 8 focuses on international scanning, looking at the stimuli that motivate political analysis and sources of information about political environments abroad. Chapter 9 is concerned with the critical issue of the utilization of political assessment in strategic planning and decision making. Chapter 10 reviews the major findings and suggests general conclusions.

2
Organizations and Environments

The emergence of the political assessment function within international firms may be approached from two different levels of analysis. The first comprises the evolution, organization, and performance of the function itself. The second approach is more general; it examines the function as an example of organization-environment interaction, of a change in strategy and structure resulting from changes in perceptions of the environment. I follow both approaches in this book in the hope that the reader will find the process to be synergistic. Generalization should inform description and analysis, and application should illuminate and enrich theory.

The more general organization-environment approach may be summarized as follows. An organization is an open system linked to its environment through flows of information processed by one or more of its members. Environments are inherently subjective; they are as perceived by individuals whose roles place them at the organization's boundary. Perceptions of environments are determined by their causal texture, by organizational factors such as strategy and structure, and by individual cognitive processes.

All organizations scan environments perceived as relevant, process and transmit the derived information internally, and incorporate environmental evaluations into planning and decision making. Performance of this function, and specifically the degree to which it is explicit, formalized, and institutionalized, depends on managerial perceptions of the probability that costly contingencies will arise from the environment. That probability, in turn, is a function of the interaction of environment and organization.[1]

---

1. Although the process is clearly reciprocal, the model is unidirectional at the boundary of the organization, as it is concerned only with the impact of the environment

In this chapter I draw upon organization-environment literature to develop a conceptual framework for analysis of the emergence of the political assessment function. Three general topics are discussed: the nature of organizational environments; how organizational boundaries are spanned to obtain environmental information; how that information is processed and communicated within the organization.

THE ORGANIZATIONAL ENVIRONMENT

OPEN SYSTEMS

There is little need to argue that organizations in general, and business firms in particular, function as systems open to their environments (Aldrich, 1979; Beckhard and Harris, 1977; Lawrence and Lorsch, 1967; Miles, 1980; Meyer and Associates, 1978). As Thompson (1967:6) notes, "the complex organization is a set of interdependent parts which taken together make up the whole . . . which in turn is interdependent with some larger environment."

An open systems perspective implies that organizations must adapt to their environments[2] and that environmental interaction is a significant factor in the development and functioning of the organization (Beckhard and Harris, 1977; Meyer and Associates, 1978). Once an open systems point of view is accepted, "the nature of environment . . . becomes a critical area of study. The behavior of an organization is contingent upon the social field forces in which it occurs and must be understood in terms of the organization's interaction with that environment field" (Katz and Kahn, 1978:3).

---

upon the firm. My primary concern is the processing of environmental information—assessment, evaluation, and integration into strategic planning and decision making—rather than the appropriate strategic response. In making this statement I am not denying the importance of the firm's impact on the environment; I am simply defining the scope of my investigation. I have earlier (Kobrin, 1977) published an analysis of the impact of foreign investment on social modernization.

2. The organizational-environmental fit, however, is contingent rather than uniquely determined. That is, whereas there may not be a single optimal strategy or structure that "best fits" with any given environment, certain strategies and/or structures are more effective than others. See Galbraith and Nathanson (1978).

ENVIRONMENTAL STRUCTURE

The literature describes a number of typologies developed to impose structure on what has been called the causal texture of the environment, that is, "the extent and manner in which the variables relevant to the constituent organizations (organisms) are, independently of any particular part, causally related or interwoven with each other" (Emery, 1967:218). The variables involve either specification of dimensions (Child, 1972; Duncan, 1972; Katz and Kahn, 1978), ideal types (Emery and Trist, 1965), or both (Aldrich, 1979). Accepting the risk of oversimplification in the interests of parsimony, I characterize the relevant environment in terms of two dimensions and a condition that arises from interaction between them. The typology, though neither exhaustive nor original, is sufficient for my purposes.

The two dimensions are complexity and dynamism. The condition is a turbulent field. The first dimension, which is scaled in terms of relative homogeneity and relative heterogeneity, concerns the number of environmental components and their degree of similarity or difference (Aldrich, 1979; Child, 1972; Duncan, 1972). It has both a quantitative and a qualitative aspect. The complexity of an organization's environment may be envisioned as a two-by-two matrix with one axis scaled in terms of the number of relevant elements and the other in terms of the relative homogeneity or heterogeneity of the elements in the field. Complexity increases as one moves toward an increase in the number and the heterogeneity of elements.

The second dimension has to do with stability or variability. It has been defined (Child, 1972) as the frequency of change in environmental elements, the degree of difference entailed in each change, and a second derivative, the variability of change itself. Other conceptions of environmental dynamism are similar (Aldrich, 1979; Duncan, 1972; Katz and Kahn, 1978). Thus the organizational environment is perceived as more dynamic if the frequency of change increases and/or if the changes that take place are more significant. Other things being equal, dynamism is greater to the extent the rate of change is more variable.

Turbulent fields entail dynamic processes that emerge as an unplanned and often unforeseen result of interactions of component systems; they are autochthonous (Emery, 1967). They involve discontinuities where changes in the nature of the environment are difficult to predict either from change along its individual dimensions or from the actions of individual organizations. Emery (1977:14) suggests that one factor leading to the emergence of turbulent fields is the growing interdependence among all sectors of society: "The productive sector is increasingly enmeshed in social responsibilities as citizens assert their role not just as producer but as consumer, inhabitant and as a social and political entity." Turbulent fields result from interactions among environmental elements which produce results that are difficult to foresee. They entail processes that have been described in the literature of catastrophe theory as "sudden transformations and unpredictable divergences, which call for [mathematical] functions that are not differentiable" (Zeeman, 1976:65).

I argue in chapter 4 that the emergence of the political assessment function is an adaptive response to increased complexity, variability, and turbulence in the environment of the international firm. As organization-environment interaction takes place through individual cognitive processes, however, it is subjective perceptions of environmental change, rather than that change itself, which are important.

THE SUBJECTIVE ENVIRONMENT

The organizational environment is inherently subjective. In fact, all human perceptions of reality are basically subjective. Hannah Arendt (1977:108) has put it well:

> Nothing that appears manifests itself to a single view capable of perceiving it under all of its inherent aspects. The world appears in the mode of it-seems-to-me, depending on particular perspectives determined by location in the world as well as by particular organs of perception. Not only does this produce error, which I can correct by changing my location, drawing closer to what appears, or by improving my imagination to take other perspectives into account; it also gives birth to true semblances—that is true deceptive appearances, which I cannot correct like an error, since they are caused by my permanent location on the earth and remain bound up with my own existence as one of the earth's appearances.

At a less abstract level it is clear that all individual perceptions of reality, including organizational environments, are strongly influenced by one's assumptions about what one is perceiving. In his classic paper on subjective rationality, Simon (1955:101) differentiated between givens

or constraints within which rational adaptation must take place and behavior variables, noting that the latter refer to the organization and the
former to the environment. He goes on to say, however, that "if we
adopt this viewpoint, we must be prepared to accept the possibility that
what we call 'the environment' may lie, in part, within the skin of the
biological organism. That is, some of the constraints which must be
taken as givens . . . may be physiological and psychological limitations
of the organism."

At the heart of the problem are the difficulties encountered in attempts to discover reality inductively. The individual or group must
somehow organize a limited number of observations into a coherent view
of the whole. This process of organization and interpretation is heavily
dependent on a priori theories and beliefs (Starbuck, 1976). One's perception of reality is, to a large degree, a function of what one has come to
expect reality to be like. Perceptions result from the interaction of information, prior experience, and individual cognitive processes.

THE TASK ENVIRONMENT

If the environment is subjectively perceived, and if perceptions are
colored by individual, organizational, and environmental characteristics,
it is reasonable to expect perceptions of the same objective environment
to vary among individuals, units within organizations, and entire organizations. "The same environment one organization perceives as unpredictable, complex and evanescent, another organization might see as static
and easily understood" (Starbuck, 1976:1080).

In part, such variance depends on how the relevant or task environment is defined. Organizations exist as open systems, but if the openness
is complete the organization will cease to exist as a distinct entity (Katz
and Kahn, 1978). The organization is circumscribed by boundaries even
if they are diffuse and permeable; Starbuck (1976) compares them with
those surrounding a cloud or a magnetic field.

Nevertheless, viewing the environment as a residual (i.e., everything that is not the organization) is also unsatisfactory, as it does not distinguish between what is potentially relevant and what is "just out there"
(Miles, 1980). As Simon (1976a, 1978) notes in a more general context,
the number of considerations potentially relevant to an organization is so
large that only the more salient are within the organization's "circle of

awareness" at any given time. Decision makers are content to disregard factors that seem to be irrelevant. In the context of the issue at hand, managers are concerned with the task environment. They are concerned with the subset, or that "part of the total environment . . . which [is] potentially relevant to goal setting and goal attainment" (Dill, 1957:410). The relevant environment encompasses physical and social factors taken directly into account in decision making (Duncan, 1972). Thus organizations are not concerned with the totality of the physical and social environment in which they exist and operate, but with that portion or area relevant to organizational strategy. The scope of the relevant or task environment is defined subjectively; it is as perceived by managers (Downey and Slocum, 1975; Duncan, 1972; Starbuck, 1976).

To the extent that individuals, units, and organizations have different goals, or even different means for attaining the same ends, their task environments are different. In large part, however, the variance in relevant environments arises from differences in perceptions. As Dill (1962:106) concludes, "Individuals and subgroups within organizations do not have the same task environments. . . . Instead of representing a common exposure to a common environment, the actions that they take in interaction with one another represent the direct confrontation of different exposures."

Perceptions of task environments vary across both space and time. Different individuals, and different organizational subunits, perceive, and through their perceptions exist, in very different environments at any point in time (Aldrich, 1979; Cyert and March, 1963; March and Olsen, 1979). The same unit exists in different environments over time as a result of changes in individuals, organizations, or environment (Dill, 1962; Thompson, 1967).

These differences in perceptions reflect differences not only in information but also in individual and organizational experience and cognitive processes. They reflect differences in a priori assumptions about the structure of reality. Thus, even if given exactly the same information about the environment, two organizational subunits can exist in two very different task environments at the same time. Perceived task environments are a function, at least in part, of such organizational variables as strategy, position in the hierarchy, history, and the like.

ENACTED ENVIRONMENTS

In fact, it can be argued that relevant organizational environments are actually created through individual and organizational perceptions (Weick, 1969). In a review of the organization-environment literature, Starbuck (1976:1069) concludes that organizational environments are largely invented by the organizations themselves: "Organizations select their environments from a wide range of alternatives and then subjectively perceive the environments they inhabit."

I am not arguing that environments do not exist objectively. They do, of course, and they have real attributes (Downey and Slocum, 1975). The organizational environment, however, is created or enacted in the sense that it is as perceived by the organization at any given point in time. Furthermore, the range of perceptions consistent with effective organizational performance, or perhaps even with organizational survival, is finite. The organization is directly affected by distorted or dysfunctional perceptions of the environment, but that is not to say that a given environment uniquely determines a single organizational outcome. Rather, it implies that all organizational alternatives are not equally effective (Galbraith and Nathanson, 1978). Miles, Snow, and Pfeffer (1974:249) argue that "a wide range of perceived environments may be tolerable for lengthy periods in many real circumstances." In fact, Snow and Miles found major differences in perceived environments in the same industry (textbook publishing), more than one of which were consistent with successful performance (reported in Miles, Snow, and Pfeffer, 1974).

NATURAL SELECTION MODELS

A view of the environment as information perceived by organizations is not universally accepted in the literature. A number of authors have proposed a natural selection or ecological model of organizational change in which the environment is viewed in terms of resources for which organizations compete. The model is based on the assumption that organizations or organizational forms "fitting" the environment are positively selected and survive, while others fail or change (Aldrich, 1979). Proponents of the natural selection model agree that perceptions of organizational environments are subjective, but they argue that the factors discussed above, such as the difficulty of building inductive models and the importance of a priori assumptions, severely hamper an organization's ability to respond strategically to environmental change. Thus, at the extreme, one might argue that both the source of variation in organizational strategy and structure and the process through which information about the environment is obtained are of little importance.[3]

It is not my intention to engage in an extensive discussion of the relative merits of the resource and information flow views of the environment, but two points should be made. First, it is obvious that acceptance of a pure natural selection model would not be consistent with the emergence of political assessment as a new managerial function. Second, the choice is not either-or; one can take a position somewhere between the poles of pure natural selection and strategic choice. Perceptions of relevant environments by decision makers are just one source of variation in organizational strategy and structure. As Aldrich (1979:122) notes, a view of the environment as an information flow "supplements the perspective on environments as consisting of resources by including the *perception of information* as an intervening link between environments and resulting organizational activities" (emphasis in original). I am therefore somewhat agnostic with regard to the ecological model.

To summarize, my basic assumption is that the relevant environment is subjective; it is perceived by individuals and organizations. A correlate of that assumption is that organizations face multiple task environments. All theorists do not accept perceptions as the only linkage between environments and organizational strategy and structure, but most of them would agree that perceptions are an important intervening variable. In this study I am concerned with the collection, processing, and utilization of information about political environments. It is assumed that perceptions of the environment affect organizational strategy and, following Chandler (1962), through strategy, structure.

SPANNING THE ORGANIZATIONAL BOUNDARY

Conceiving organizations as interacting with their environments is analogous to conceiving nations as making war and conducting diplomatic relations. Both are nonoperational abstractions. Members of orga-

3. See Aldrich (1979) and Meyer and Associates (1978) for more detailed discussions of the population ecology model. Child (1972) presents a dissenting model of strategic choice.

nizations, either as individuals or as part of a group, cross or span organizational boundaries and interact with the environment.

It is clear that organizational boundaries are not entities that can be established spatially in three dimensions. The problem is not merely that they are diffuse and permeable. They must be established in terms of individual psychological and perceptual distances. Although the definition contains an obvious tautology, it is reasonable to define organizational boundaries in terms of individuals who interact directly with environments. Given that the interactions involve perceptions, and given the multiple and segmented nature of task environments, it is reasonable to assume that the locus of organizational boundaries will vary across time and issues. Whether or not a given individual functions at any specific point at the organizational boundary depends, at least in part, on which aspect of the environment is of concern.

Furthermore, if organizational boundaries are to have meaning, all members of the organization cannot be located there. At least some members operate at the technical core (Thompson, 1967), sealed off, at least partly, from environmental influences. They may need data about the environment, but they do not directly perceive the environment. They must rely on the perceptions of others.

March and Simon (1958) note that, because of specialization, most information enters an organization only at specific points. Direct perception of external environments is limited; what is communicated internally is inferences drawn from a body of evidence rather than the evidence itself. March and Simon call this editing process "uncertainty absorption." It follows that changes in the organization's model of the external world can take place only at points of uncertainty absorption, that is, where inferences are drawn from perceptions of external environments.

THE BOUNDARY SPANNING FUNCTION

The points at which uncertainty absorption takes place—where the organization is directly linked to the environment—may be viewed in terms of roles filled by members of the organization or of functions performed by them. These roles and functions are described as "boundary spanning roles" or "boundary spanning activity" in the literature (Adams, 1976; Aldrich, 1979; Aldrich and Herker, 1977; Jemison, 1979; Leifer and Delbecq, 1978; Leifer and Huber, 1977; Organ, 1971). The concept of the boundary spanner is straightforward. A boundary spanner is an individual whose activities place him or her at the boundaries of the organization and whose responsibilities include environmental interaction (Adams, 1976; Leifer and Delbecq, 1978).

Boundary spanning responsibilities are inherent in the roles of sales personnel, purchasing agents, market research analysts, corporate economists, governmental affairs experts, and political analysts. Boundary spanning may also be viewed, however, as a function that exists independently of any given role (Leifer and Delbecq, 1978). The distinction is significant. First, numerous individuals may perform boundary spanning functions regardless of their formal organizational roles. Boundary spanning may be nothing more than a manager's skimming the headlines of the morning paper or listening to a television news program. Yet that input may markedly influence the company's investment decision making.

Second, even if formal boundary spanning roles have not been established, it is, with regard to elements of the task environment, a universal function (Aldrich, 1979). If an aspect of the environment is perceived as germane to the establishment and achievement of goals, it must be taken into account in planning and decision making. Whether or not responsibilities for environmental assessment have been formally assigned, environmental evaluations are always incorporated into the decision process, if only by the decision makers themselves in an implicit and intuitive way.

The functions of boundary spanners include the acquisition and processing of information, external representation of the firm, internal representation of the environment, and the control and/or facilitation of physical inputs and outputs (Adams, 1976; Aldrich and Herker, 1977; Jemison, 1979; Katz and Kahn, 1978). Obviously I am primarily concerned with the acquisition and processing of information. Miles (1980) notes that the information processing and "gatekeeping" function of boundary spanners comprises three subtasks: interpreting environmental information in terms of organizational opportunities and constraints; translating this information to make it comprehensible to decision makers; choosing what environmental information should be communicated internally and when it is appropriate to do so. All three subtasks are crucial elements in the political assessment function.

Boundary spanning has unique characteristics which may lead to role conflict among those who perform the function and may affect the relationship between boundary spanners and other members of the organization. These characteristics derive from the singular structural relationship of boundary roles to other organizational roles and from the need for constant interaction with external actors (Adams, 1976; Organ, 1971). First, individuals occupying boundary roles are more distant psychologically from other members of their organizations than those members are from one another. Second, their proximity to the external world and the role conflict generated by their exposure to two sets of values and norms arouse suspicion in other members of the organization (Adams, 1976; Organ, 1971). Boundary spanners must often serve as change agents within the organization, reflecting aspects of the external environment which have an impact on the organization as presently constituted.

American expatriate managers of subsidiaries abroad exemplify the ambivalent relationship between boundary spanners and those closer to the core of the organization. Such managers are valued as the organization's representatives in host countries and also as a primary source of information about their respective local environments. Corporate management, however, is often concerned that these managers will "lose perspective" and identify with the local subsidiary and/or the host country rather than carry out the objectives of the global firm. As a result, American managers abroad typically are transferred quite frequently to prevent their "going native," a prospect less than desirable from the point of view of the organization as a whole.[4]

EVOLUTION OF THE BOUNDARY SPANNING FUNCTION

INSTITUTIONALIZATION

Institutionalization entails both differentiation and formalization. Differentiation means specialization of role and function. In social organizations it takes form as a "move toward the multiplication and elaboration of roles with greater specialization of function" (Katz and Kahn, 1978:29). Differentiation includes both occupational specialization and the emergence of separate subunits or divisions (Aldrich, 1979), and the degree to which it is implemented can be gauged by such factors as oc-

4. European companies, in contrast, usually keep their expatriate managers in place for longer periods of time. Obviously there are other important reasons for the rotation of American managers, including the need to give them breadth of experience.

cupational titles, job descriptions, division of labor, technical languages used, and academic degrees (Katz and Kahn, 1978; Miles, 1980). Formalization entails increasingly explicit expectations about both the performance of functions and the activities associated with organizational roles: "The clearer, more detailed, and more unequivocal the specifications are for the performance of individual roles and units' tasks, the greater the formality of structure" (Miles, 1980:23). Formalization is measured in terms of the extent to which expectations about means and ends are complete.

Institutionalization also implies that a newly differentiated function is integrated into the organization. It embraces well-established and relatively permanent structures that are accepted as an integral part of the organization. This last point is critical to this study.

The evolution of a new managerial function requires a stimulus exogenous to the process itself; it is most unlikely to arise spontaneously. If one accepts the basic premise of subjective rationality (Simon, 1955, 1956, 1978)—that organizations satisfice rather than optimize—it follows that an organization will not search for new alternatives unless its present course of action is unsatisfactory (Cyert and March, 1963). Organizations that satisfice consider action only when inaction does not satisfy the criteria in question: ". . . if there is no safety problem . . . there need be no safety action" (March and Simon, 1958:176).

Similarly, Chandler (1962) argues that changes in structure of an organization follow or result from changes in strategy. The causal linkage is reactive rather than proactive. Changes take place when the existing structure becomes dysfunctional and no longer facilitates the achievement of objectives. Chandler posits that changes in strategy ultimately are caused by changes in the organization's environment, by new opportunities and needs created by changing population, income, and technology.

It is clear that one must look to the environment to find the primary causal explanation for the establishment and formalization of boundary spanning roles (Adams, 1976; Aldrich, 1979; Aldrich and Herker, 1977; Jemison, 1979; Lawrence and Lorsch, 1969; Leifer and Delbecq, 1978; Meyer and Associates, 1978; Thompson, 1967). "The general principle underlying these generalizations [concerning the impact of environmental conditions on boundary role differentiation] is that of isomorphism between environmental characteristics and organization's structure" (Aldrich, 1979:256). It is much too facile, however, to argue that the relationship is unidirectional, flowing from environmental change to organizational strategy and structure.

The change that is immediately material comes from perceptions of the environment rather than from the environment itself. Whereas one would expect the two to be correlated, changes in perceptions of the task environment can result from changes in subject as well as in object, from changes in organizational strategy and individual cognitive processes as well as from changes in the causal texture of the environment. The formalization of boundary spanning roles depends upon organizational recognition or perception of potentially significant contingencies arising from the environment. In fact, Aldrich (1979) argues that the existence of boundary spanning roles, per se, is an important guide to the environmental contingencies that management perceives as important.

Changes in the organization's task environment are the stimuli for formalizing the boundary spanning function. Such changes are likely to be perceived indirectly. Managers observe strategic problems encountered in achieving organizational objectives, either absolutely or relative to other firms. The crucial point is that the development and the institutionalization of a new managerial function are most likely to be reactive phenomena; functions emerge in response to a need to develop procedures to handle new problems (Simon, 1976a).

ENVIRONMENTAL FACTORS AFFECTING INSTITUTIONALIZATION

There is widespread agreement that the tendency to differentiate and formalize boundary spanning roles is stronger when environments are perceived as variable, heterogeneous, and turbulent: "The more heterogeneous the task environment, the greater the constraints presented to the organization. The more dynamic the task environment, the greater the contingencies presented to the organization. Under either condition, the organization seeking to be rational must put boundaries around the amount and scope of adaptation necessary, and it does this by establishing structural units specialized to face a limited set of constraints. . . . The more constraints and contingencies the organization faces, the more its boundary spanning component will be segmented" (Thompson, 1967: 73). (See also Adams, 1976; Aldrich, 1979; Leifer and Delbecq, 1978.)

The causal argument has two components. First, the transition from a random to a clustered environmental structure (Emery and Trist,

1965) generates an isomorphic response on the part of the organization. As environments become more segmented and differentiated (i.e., more heterogeneous), organizations respond by segmenting and differentiating boundary spanning roles functionally to correspond to segments of the task environment (Thompson, 1967).

Second, as environments become more heterogeneous, variable, and turbulent, perceived uncertainty increases. The segmentation and formalization of boundary spanning roles are an organizational response motivated by the need to acquire additional information to reduce uncertainty (Lawrence and Lorsch, 1967; Leifer and Delbecq, 1978; Thompson, 1967). In other words, institutionalization of boundary spanning roles is an adaptive reaction by organizations. As noted above, it depends upon the recognition by management of contingencies affecting the firm which may be generated by changes in the task environment. The phrase "recognition by management" is crucial. Of primary concern are changes perceived in the task environment as arising from changes in environmental relationships or from changes in organizational strategy which enlarge the scope of the task environment. Thus the formalization of boundary roles depends in part on changes in the perceived nature of the task environment, which in turn depends on interaction between changes in the causal texture of the environment and changes in organizational strategy and structure.

ORGANIZATIONAL FACTORS AFFECTING INSTITUTIONALIZATION

Given changes in the perceived task environment, it can be argued that the emergence and formalization of boundary spanning roles are a function of organizational factors such as size, strategy, and technology. The process of boundary role formalization may diverge in two firms whose perceptions of the task environment differ solely because of differences in structure and strategy.

The tendency to differentiate boundary spanning roles, as well as the tendency to differentiate organizational roles in general, is partly a function of size (Aldrich, 1979; Aldrich and Herker, 1977). Smaller organizations, relative to larger-scale units, tend to utilize simpler structures and to limit the differentiation of roles and functions. The smaller firm is likely to be more flexible and better able to respond rapidly and efficiently to environmental change. A small firm is also likely to make better use of informal flows of information than is a larger one whose hierarchical structure is more complex.

The industrial environment of the firm is also a relevant factor. Technological development entails both innovation and imitation, but the latter is by far the major factor in the process of diffusion (Rogers, 1971). The formalization of boundary spanning roles in any given firm is likely to be markedly affected by developments in other firms within its frame of reference. Organizations tend to establish new roles and units "already given meaning in the wider environment . . . in other similar organizations" (Meyer and Associates, 1978:356).

The propensity to institutionalize the boundary spanning function is dependent upon perceptions of potentially significant contingencies arising from the environment. The probability of significant contingencies results, in turn, from organizational vulnerability to environmental processes and the cost of such contingencies should they occur. Other things being equal, vulnerability and cost depend upon such organizational characteristics as growth and product strategy, technology, industrial sector, and the like. For example, an innovative and potentially valuable technology that can be contained within the organization is likely to provide a source of power that lowers vulnerability to certain types of environmental change. Similarly, the potential cost of contingencies varies among organizational subunits in terms of their potential for loss, both as autonomous entities and, more important, as contributors to the organization as a whole. Since organizational factors affecting the institutionalization of boundary spanning can be discussed more effectively in a specific context than in the abstract, further discussion is delayed until institutionalization of the political assessment function is taken up in chapters 4 and 5.

THE PROCESSING OF ENVIRONMENTAL INFORMATION

One of my major theses is that the basic problem organizations face in dealing with external environments is one of managerial process and not simply one of sources of information and forecasting methods. The scarce resource is not information but the capacity to process it (Simon, 1976*a*).

I proceed from a view of the external environment as information that is available, or could be made available, to the organization. Since the information coming from the environment is, at best, raw data, a "major organizational function . . . involves evaluation, interpreting and combining inputs into formulations of tasks for the organization to perform" (Dill, 1962:98). Raw information must be acquired, processed, selected, translated, and transmitted in a form that satisfies the requisites of specific organizational tasks. It must also eventually be integrated into the larger managerial process; it must be utilized in planning and decision making.

As pointed out earlier, the organization's task environment is subjectively perceived by members of the organization. Furthermore, the perceptions are those of individuals whose function requires them, either implicitly or explicitly, to scan the relevant environment. The scanning function has two major components: input of information across organizational boundaries and filtering of that information and transmitting it to its ultimate user (Aldrich and Herker, 1977; Katz and Kahn, 1978; Leifer and Delbecq, 1978; March and Simon, 1958).

Filtering, in turn, has two aspects. The first follows directly from the subjective nature of perception. Perception of the objective environment is colored by organizational and individual behavioral and cognitive characteristics. Organizations selectively receive inputs from the environment, reacting only to information systems to which they are attuned (Katz and Kahn, 1978). Boundary spanners perceive the environment subjectively and thus selectively; what they see depends upon where they sit and who they are. The input process, then, involves the filtering of information through the perceptions of individuals in boundary roles.

The second aspect of filtering is related to organizational communication. It is what March and Simon (1958) call "uncertainty absorption." Raw data in the form of direct perceptions of the environment enter the organization only at specific points on its boundary. These direct perceptions are first summarized by boundary role personnel and then transmitted to the rest of the organization: "The vast bulk of our knowledge is not gained through direct perception but through the second-hand, third-hand, and nth-hand reports of the perceptions of others, transmitted through the channels of social communication" (March and Simon, 1958: 153). The process of uncertainty absorption "takes place when inferences are drawn from a body of evidence and the inferences, instead of the evidence itself, are then communicated" (March and Simon, 1958:165). Thus filtering encompasses both perception and communication: what one sees and what one says about what one sees.

The process of filtering markedly increases the importance and the potential organizational power of boundary role personnel (Adams, 1976; Aldrich and Herker, 1977; March and Simon, 1958; Organ, 1971). Filtering is not merely a structural characteristic of the boundary spanning process which serves as a potential source of noise or even distortion in the system. It is also a major responsibility of boundary role personnel. That function entails, or should entail, selection and interpretation. It would be dysfunctional for boundary spanners to serve as indiscriminate vacuum cleaners sweeping up all information available in the environment. They must exercise choice and judgment, selecting data that will help to attain organizational objectives. Furthermore, it would also be dysfunctional for them to transmit information in the form of raw data; some interpretation, editing, and coding are obviously required. Filtering, though functional in terms of the efficient achievement of organizational goals, also serves as a potential source of power for boundary role personnel. This fact has several important ramifications for this study.

Environmental scanning is rarely the only responsibility of boundary role personnel. Purchasing agents are responsible for obtaining needed inputs at a reasonable price as well as for reporting changes in technology or in organizations. As sales personnel are primarily expected to sell the product, for them environmental scanning is a secondary, though important, function. Managers of subsidiary companies of an international firm are basically responsible for "running the business." Although their duties include reporting on events in the political environment, that is not their primary function. General managers are seldom rewarded directly for environmental spanning. They are rewarded for the achievement of objectives. Boundary spanning is an art that requires a great deal of judgment, but it is far from clear that all boundary spanners are recruited or rewarded on the basis of their expertise in selecting and summarizing environmental information.

An important consequence of uncertainty absorption is that only those located at the organizational boundaries can examine the "evidence" directly. Managers who receive communications from boundary spanners receive inferences drawn from perceptions of evidence, rather than the evidence itself. The ability of the recipient of such communications to judge their correctness is thus severely limited (March and Simon, 1958). If the recipient accepts the communication, he or she must accept it as it stands. "To the extent that he can interpret it, his interpretation must be based primarily on his confidence in the source and his knowledge of the biases to which the source is subject, rather than on a direct examination of the evidence. . . . Hence, by the very nature and limits of the communication system, a great deal of discretion and influence is exercised by those persons who are in direct contact with some part of the 'reality' that is of concern to the organization. Both the amount and the locus of uncertainty absorption affect the influence structure of the organization" (March and Simon, 1958:165).

The multiple responsibilities of individuals in boundary spanning roles may cause them to make biased assessments. As environmental assessment and evaluation probably do not constitute their major function, their assessments are not likely to be completely objective and independent. They are influenced by the assessors' other functions and larger objectives.

Filtering or bias thus arises from two phenomena: perceptual differences among individuals or subunits, and "attempts to manipulate information as a device for manipulating the decision" (Cyert and March, 1963:67). Katz and Kahn call the selective absorption and transformation of information "coding": "The nature of the system imposes omission, selection, refinement, elaboration, distortion, and transformation on the incoming communications" (1978:433).

Another important aspect of intraorganizational communication is the attempt to increase efficiency by developing a technical vocabulary and classification schemes. As March and Simon (1958) note,[5] it is difficult to communicate about intangible and nonstandardized objects that are not easily ordered within a system of classification. "Hence, the world tends to be perceived by the organization members in terms of the particular concepts that are reflected in the organization's vocabulary. . . . the heaviest burdens are placed on the communication system by the less structured aspects of the organization's tasks, particularly by activity directed toward the explanation of problems that are not yet well defined" (March and Simon, 1958:164).

The tendency to develop a specific language affects the locus of un-

5. March and Simon call this phenomenon reification.

certainty absorption. According to March and Simon, the more complex the data and the less adequate the organization's language, the closer to the source of information uncertainty absorption is likely to take place and the stronger the tendency to summarize at each step in the process. An organizational language also inhibits communication about new or unstandardized situations, which cannot easily be described in terms found in the operating vocabulary.

INFORMATION FLOWS IN THE INTERNATIONAL FIRM

The problems of processing and transmitting information are exacerbated in the extended system of communications characteristic of the international firm (Brooke and Remmers, 1978). Fayerweather (1978) detects four "gaps" that affect the process. First, the international system links different cultures. Groups differ in attitudes, values, and social mores. Second, the sender and the receiver of communications are often of different nationalities. Third, managers of multinational firms are constantly making decisions in one environment based upon stimuli arising in another. It is difficult not to interpret signals in terms of their meaning in the receiver's more familiar home environment. Fourth, even in the era of jet transportation, satellite communications, and computer technology, it is still easier to deal with a subsidiary in Des Moines than with one in Dakar.

All the problems associated with filtering are likely to be aggravated in the multinational context. The point where uncertainty absorption takes place may be far distant from the user's location, not only geographically but also culturally and ethnically. The user of information must try to understand an environment where events have widely different meanings based on observations made by individuals whose nationality and culture, whose values, attitudes, cognitive processes, and patterns of interpersonal communication, are at variance with his or her own.

In addition to communication gaps, the very nature of the multinational corporation exacerbates problems associated with filtering. Subsidiary managers who value independence and autonomy may attempt to manipulate the decision by manipulating the information they transmit. Because international corporations function at the global level, corporate management needs much more information than is pertinent at the local level. Brooke and Remmers (1978) report that subsidiary managers assert their independence and lower their visibility by limiting the data they transmit to headquarters. Sometimes they justify such efforts by quoting local laws and customs: "This and other local knowledge provided a bargaining base to maintain some of the power in the subsidiary eroded by centralizing pressures" (1978:129). It is reasonable to assume that information about the political environment is particularly susceptible to this kind of reasoning.

3

The Relevant Environment: Political Risk and Political Assessment

Political risk may be defined as potentially significant managerial contingencies generated by political events and processes, but that statement begs a number of important questions. First, and perhaps the least tractable, is the scope of the relevant environment in terms of the specific meaning attached to "political events and processes." Second is the precise nature of the relationship between the political environment and the firm. Third, defining political risk in terms of contingencies suggests the presence of uncertainty.

THE POLITICAL ENVIRONMENT

The common functional divisions of the external environment (e.g., political, social, legal, cultural, economic) are analytical abstractions that break down at the level of experiential reality. Since society exists in its interrelated entirety, precise definition of specific aspects of the external environment is difficult. For example, referring to politics, Lasswell and Kaplan (1950:xvii) conclude that the "power process is not a distinct and separable part of the social process, but only the political aspect of an interactive whole." A number of authors argue that the two major aspects of a firm's environment, politics and economics, are not distinct and separate, but rather interactive and reciprocal. (See Gilpin, 1975; Bergsten, Keohane, and Nye, 1975; Lindblom, 1977.) Lindblom, in fact, goes so far as to claim that the difference between the two may be entirely perceptual. The same event may be seen as primarily political or primarily economic depending on the observer's training and orientation.

Politics includes two related concepts. First, "the political process is the shaping, distribution and the exercise of power" (Lasswell and Kaplan, 1950:39). Second, certain processes and events attempt "to influence significantly the kind of authoritative policy adopted for society" (Easton, 1968:127). The two are different sides of the same coin; the purpose of attempts to attain, keep, increase, or exercise power is to influence authoritative policy. Events are political in that they reflect such attempts, either by individuals or by groups. "Authoritative" is the crucial notion as it allows one to distinguish between social or religious and political aspects of society: it differentiates between moral suasion and the force of law.

Since the task environment is defined in terms of its relevance to managerial strategy, the main focus of political events and processes that concern international firms is economic. Still, a broad range of political phenomena are potentially relevant. Investors may be caught in the web of "high politics"; they may feel the effects of regular or irregular changes in regime; they are often the object of routine policymaking.

International firms have been directly affected by the military-security concerns of host states. Certain sectors, such as communications media and defense-related industries, are often restricted to local nationals. In time of war, assets located in states in conflict with a firm's home country have been confiscated; in both world wars, the property of German firms in the United States was seized.

Regular and irregular changes in government, ranging from an election to a coup or revolution, may be partly determined by economic events and thus bring about changes in policy toward foreign investors. For example, shifts in political-economic ideology following an election (as in Chile in 1971) or a revolution (as in Cuba in 1959) may lead to the expropriation of most, if not all, foreign-owned firms.

Despite the often dramatic impact of military-security affairs or of changes in regime, I contend that the most important source of politically generated managerial contingencies is routine policymaking. In virtually all countries that attract significant foreign investment, policymaking is a fairly open process in which outcomes result from the interaction of social groups. Economic policy reflects the interests and relative power of various branches of government, labor, local industrialists, the military, consumer groups, and other actors.[1]

1. Root (1972) attempts to distinguish between political and economic risks in similar terms. He notes that political events either result from government action or bear on a

The political power of interest groups—labor and management in declining industries, for example—impedes the implementation of a rational economic trade policy, thereby causing the continued protection of inefficient firms. Similarly, the imposition of the Steel Trigger Price System by the United States[2] was determined both by balance of payments difficulties and by political pressure from such groups as management and labor in the industry and other interests in steel-producing areas concerned about possible deterioration in the industry's competitive position. The determination of policy toward foreign investors is political in much the same sense. Although economic analysis often plays an important role in defining the problem and in limiting possible responses, policymaking is inherently political. Managerial contingencies arising from changes in the demand for products or the supply of factor inputs, which are primarily economic in nature, are not of immediate concern here.

Impacts on demand caused by technological changes, competitors' actions, or shifts in consumer preferences are not usually thought of as politically generated. Yet the picture changes when disintegration of the market structure results from widespread disorder and violence, as in Lebanon during the civil war, or from the banning of certain products by a politicized religious revolution, as in Iran in 1979–80. Similarly, disruptions of the labor supply by strikes over wages and benefits or other work-related issues are economic in origin, whereas widespread general strikes, as in Poland in 1980 and in Nicaragua in January 1978 to protest the Samoza regime, are clearly political.

Still, the distinction between political and economic contingencies is far from clear-cut. For example, price controls imposed to control inflation seem to be largely economic, but their implementation is rarely free of political overtones, reflecting power relationships within society. For example, one of the firms interviewed for this survey expressed concern that Brazil would control the prices set by the final producers, which in the main are foreign-owned, but not the prices set by domestic suppliers.

---

nation's political authority. In a second paper, Root (1976:4) makes a further attempt at a distinction: "An uncertainty is political if it relates to (a) a potential government act . . . , or (b) general instability in the political/social system."

2. Trigger prices were imposed in January 1978. The mechanism, designed to forestall antidumping action by United States producers, set trigger prices above the cost of production of imported steel. As long as imports were priced above the trigger prices, which were reviewed quarterly, they were to be free from antidumping action. The trigger prices were suspended in early 1980 as a result of an antidumping petition filed by U.S. Steel (International Letter, Federal Reserve Bank of Chicago, March 28, 1980).

Thus changes in the socioeconomic system, irregular changes in regime, attempts to alter the industrial system, and attempts by labor groups, local entrepreneurs, or "stakeholders" in a given industry to increase their "share of the pie" through the exercise of political power—all are matters of concern to foreign investors. The possibility that managerial contingencies will arise from such events and processes is known as political risk. Before examining the concept in depth, I first review the existing literature.

PREVIOUS ATTEMPTS AT DEFINITION[3]

My concern is the impact of the political environment on industrial firms, and not the impact of politics on cross-border lending by financial institutions, which is a related but distinct problem. In that context the subject of country risk has drawn a good deal of attention in recent years and has developed a large literature of its own.[4]

Although the term "political risk" appears frequently in the literature, agreement about its meaning is limited to an implication of unwanted consequences of political activity. Academic definitions of political risk fall into two major groups, whose differences, though substantial, are subtle rather than dramatic.

Political risk is usually conceived of in terms of governmental or sovereign interference with business operations. The definition given by Weston and Sorge (1972:60) is representative: ". . . political risks arise from the actions of national governments which interfere with or prevent business transactions, or change the terms of agreements, or cause the confiscation of wholly or partially foreign owned business property." Smith (1971:9), constructing a model based on power elites, asks: "Would the challenging pre-elite group be favorably disposed towards continued foreign investment?" Similarly, Eiteman and Stonehill (1979), defining political risk in terms of conflict between corporate goals and national aspirations, develop a typology based on forms of host government interference with foreign business. Aliber (1975), Baglini (1976), Carlson

3. Parts of this chapter, including the section on definitions of political risk, are based on my earlier review of the literature (Kobrin, 1979).
4. The literature on the risks faced by international lending institutions is extensive. See Walter (1980) for a good review.

(1969), Channon (1978), Greene (1974), and Lloyd (1976) all, either explicitly or implicitly, define political risk as government interference with business operations.

The second group of authors define political risk in terms of specific events, such as political acts, constraints imposed on firms, or a combination of the two. Rodriguez and Carter (1979) concentrate on expropriation (partial or total) and exchange risk in less developed countries. Van Agtmael (1976) focuses on instability, nationalization (total and "creeping"), and external political change. Hershbarger and Noerager (1976) list property damage, expropriation, government interference with existing contracts, exchange controls, discriminatory taxation, and regulation. Zink (1973), in defining political risk, differentiates between events related to system stability, which are detrimental to all business enterprises, domestic and foreign, and events stemming from host government policy, which affect only foreign investors. Nehrt (1970) suggests that the investment climate comprises both a business climate (economic, social, and administrative) and a political climate, defined as the risk of creeping expropriation and of future direct competition from public enterprises. Daniels, Ogram, and Radebaugh (1979) see political risk as a change in the political environment leading to deterioration of operating positions; they specify events that can cause such a change.

Thus, political risk is usually defined in terms of events occurring in the environment (e.g., an irregular change in regime) or at the junction of environment and firm (e.g., expropriation) which are typically associated with acts of government. Haendel, West, and Meadow (1975:xi) describe political risk as the "risk or probability of occurrence of some political event(s) that will change the prospects for the profitability of a given investment." Root (1972:355) defines it as the "possible occurrence of a political event of any kind (such as war, revolution, coup d'état, expropriation, taxation, devaluation, exchange controls and import restrictions) at home or abroad that can cause a loss of profit potential and/or assets in an international business operation." Robock (1971:7) suggests an operational definition:

> . . . political risk in international business exists (1) when discontinuities occur in the business environment, (2) when they are difficult to anticipate and (3) when they result from political change. To constitute a "risk" these changes in the business environment must have the potential for significantly affecting the profit or other goals of a particular enterprise.

POLITICAL RISK

Past Precedent

Recent dramatic events in Iran, beginning with the overthrow of the shah in 1979, brought forth numerous articles on political risk in the business press.[5] A good example is a piece in *Dun's Review*, entitled "Doing Business in Unstable Countries" (March 1980:49), which argues that the political climate in many Third World countries has proved to be a serious drawback to foreign investment: "American factories have been bombed in Bolivia, expropriated in Ethiopia and shut down completely in El Salvador. American executives have been kidnapped in Argentina and assassinated in Mexico." *Fortune* (Kraar, 1980:86) approached the topic in a pessimistic vein: "Over the past decade, American corporations have been discovering one supposedly rich foreign market after another —only to have their hopes dashed or diminished by unexpected political changes or upheavals. But it remained for the revolution in Iran, which exposed U.S. firms to potential losses totaling $1 billion, to drive home the lesson in global survival." *Industry Week* (March 3, 1980:21) quotes a government official as saying that the "Iranian confrontation, as well as the political volatility in some other countries, has made American firms much more conscious of the non–commercial risks they face in doing business overseas."

These and many other articles stress the threat posed by major discontinuities, such as the revolutions in Iran and Cuba and widespread political violence in Argentina and El Salvador. The prevailing concern is embodied in the question, "Who's next?" The only contingency considered is a major dramatic discontinuity, accompanied by violence, conflict, and sharp shifts in ideology, which stirs up "waves of economic nationalism."

Although the Cuban and Iranian revolutions have undeniably created major problems for American firms, to focus solely on dramatic discontinuities is misleading and counterproductive. All managerial contingencies arising from political events or processes are of concern but, despite the impact of the turmoil in Iran, the devastating effects of the civil war in Lebanon, and mass expropriations in Cuba, Chile, and Ethi-

5. The following articles are examples: "Businesses Scour Foreign-Risk Forecasts Despite Doubts about Validity of Ratings," *Wall Street Journal* (March 7, 1980); "Political Risk Analysts: As World Turns Firms Need Own Intelligence," *Los Angeles Times* (February 17, 1980); "The Multinationals Get Smarter about Political Risks," *Fortune* (March 24, 1980); "Doing Business in Unstable Countries," *Dun's Review* (March 1980).

opia, it can be argued that major discontinuities account for only a small proportion of the total.

The broad range of contingencies that arise from the political-economic environment are ordered along two dimensions. The first involves Robock's (1971) distinction between macro risks, or environmental events, which affect all foreign firms in a country, and micro risks, which are specific to an industry, a firm, or even a project. The second differentiates between contingencies that affect ownership of assets, such as full or partial divestment, and those that affect operations, ultimately constraining cash flows or returns. Potential contingencies include macro risks, such as mass expropriation; nondiscriminatory measures, such as changes in taxation, price controls, and environmental regulations; and constraints aimed directly at foreign firms, such as limitations on the repatriation of capital, restrictions on expatriate employment and foreign ownership, and local content regulations.[6]

Most politically generated contingencies present micro rather than macro risk, and, increasingly, most affect operations rather than ownership. In most instances, political events do not lead to major discontinuities or to violence; they may not even bring about a change in regime. Nevertheless, they do initiate significant changes in policy toward some foreign investors, and thus create political risk. Although such changes may involve full or partial expropriation, they more typically entail price controls, restrictions on expatriate employment, local content regulations, or other regulatory constraints.

THE INVESTMENT CLIMATE

Many of the managers interviewed for this study perceive political environments and their potential impact on firms subjectively or intuitively, expressing concern about the "investment environment" or the "business climate" in a given country. More specifically, political instability abroad is the major concern of managers and it appears to serve as a proxy for uncertainty about the political environment in general.

The idea that an investment climate exists posits the existence of

6. Local content regulations require that a given proportion of the final product, in terms of value or some physical measure, be produced within the host country. The regulations, which are common in countries such as Mexico and Brazil, are designed to stimulate industrialization by forcing local manufacture rather than simply assembly of parts produced abroad.

macro risk: political events and processes that affect all foreign firms directly. The expropriation of all foreign firms in Cuba after 1959 and in Ethiopia after 1974 was inherent in the revolutionary change from a market to a socialist political-economic system. Similarly, civil war and violence in Lebanon destroyed both market and infrastructure. Although the situation in Iran is not so clear-cut, the turmoil and disruption following the overthrow of the shah in 1979 made it extremely difficult, at least for American firms, to conduct operations.[7]

I contend that situations of macro risk are the exception rather than the rule. First, there is a clear distinction between political instability and political risk. Second, the number of major discontinuities that significantly affected the operations of foreign firms in the past three decades is limited. Third, in the vast majority of instances the impact of politics on firms varies widely, even given the same environmental scenario; it is a function of industry-, firm-, and even project-specific characteristics. The relationship between environment and firm varies in accordance with strategy, organizational structure, and managerial style. General concepts, such as *the* investment climate of a given country, therefore have meaning only in limited and atypical situations. Most managerial contingencies are generated by the interaction of the organization and the political environment.

POLITICAL INSTABILITY AND POLITICAL RISK

The distinction between political instability and political risk is clear. Robock (1971:8) concludes that "political fluctuations which do not change the business environment significantly do not represent risk for international business. . . . Political instability, depending upon how it is defined, is a separate although related phenomenon from that of political risk." Political instability may not result in managerial contingencies, and contingencies certainly arise in the absence of instability.

Political violence or instability are not necessarily linked to the operations of foreign-owned firms. For example, a coup effecting an irregular change in government may simply be a means of changing ruling elites in the absence of well-developed institutions such as political par-

---

7. It should be noted, however, that even conditions of macro risk do not necessarily affect every firm operating in the country. One respondent said that his firm successfully conducted business throughout most of the civil war in Lebanon until a stray shell hit its office building and destroyed customer sales and service records.

ties. The change, whether violent or nonviolent, is often simply a substitution of personnel rather than a shift in ideology or even policy. Foreign firms have operated successfully in unstable or even violent environments. A notable example is Gulf Oil in Angola, where civil war in 1975 and the emergence of a Marxist government dominated by the Popular Movement for the Liberation of Angola signaled a major discontinuity, accompanied by widespread political violence and a shift in ideology. Nevertheless, Gulf correctly foresaw that these political events would not hamper its production of oil.

Discontinuities in the political environment may actually lessen the probability of political risk. After the Peronist regime was overthrown in Argentina, the government's attitude toward foreign investment became more positive; in fact, previously expropriated firms were returned to their owners. Similar policy shifts occurred after the demise of Sukarno in Indonesia and the violent overthrow of Allende in Chile. Most empirical studies have not been able to establish a simple relationship between political instability or conflict and foreign direct investment.[8]

ENVIRONMENT AND FIRM

To generalize, events that occur in the environment must be distinguished from impacts on a firm's operations. As noted in chapter 2, open systems theory does not negate the existence of a boundary between the environment and the organization, regardless of how permeable and diffuse that boundary may be. Events that take place in the external environment may affect the firm, either directly or indirectly, but they are not events within the firm.

The environment has a direct effect on a firm when external events are the proximate cause of an impact on the firm's operations and ultimately on its cash flows and returns. The effect is indirect when political events lead to intervening processes that are the direct and proximate cause of impacts on the firm's operations. The distinction is imprecise because "intervening processes" themselves are found in the environment, or at the firm-environment border, but it is nevertheless significant. The point is that environmental processes and impacts on the firm are separate and distinct phenomena and that the causal relationship between the

8. See Green (1972), Kobrin (1976a, 1978), Root and Ahmed (1979), and Thunell (1979) for examples of attempts to test empirically the relationship between political conflict and instability and flows or stocks of foreign direct investment.

two must be proven and not assumed. Impacts on foreign firms, negative or positive, are not inherent in all, or even most, events that take place in the political environment.

The instances of widespread violence, instability, and social revolution directly affecting the operations of foreign firms in the past three decades are few in number. Analysis of one specific impact, expropriation, provides an example.[9] A study of more than 1,500 expropriations between 1960 and 1976 in 76 less developed countries (Kobrin, 1980) categorized the seizures as mass or selective. A mass expropriation was the wholesale taking of foreign firms after major political change; in the selective takings, some foreign-owned firms were expropriated for specific reasons. Only in mass expropriation is there a direct link between macro political change and foreign firms. Selective expropriation is a policy instrument designed to achieve a specific objective. The study reveals that in only 8 of the 76 countries (Algeria, Angola, Chile, Ethiopia, Indonesia, Mozambique, Peru, and Tanzania) could expropriations during the seventeen-year period be characterized as mass and as ideologically motivated. In the other 68 countries, selective expropriations of firms in a single industry, or even of certain firms within an industry, were not generally directly linked to instability or conflict.

GOVERNMENT POLICY AS AN INTERVENING VARIABLE

My contention, though difficult to support empirically, is that in most instances political instability and violence do not directly affect foreign enterprises. Instead, they lead to changes in the host government's policy vis-à-vis foreign investors. That is, basic changes in the political environment alter the relative power or the objectives of various groups, including the current regime, the opposition, labor, students, and the like, which have a stake in governmental policy toward foreign-owned firms. The effects of conflict—for example, an attempted or a successful coup—are more likely to be felt through the medium of changes in government policy than directly as plant bombings, assassinations of execu-

9. Expropriation is only one example of the impact of the political environment on foreign firms, and not necessarily the most important example. Kobrin (1980) estimates that roughly 5 percent of foreign firms have actually been expropriated in the less developed countries. But expropriation, as a tangible, public event, is the one "constraint" for which reasonably good data are available. The following discussion is based on Kobrin (1980).

tives, the impact of turmoil and disorder on inputs and outputs, or even mass expropriation.[10]

Political instability and conflict are not necessary or even frequent prerequisites to constraints imposed on foreign firms as a result of changes in the political environment. Price controls, limitations on foreign ownership and employment, local content regulations, partial or complete expropriation, exchange and import controls, remittance restrictions, and the like may result from the regular functioning of the political process owing to losses or gains in the regime's power or to changes in the character and power of the opposition or of interest groups. Of primary concern are shifts in relationships within the political environment which alter governmental policy toward foreign investors. For example, recent pressure by Brazilian industrialists for restrictions on foreign ownership reflects a number of environmental factors, ranging from economic conditions to political liberalization and decreased power of the military government. Whereas few if any observers of Brazil (in 1981) expect widespread conflict and instability in the short- to mid-term future, many look for significant changes in the conditions under which foreign firms operate.[11]

MICRO RISK

Potentially significant contingencies arising from the political environment are likely to be industry-, firm-, or project-specific. That is, political risk is usually micro risk in that it results from the interaction of organization with environment. The proposition that impacts upon firms are a function not only of political events but also of organizational strategy and structure is well supported by empirical evidence. In an earlier study (Kobrin, 1980) I show that vulnerability to expropriation varies widely in respect to industrial sector, level of technology, and ownership structure. Sensitive sectors—natural resources, banking, insurance, utilities—are significantly more likely to be expropriated than are manufacturing and trade, in which firms tend to be smaller and to exercise less direct control over areas basic to the economy. Within the manufacturing

10. See Kobrin (1978) for a further elaboration and an empirical test of this argument.
11. See, for example, "Will Foreign Bankers Blow the Whistle on Brazil?" *Business Week* (November 19, 1979); "Oh Brazil," *The Economist* (August 4, 1979), and *Latin American Economic Report* (various issues, 1979).

sector, firms in technologically intensive industries are significantly less vulnerable than firms whose technology is mature and widely available. The former presumably are regarded as making a valuable contribution to the host society in terms of a transfer of needed resources and have substantial bargaining power. The opposite is true of firms in the latter category.

OPERATIONS VERSUS OWNERSHIP

Managerial contingencies of concern in the future are more likely to be those that affect operations, and ultimately cash flows and returns, than those that affect ownership of assets. Preliminary evidence for the period 1976–1979 suggests a sharp decline in the incidence of expropriations in less developed countries (LDCs) after 1975.[12] The virtual completion of expropriation in major extractive industries, such as petroleum, contributed significantly to the decline, however the improved ability of host governments to control behavior through regulation is a major factor. Because many LDCs have markedly increased confidence in their ability to alter the package of costs and benefits associated with foreign direct investment (FDI) to their advantage, they prefer regulation to expropriation. Although expropriation is an attention-getting dramatic event, its incidence is much more limited than commonly believed. In my 1980 paper I estimated that expropriation affected only 5 percent of all firms in LDCs, though it was more pervasive in some sectors than in others.

In summary, political risks are contingencies arising from the political environment, not political events and processes per se. Political events must be regarded as cause, not effect, and hence they are of concern only insofar as they affect managerial strategy. The concept of the investment environment in a given country has limited utility. The impact of most political events varies from firm to firm and from project to project; it is increasingly more likely to take the form of constraints imposed on operations rather than of termination of ownership. Contingencies arise from the interaction of environmental factors and the firm's strategy and structure.

12. The preliminary results are based on an updating of the data base conducted in conjunction with preparation of a technical paper compiled for the United Nations Center on Transnational Corporations, to be published in 1982.

UNCERTAINTY AND POLITICAL RISK

It has been argued that uncertainty is perhaps the crucial variable linking the environment to organizational strategy and structure (Downey, Hellriegel, and Slocum, 1975; Duncan, 1973; Huber, O'Connell, and Cummings, 1975; Lawrence and Lorsch, 1967). Thompson (1967:159) goes further: ". . . uncertainty appears as the fundamental problem for complex organizations, and coping with uncertainty as the essence of the administrative process."

The nature of change in the external environment (continuous or discontinuous) and managers' perceptions of that change (certainty, risk, and uncertainty) have been important elements in previous attempts to define political risk. Robock (1971), who is particularly concerned with discontinuities, excludes gradual and progressive changes in the environment, which are neither unexpected nor difficult to anticipate. Root (1972, 1976) and Haendel, West, and Meadow (1975) explicitly define political risk in terms of uncertain future events. The latter, for example, distinguish between risk and uncertainty in terms of adequacy of information. It would not be unreasonable to paraphrase Thompson and state that coping with uncertainty is the essence of the political assessment problem. In this connection, however, I contend that managers' uncertainty flows from limited experience rather than from a high incidence of discontinuous environmental change.

A basic assumption of the behavioral theory of the firm—that of subjective rationality—is that the link between models of reality and reality itself is experience. That link is tenuous, however. "Environmental actions and events are frequently ambiguous. It is not clear what happened, or why it happened. Ambiguity may be inherent in the events, or be caused by the difficulties participants have in observing them. The complexity of, and change in, the environment often overpowers our cognitive capacity" (March and Olsen, 1976:8).

The fact that widespread concern about political environments has emerged only recently suggests that most managers of United States–based international firms have had limited experience in this area, in terms of both actual constraints and abstract conceptualizations of the comparative political process. They therefore exhibit uncertainty about the current state of the political environment and its relationship to the firm, as well as about the impacts of future events. They also face ambiguity of preference for possible outcomes.

THE NATURE OF CHANGE

By its very nature discontinuous change is more difficult to predict than continuous change. Environmental discontinuities clearly increase the difficulty of political assessment. Nevertheless, continuous change in political environments, and even relatively certain events, do affect the firm and therefore require assessment or evaluation and demand a strategic response. Determination of the nature of change (and of the certainty of the event) is, in fact, one of the objectives of the analytical process. It is to some extent guided by the amount of information available to the observer. Continuous change may make the analytical task easier, and a low degree of uncertainty may limit the amount of business risk, but in neither instance is the need for assessment of the political environment eliminated. An accurate analysis of the current environment is essential to any forecast, regardless of the nature of future change. Whether an expropriation is fairly certain (e.g., resulting from a fade-out agreement),[13] whether it is predictable on the basis of current trends (e.g., when it is the stated policy of a political party that has regularly increased its percentage of the vote), or whether it follows a discontinuity (e.g., the revolution in Cuba), its effect on the firm is the same after the fact, all else being equal.

Environmental discontinuity significantly increases the difficulty of political assessment, but uncertainty in another sense is fundamental to the problem. Managers are uncertain about the current nature of the existing political environment and about its potential impact on foreign firms. Discontinuous change is neither necessary nor sufficient to create political risk.

UNCERTAINTY DEFINED

The technical distinction between certainty and uncertainty turns on the nature of outcomes of future events. Certainty means that a single outcome can be unambiguously associated with a given event; uncertainty, that one cannot unambiguously specify the outcome of an event. The problem is considerably more complex than that, however. Once one moves away from certainty, which is an ideal construct in this con-

13. A fade-out agreement specifies planned divestment of equity ownership at some point in the future as a condition of initial entry by a foreign direct investor. For example, the Andean pact required that all new foreign investors agree to sell 51 percent of their equity to local investors within 15 years in all but the poorest Andean countries, where the time period was increased to 20 years (Robinson, 1978).

text, a number of states of reality fall under the rubric of uncertainty. Distinctions among them are made on the basis of such factors as one's ability to enumerate a mutually exclusive and complete set of outcomes and to assign probabilities to those outcomes and one's confidence in the estimates.[14]

The basic dichotomy between risk and uncertainty is associated with Knight (1971). Risk implies that, while a single outcome cannot be unambiguously associated with a given event, one can specify all possible outcomes and establish an "objective" probability distribution. Two classic examples of risk are a roll of the dice and the offering of life insurance. In both instances all possible outcomes are known. In the former, probabilities can be assigned through a priori calculation. For the latter, a probability distribution can be established from statistics such as age, profession, family history, physical condition, and the like.

For the vast majority of business decisions the state that Knight defines as risk is also an ideal construct. First, most business decisions, and certainly FDI decisions, are unique events. They can be neither repeated nor divided; they cannot be treated as one of a series of experiments and pooled. Second, the decisions of interest here are made by human beings in a complex environment. Situations where all, or even all important, alternatives can be specified are rare. Third, as decisions are made in the present, possible outcomes must be imagined outcomes, existing subjectively in the mind of the decision maker. Shackle (1969:10) states the matter clearly: ". . . the outcomes, by comparison of which a decision is made, are fragments of the individual mind (no matter whether in some later activity they shall be observed to have come true . . .)."

Both certainty and risk therefore have little application to most managerial decisions with which we are concerned. Managers operate in the realm of uncertainty where knowledge of the complete set of outcomes associated with any event/decision and the ability to assign objective probabilities are virtually nonexistent. Still, uncertainty is not complete, and managers can make some judgments about outcomes and their likelihood of occurrence. Complete uncertainty entails what Shackle calls a "powerless decision" and it clearly is not of interest. What is of interest is uncertainty that is both subjective and bounded.

14. This discussion is based in part on Kobrin (1979). Business risk is defined in terms of the variation of a firm-specific variable, such as cash flows or returns, about its mean (Rodriguez and Carter, 1979). In insurance terminology, risk may be pure or speculative. The former implies only the possibility of loss or no loss (e.g., a fire or a fraud), whereas the latter implies the possibility of gain as well as loss (Kelly, 1974).

UNCERTAINTY IS SUBJECTIVE

March and Simon (1958:139) summarize their subjective theory of rational choice in terms of two fundamental characteristics: "(1) Choice is always exercised with respect to a limited, approximately simplified 'model' of the real situation. . . . (2) The elements of the definition of the situation are not 'given'—that is, we do not take these as data of our theory—but are themselves the outcome of psychological and sociological processes, including the chooser's own activities and the activities of others in his environment." The "givens" are not objectively manifest as a function of the decision situation but are subjective; they are premises accepted by the decision maker (Simon, 1976b; see also Simon, 1955, 1956, 1978). Uncertainty is itself subjective in a more profound sense than is implied by an individual estimate of probabilities. It is subjective in the sense that the decision situation, including environmental events and their impact on the organization, cannot be defined objectively; the situation is as perceived by the decision maker. "Uncertainty, however, exists not in the outside world, but in the eye and mind of the beholder" (Simon, 1976b:142).

The literature reflects general agreement that uncertainty is subjective, that it is a behavioral variable which is a function of individual and organizational perceptions rather than the objective environment. For example, in a critique of the contingency theory literature[15] Downey, Hellriegel, and Slocum (1975:614) conclude that "uncertainty may be thought of as an attribute of an individual's behavioral environment rather than an attribute of the physical environment."

To be sure, uncertainty is not independent of the environment. An environment clearly exists apart from individual perceptions—the tree falls whether or not the event is seen or heard. Nevertheless, individual and organizational reactions to environments in general, and to uncertainty in particular, are individual and organizational perceptions. Reviewing a number of studies of individual perceptions of uncertainty, Downey, and Slocum (1975:567) conclude that "specific attributes of physical environments tend to elicit similar perceptions of uncertainty by individuals. These similar perceptions of uncertainty by individuals, however, stem from similarities in individual perceptual processes rather than

15. See Lawrence and Lorsch (1967) and Duncan (1972) for an introduction to contingency theory.

from the existence of uncertainty as an attribute of the physical environment." Uncertainty is subjective in the sense that it is as perceived by the subject; it flows from individual experience and cognitive processes and organizational characteristics, as well as from environmental contingencies.

THE POLITICAL ASSESSMENT PROBLEM

Definitions of uncertainty in the literature coalesce around three contingencies: (1) lack of knowledge or information about environmental processes and relationships; (2) difficulty in specifying or inability to specify relationships between environmental and organizational-specific factors (How will environmental variables actually affect the firm?); (3) inability to specify the outcome of a specific event or decision. The net result is a problem of complex and compound probabilities, chiefly the probable impact of the environment on a firm-specific variable when an estimate of the future environment is based on a subjective understanding of the current state of affairs. (See Downey and Slocum, 1975; Duncan, 1972; Lawrence and Lorsch, 1967, among others.)

Uncertainty is used broadly to include knowledge of what is, as well as knowledge of what will be. Any prediction or forecast must be based on hypotheses about change; an understanding of the current state of affairs must be presumed (Armstrong, 1978). Barefoot empiricism aside, forecasters must understand causal relationships among environmental elements and the relationship between the environment and the process in question. Understanding current environments is considerably more difficult in political assessment than in most business forecasting.

Downey, Hellriegel, and Slocum (1975) note that the attributes of the physical environment are two steps removed from perceptions of uncertainty. In the first step, perception of environmental attributes "involves less than one-to-one mapping." The second is the manner in which perceived attributes elicit perceptions of uncertainty. This leads to an attempt to define uncertainty more precisely in the context of the political environment of international business.

Managers in international firms assessing political-environmental uncertainty experience difficulties in understanding the nature of political processes and their relationship to the organization. Thus it is hard for them to specify outcomes and assign probabilities for (1) events in the political environment and (2) impacts of the environment on the operations of their firms. Both are significantly affected by organizational and individual factors. What is of concern is managerial perceptions of the environment and of the likely impact of the environment on the firm's operations. For several reasons, such perceptions are more likely to be influenced by individual cognitive processes in this area than in other managerial functions. First (for reasons discussed in chapter 4), the need to come to grips with politics on other than an intuitive basis is rather new to American managers. Few of them have developed the same abstract or conceptual understanding of politics as a process as they have of basic business processes (marketing or finance) or even of economics. This is exacerbated by the comparative nature of the political problem. Second, in international business, stimuli arising in a different social and political culture must be interpreted. Managers, as human beings, view the world through ethnocentric glasses. These two problems are not independent.

Managers find it difficult to evaluate the various elements in political environments of host countries and the causal relationships among elements. They tend to interpret elements (e.g., legislatures and bureaucrats) and their relationships (e.g., establishment of regulations affecting foreign investors) in the context of the investor's home country. Managers also face a problem in developing a conceptual model of the process through which political events affect projects. First, few data have been accumulated on the historical relationship between environments and constraints imposed upon firms. Second, the dependent variable—potential contingencies arising from the environment—is largely a function of the characteristics of the project itself. It is difficult to generalize; determining the nature of potential constraints is as important a part of the analytical problem as is prediction of their possible occurrence.

A great deal of uncertainty thus exists about the nature of political environments and about the relationship between environmental events and the firm's operations. A manager interpreting the political process in terms of prior experience may easily misinterpret the texture of the investment environment and the probability that constraints will be imposed.

Although subjective uncertainty is a fundamental component of the political assessment problem, the nature of the environment cannot be ignored. The characteristics of the political environment tend to increase subjective uncertainty in the sense of both the variance of the probability distribution and the degree of confidence in one's estimates (Aharoni, 1966, makes this distinction).

In chapter 4, I argue that recent changes in the nature of the political-economic environment, combined with internationalization of the enterprise, have increased complexity, variability, and turbulence in the environments of American international firms. There is little question that increases in complexity and variability of organizational environments lead to increases in perceived uncertainty (Aldrich, 1979; Leifer and Delbecq, 1978; Thompson, 1967). The relationship between uncertainty and a turbulent field is definitional; Emery (1977:10) concludes that the forces that give rise to turbulence can "trigger off social processes of which they had no forewarning, in areas they had never thought to consider and with results they had certainly not calculated on."

UNCERTAINTY AND DECISION MAKING

To this point, I have dealt with uncertainty in terms of problems encountered in assessing potential managerial contingencies generated by political events and processes. Uncertainty also enters into the decision-making process in a related, but quite different, sense. Managers are uncertain of their preferences for outcomes of events.

March (1978) notes that rational choice is based partly on guesses about future consequences of current actions and about future preferences for those consequencs. To the extent that decision makers encounter difficulty in specifying outcomes, preferences remain ambiguous. If you know that something is likely to happen but you are not sure exactly what shape it will take (or even which alternative shapes are probable), it is difficult to come up with a transitively ordered set of preferences. The problem deepens when causal relationships are unclear and past experience is difficult to interpret. As Cohen, March, and Olsen (1972:1) note, preferences are "discovered through action as much as being the basis of action."

Preferences are indeed problematic. Decision makers, almost universally, prefer achievement of increased profits, sales, or growth. But, at the next level of analysis, would expropriation be preferred to strict price controls combined with local content regulations? The question is difficult to answer, for several reasons. First, few managers have had a substantial experience with either alternative; the need to deal with politically imposed constraints is a novel aspect of corporate life. Though some managers have had more experience than they would have preferred with expropriation and local content regulations, they have not had the opportunity to observe a large enough set of events to provide a reasonable basis for generalization. The determinants of events such as expropriation, and even their impact on firms, are far from clear. Second, events such as possible expropriation stand as symbols for a diffuse array of unpleasant outcomes. Again, experience with political environments has been limited and environment-firm relationships are only partly understood. A manager cannot be sure exactly what expropriation would mean to the firm; it may serve as a code word for a set of diffusely perceived but unwanted consequences.

In summary, organizations and decision makers facing uncertainty and ambiguity have difficulty in specifying outcomes of events, in assigning probabilities to these outcomes, and in determining preferences for them. Managers are unsure of the future state of the political environment, the constraints and/or opportunities that will be presented, and the effect of those constraints on firms. Political assessment involves difficulties encountered both in current analysis and in forecasting. The problem flows from ambiguities based on historical experience, current relationships, and future events. It is difficult to perceive the future when past and present are only imperfectly understood.

SUMMARY: POLITICAL RISK

Political risk has been defined broadly as potentially significant managerial contingencies generated by political events and processes under the following circumstances.

1) The relevant political environment is defined in terms of process: attempts to exert power to influence authoritative policy. Contingencies resulting from impacts of the normal functioning of economic processes on supply and demand are excluded.

2) The significance of contingencies is determined by their potential effect on the magnitude and distribution of cash flows.

3) Environmental events and managerial contingencies are distinct and separate phenomena and the relationship between them must be proven rather than assumed; that is, political instability is not political risk.

4) The relationship between the political environment and the firm's operations may be direct or indirect and negative or positive. In most instances government policy provides the linkage between environment and impacts of the organization.

5) It is the potentiality of impacts on the firm rather than the nature of environmental change which is of concern. Political risk results from continuous as well as discontinuous change. It is assumed that the former, the routine functioning of the political process, accounts for the vast majority of impacts.

6) Political risk is more likely to be micro than macro. That is, contingencies are likely to be firm- or even project-specific and are likely to result from the interaction of organizational strategy and structure with the environment, rather than from political events that affect all foreign firms in a given country.

7) Managerial contingencies are increasingly likely to take the form of constraints on operations rather than on ownership of assets.

8) It is managerial perceptions of the political environment and likely impacts on the firm's operations which are of concern. Uncertainty thus plays a critical role. There is considerable uncertainty about the current state of the political environment, about its relationship to the firm, and about the outcomes of future events. Ambiguity also exists, as managers have difficulty in ordering preferences for outcomes.

4

The Political Environment and the International Firm

More than half of the firms surveyed for this study have attempted explicit assessment of political environments, and more than a third have begun to institutionalize the function. These results contrast sharply with Root's (1968*b*) findings of a decade earlier, when he saw no evidence of systematic evaluation of political risks abroad. Following Aldrich (1979), I argue that the relatively rapid emergence of boundary spanning (i.e., political assessment) roles in a substantial minority of firms indicate that managers perceive a significant increase in the probability of potentially costly contingencies arising from the political environment.

In organizational terms, the domain of the task environment (which is defined subjectively) has expanded to include political factors abroad. In the past three decades, political events and processes have become directly relevant to strategic planning and decision making. In this chapter I suggest that the expansion of the task environment results from two interrelated postwar trends: (1) the internationalization of production and (2) secular changes in the political–economic environment. (In chapter 5, organizational determinants of the institutionalization of the political assessment function are analyzed in depth.)

The expansion of the task environment is perceived by managers along two interdependent dimensions. First, political factors abroad are more likely to affect directly the attainment of corporate objectives. Second, the interaction of changes in the firm and in the external environment has increased the heterogeneity, variability, and turbulence of the task environment and thus the degree of perceived uncertainty.

THE NATIONAL FIRM

Political factors have never been irrelevant to American business firms. From Alexander Hamilton's import substitution policies to the antitrust activity at the turn of the century and the transition to a mixed economy under the New Deal, the political and social environment has had an impact on corporate goal setting and decision making. Through the late 1960s, however, political factors were not routinely a part of the task environment of domestic firms. They were directly relevant to strategic planning and decision making only in exceptional circumstances.

The political environment has always been part of the external environment surrounding business firms. So has use of the English language, however. In other than exceptional circumstances—the attempt to penetrate the Hispanic market in the Southwest, for example—language was not regarded as relevant to decision making. Language existed as an environmental parameter, rather than as a variable. Politics did also, for several reasons.

First, the American political system has been remarkably stable over time. No irregular transition has ever occurred in either the executive or the legislative branch. When a president has been unable to finish his term in office—through death, assassination, or resignation—succession has followed an orderly constitutional procedure. A wide variety of interest groups have access to the system through institutionalized input processes such as political parties and lobbying. Certainly through the late 1960s, instances in which groups attempted to express discontent irregularly (e.g., through violent or nonviolent demonstrations) were the exception rather than the rule.

Second, the American political process has not been characterized historically by major ideological differences on economic questions. Despite interparty disagreements from the New Deal through the late 1960s on such issues as Keynesian theories, the rights of labor, and social welfare legislation, neither major party seriously suggested socialization of the "commanding heights" of the economy or the institution of national planning. Despite disagreement about how "mixed" our mixed economy should be, basic reliance on a market system and the private sector was generally accepted. Regardless of campaign rhetoric, business could expect a reasonable continuity in policy even when the other party came to power.

Third, and again through the mid-1960s, the economic system of the United States was well insulated from events in other countries. From 1960 to 1965, for example, exports amounted to only 5.9 percent of the gross national product (GNP). Total foreign investment (direct and portfolio) accounted for only 6.7 percent of gross domestic investment.[1] In the mid-1960s imports of petroleum were moderate, amounting to only 22 percent of consumption (Stobaugh and Yergin, 1979). Although American firms were engaging in rapid and pervasive international expansion, they were operating in an international economic system that was clearly dominated by the United States. From the Bretton Woods agreement in 1944 through the devaluation of the dollar and the end of convertibility into gold at a fixed price in 1971, the United States clearly established the rules for the international economy. In that period the United States was a hegemonic power.

In general, though the business environment included a major political component, political factors were not usually directly relevant to planning or decision making. Policy changes tended to be of degree rather than of kind. Furthermore, most domestic firms are managed by American citizens, raised and educated in the United States, who possess an intuitive understanding of American politics. Regardless of occasional serious errors, they know how the system works and how to relate to it.

The fact that the firm's task environment did not, prior to international expansion, routinely include political factors has important implications for the evolution of the political assessment function. Managers lacked a domestic base of experience upon which to draw when they realized the need for explicit and formal environmental analysis abroad. For the vast majority of American firms, especially those engaged in manufacturing, the emergence of political analysis as a necessary function marked a discontinuity in managerial procedures and organizational structure.

INTERNATIONALIZATION OF THE FIRM

Although a number of United States firms established operations abroad quite early,[2] broad-scale international expansion is a fairly recent

---

1. *Survey of Current Business*, various issues, 1960–1965.
2. Mira Wilkins (1970) reports that American industrial concerns had opened branch factories in England as early as the 1850s and, "by the 1880s and 1890s, there began on a substantial scale the emergence of modern multinational enterprises, enterprises with inter-

phenomenon, especially for manufacturing firms which ventured abroad much later than resource-based companies or utilities.[3] Foreign direct investment (FDI)—that is, sufficient equity ownership of subsidiaries in other countries to provide a degree of managerial control—totaled less than $12 billion in 1950. By 1978, FDI had risen to more than $168 billion, an average annual growth rate of 9.6 percent. Manufacturing FDI grew from $6.3 billion in 1955 to $19.2 billion in 1965 and $65.6 billion in 1978.[4] Growth in terms of the proliferation of subsidiaries is equally impressive. In 1960 the 186 companies that met the Harvard Project's criteria for a multinational enterprise (as of the mid-1960s) had a total of 4,796 subsidiaries abroad. By 1975 that number had risen to 11,198.[5]

There has been a qualitative as well as a quantitative transformation of international business. American multinational corporations (MNCs) of the 1960s and 1970s are superficially similar to the early ventures of Singer, Ford, and United Fruit, consisting of a cluster of firms of diverse nationalities, some or all of whose equity is held by the American parent. The significant difference is that in the modern MNC the subsidiary firms follow a common strategy and are under the control of a centralized management (Vernon, 1971*b*).

The modern MNC functions as an integrated global system: it achieves its system-wide objectives through global mobilization and allocation of resources. International enterprises during the early twentieth century did transfer resources and even strategies across national borders, but global integration was beyond their reach. What has made the difference is the radical transformation of communications and transportation technology after World War II; Brzezinski (1970) called it the "technetronic revolution." The modern MNC is the child (and, to some extent, the parent) of jet planes, satellite communications, and high-speed computers.

---

related marketing and manufacturing facilities in several nations." By the start of World War I such well-known firms as Eastman Kodak, General Electric, Singer, and International Harvester, to say nothing of Standard Oil of New Jersey, had substantial direct investments abroad (Wilkins, 1974; see also Wilkins, 1970, for a history of United States international business from the colonial era through 1914).

3. For example, 58.5 percent of the manufacturing firms that responded to the mail survey first ventured abroad after World War II, and 14.0 percent, after 1965.

4. *Survey of Current Business*, various issues, 1950, 1955, 1978.

5. The Harvard Project's sample includes American firms that appeared in the *Fortune* 500 listing (1963 or 1964) and held 25 percent or more of the equity of manufacturing enterprises in six or more foreign countries. See Vaupel and Curhan (1969) and Curhan, Davidson, and Suri (1977).

Internationalization is reflected both in physical expansion abroad and in strategic evolution toward increased centralization of control, coordination, and rationalization. In its early stages, international expansion was expansion into the uncharted territory of unfamiliar, and perhaps foreboding, foreign environments. The individual firm was a loose confederation of autonomous subsidiaries linked to the parent through a rather primitive system of financial control. Perlmutter (1969) characterized this organizational structure as polycentric. (See also Stopford and Wells, 1972.)

As international operations become more important, managers begin to realize the potential returns from worldwide integration. According to Robinson (1978:669), "Although inclined . . . to permit substantial autonomy to their associated firms, the multinationals, as they mature and gain international experience at the center, eventually begin to accelerate the centralization process. The benefits to be derived from integrating the worldwide movement of corporate resources become increasingly apparent as the contribution to corporate profits from overseas activity mounts and as the skill to effect such integration appears in corporate headquarters."

In Perlmutter's (1969) terms, the strategy becomes geocentric. The firm operates as an integrated international system optimizing on a worldwide basis. Its subunits pursue a common objective through a common strategy. The parent firm increases its control over subsidiaries, and affiliate autonomy is correspondingly reduced. The subsidiary no longer exists as an independent entity attempting to optimize performance at the local level. It becomes a subunit in a larger enterprise that organizes its activities on a global basis. In theory at least, the rationale for the existence of the subsidiary is its marginal contribution to the attainment of system-wide objectives rather than the pursuit of local and independent goals. As Fayerweather (1978:215) concludes, "The unifying influences . . . represent a substantial portion of the basic rationale for the existence of the multinational corporation and the source of a considerable part of its competitive advantage."

In a world where all the assumptions of "perfect competition" were realities, optimization at the system level would simply require independent optimization by subunits. Indeed, in such a world the MNC could not even exist.[6] In the real world of fragmented nation-states, however,

---

6. The theory of foreign direct investment posits that foreign investors require some sort of advantage over local competitors to offset the disadvantages of unfamiliarity

which have different tax codes, different monetary and fiscal policies, and varying government regulations, independent local optimization can mean suboptimization for the MNC as a whole. A manager faces the challenge of operating a unified global system despite strong pressures for fragmentation. Such centrifugal pressures flow from environmental differences: "Fragmenting influences encourage management to tailor the operations in each country . . . to its unique combination of economics, culture and nationalism" (Fayerweather, 1978:215). Optimization at the global level may well conflict with optimization in regard to the task environment of each subsidiary. Perlmutter (1969) says the forces opposing geocentrism are environmental, including political and economic nationalism, linguistic differences, and varying cultural backgrounds.

International firms do not simply have to operate efficiently in a large number of countries. Rather, they have to work toward global or system-wide objectives by simultaneously operating in many disparate environments. The essence of the problem is an asymmetrical relationship. In theory, the firm is a unified global entity seeking to attain system-wide objectives. In reality, the firm is not global, but transnational. It achieves its objectives through access to, and operation in, a large number of different national, social, economic, and political systems. The multinational firm has to function in a world organized on the basis of sovereign national states.

EFFECTS OF INTERNATIONALIZATION

The process of internationalization tends to increase managerial perceptions of politically generated contingencies in two related ways. First, it increases vulnerability to such contingencies and emphasizes their potential costs. Second, the transformation of politics from a parameter to a

---

with the local environment and distance from home. Such advantages must generate sources of rents which can be contained over time, and thus they flow from imperfections in factor or goods markets. They can, for example, arise from technology, vertical integration, or the ability to promote branded products. Thus, in a world where the assumptions of perfect competition were a reasonable description of reality, foreign direct investment, and the equity-based multinational firm, could not exist. The foreign investor could not compete with local enterprise. See Kindleberger (1969) for a good introduction to the topic. Buckley and Casson (1976) extend the argument by hypothesizing that the multinational firm represents the substitution of administration for markets (internalization) as a result of imperfections in the markets for intermediate goods in general and knowledge in particular.

variable—as a result of internationalization—heightens the level of uncertainty in the task environment.

Contingencies generated by the political environment are more likely to hamper the achievement of objectives as the firm becomes more widespread internationally. With the enlargement of international operations, a global strategy evolves; integration and rationalization across national borders become essential if the firm is to exploit fully its potential multinationality. Although global strategy increases the pressure for unification, environmental (particularly political) differences act as constraints.

The MNC thus embodies a paradox. On the one hand, its very essence, the factor that differentiates it from the international firms that functioned from the mercantilist era through the mid-twentieth century, is strategic unification. On the other hand, a degree of suboptimization is a basic prerequisite of existence in environments that differ sharply in political-economic objectives. The unification/fragmentation conflict, the balance between global optimization and adaptation to local environments, is the fundamental managerial issue facing multinational corporations. With internationalization and the evolution of a global strategy, the relevance and the potential cost of politically generated contingencies increase.

The firm's political environment itself becomes more complex as a result of international expansion. Operating in differing political environments significantly increases the heterogeneity of the firm's environment even if each one is relatively homogeneous. Differences in tax codes, government-business relationships, antitrust regulations, methods of articulating interest and influence, political-economic philosophy, labor legislation, and the like must be taken into account when global plans are formulated. Ownership strategy, pricing and dividend policies, and even product planning must reflect the constraints imposed and the opportunities presented by disparate national environments.

Internationalization has also increased the variability of a firm's political environment, even when individual national environments are stable. Shifting patterns of business operations in various national markets increase the variability of political factors. The discovery of an important oil reserve (Mexico), the growth of market potential (Brazil), or even the opening of a new market (China) may bring about a sizable shift in sales and in profit potential across national markets. This change means a transformation of the mix of political factors with which the firm must contend even if each environment is stable.

As pointed out in chapter 2, perceptions of increased environmental complexity and variability lead to increased uncertainty. Internationalization brings clearer recognition of potential contingencies arising from the political environment because (1) those contingencies more directly affect global strategy, and (2) levels of uncertainty and thus business risk are increased.

THE POLITICAL-ECONOMIC ENVIRONMENT

The political-economic environment facing the international as well as the American domestic firm has undergone a profound transformation during the past thirty years. Like internationalization, this transformation has sharpened managerial perceptions of potentially significant contingencies arising from the political environment in two ways. First, the changes have enhanced the probability that political events and processes abroad will affect managerial strategy. Second, they have increased heterogeneity, variability, and turbulence and thus managerial perceptions of uncertainty.

Five interrelated environmental changes are major contributors to this transformation. First, politicization of economic and social aspects of life, both intra- and internationally, has increased. Second, nationalism has become a stronger force, both quantitatively and qualitatively. Third, political instability has become more pervasive. Fourth, political-economic relations between states are more complex and interdependent than ever before. Fifth, the international political-economic system has become more complex and more variable with the decline of United States hegemony in the late 1960s. Obviously these changes are not at all distinct, but separate discussion facilitates analysis.

THE POLITICIZATION OF ECONOMICS

In theory, a perfectly functioning competitive market system is consistent with complete independence between economics and politics. In practice, complete independence has never existed (Lindblom, 1977; Polanyi, 1957). At a minimum, politics provides the framework for economic activities (Gilpin, 1975), and a change in political regime may markedly alter the nature of the economic system (e.g., Russia in 1917, Cuba in 1959, and Chile in 1973).

A significant increase in the degree of politicization of the economic and social aspects of life began in the years after World War II. Most governments now accept some degree of responsibility for the socioeconomic welfare of their citizens. They intervene more frequently in the economy in order to achieve welfare objectives (Bergsten, Keohane, and Nye, 1975). As Nye (1974:154) suggests, "Most national security policies in today's world are designed not merely to insure the physical survival of individuals within a nation's boundaries, but to assure some minimal level of economic welfare."

Furthermore, a revolution in economic needs and expectations has taken place. Owing to the development of mass media, the growth of educational opportunities, and rapid urbanization, the citizens of most countries have become more conscious of the possibility of attaining higher levels of welfare. And they have mobilized to achieve that goal through political action. In the postwar era both the government and the governed have come to expect the state to bear the major responsibility for economic welfare.

In advanced industrial states, acceptance of government responsibility for achieving such objectives as economic growth, full employment, and internal and external stability, while maintaining at least minimal standards of social welfare, grew out of the depression of the 1930s and the reliance on Keynesian policies after the war. In emerging nations, demands for rapid growth, modernization, and industrialization in the face of underdeveloped economic institutions left little doubt that the government had to become involved in economic matters. Thus a global trend toward broader participation in national politics and deeper political involvement in economic activities developed. One must agree with Gilpin (1975) that in the modern world the relationship between politics and economics is reciprocal.

NATIONALISM

A second major change in the environment in the past thirty years has been a quantitative and qualitative increase in nationalism. First, the breakup of colonial empires during and after World War II doubled the number of independent nation-states. Of the 131 independent states reported in the *World Handbook*, 65 achieved independence after 1940, and 41, or 32 percent, between 1960 and 1968 (Taylor and Hudson, 1972). In late 1979, 151 states were members of the United Nations (*New York Times*, Sept. 21, 1979).

Second, there has been a qualitative increase in the assertion of "national interest," that is, in attempts to attain national objectives through autonomous national policies. In part, the increase is owing to the efforts of new states to establish an independent national identity and to legitimize central political authority, even when the population is characterized by linguistic, cultural, and political fractionalization. The qualitative increase stems also from heavier postwar emphasis on development and growth. Less developed countries have undertaken rapid modernization in an effort to catch up with industrialized countries. In a world of differing objectives and of finite resources the emphasis on growth and development has inevitably led to conflict, both between foreign investors and host states and between industrialized and nonindustrialized countries.[7]

Third, the advanced industrialized countries have shifted away from liberal policies tending to create an open international economic system and toward a neomercantilist position. It is perhaps too early to render a final judgment, but certainly the assumption that all states will benefit from the free movement of goods and economic resources across national borders is now less prevalent than it was in the early 1960s.[8]

The growth of nationalism has been accompanied by a shift in bargaining power from the MNC to the host country, particularly in developing countries. With the development of administrative, managerial, and technical capabilities has come a greater capacity for regulating foreign enterprises. Robinson (1976) concludes that a professional group of host country "entry-controllers," with transnational linkages, is emerg-

---

7. The conflict is reflected in the demand of the Third World for a "new international economic order" and resistance to that demand on the part of Western industrialized countries.

8. This point of view is bolstered by the difficulties encountered in the Tokyo round of trade negotiations completed in 1979 as compared with the Kennedy round of the 1960s. In 1977 *Business Week* (Oct. 3) reported that the timetable for negotiations was crucial as "a rapidly rising tide of global protectionism threatens to overtake the talks." After the negotiations ended, Ambassador Strauss noted that the "basic challenge . . . was to preserve the existing trade system and to improve it at a time when the domestic tolerance for the problems of international trade was declining" (Perkins, 1979:13).

ing. The concept of foreign investment as an "obsolescing bargain" with terms shifting in favor of the host country is well developed in the literature (Bergsten, Horst, and Moran, 1978; Vernon, 1971*b*, 1977).

INSTABILITY

The emergence of new nations and their drive for industrialization and modernization have increased intrastate political conflict and instability. Such conflict, often violent, is a response to the breakdown of traditional sociopolitical structures and the efforts to centralize power and legitimate national authority in the face of diverse regional or tribal loyalties (Geertz, 1963). Furthermore, there is ample theoretical and empirical support for hypothesizing a causal relationship between the process of modernization and political conflict. Political violence tends to be limited in both the most traditional and the most advanced states and to peak in states that are in the process of modernization (Gurr, 1971). It is in transitional states that newly created aspirations are most likely to be frustrated and that institutions to manage the resulting discontent are likely to be weakest. When political mobilization outpaces the development of input institutions (e.g., an open party system), the articulation of discontent may take violent forms (Huntington, 1968).[9]

INTERSTATE POLITICS

Two major changes in interstate political-economic relationships also markedly affect the international firm. The emergence of a wide variety of transnational linkages, resulting in what Keohane and Nye (1977) call "complex interdependence," has altered the nature of the state-dominated system, with its formal and institutionalized diplomatic relations. At the same time United States hegemony over the system weakened and eventually broke down.

In the traditional model of the international political system, a variety of international interests are aggregated into a single national interest which is officially articulated by a foreign minister or a department of state. States, presumed to act as coherent units, are the dominant

9. A substantial literature reporting empirical tests of hypotheses relates political conflict to economic, social, and political determinants. See Gurr (1971) and Parvin (1973) for examples.

actors in world politics (Keohane and Nye, 1977). The traditional model also posits a clear hierarchy of international political issues; military-security affairs ("high politics") dominate socioeconomic questions ("low politics").

Although the nation-state is still a major actor in international politics, the traditional (realist) model has clearly lost explanatory power[10] during the past thirty years or so. First, the postwar revolution in communication and transportation gave rise to a large number of transnational nongovernmental entities that command significant resources and operate across national borders (Keohane and Nye, 1971; Huntington, 1973). These transnational actors, of which the MNC is the prototype, transfer resources and link individuals and organizations in different countries. By increasing linkages between states, they have caused foreign policies to be articulated outside official channels. The wide variety of significant nongovernmental[11] actors—MNCs, the Vatican, the Red Cross, terrorist groups—invalidates the presumption that coherent states are the only important actors in international affairs. International relations have thus become infinitely more complex.

Second, the presumption of a clear hierarchy of issues must be questioned in a world where Japan, with limited military capabilities, is a major economic power, and Saudi Arabia has importance because of its petroleum reserves (and the wealth they generate) alone. Among the complex reasons for the emerging independence of issue areas are the reduced usefulness of military force in a nuclear age and the scarcity and unequal distribution of natural resources. The ramifications, however, are clear. International political-economic relations are more complex and variable than ever before. The number of actors and issue areas has significantly increased, as has the possibility that they are to some degree independent. Paradoxically, with a variety of domestic groups linked to their counterparts in other countries through numerous channels, nations are more interdependent than ever before. As Keohane and Nye (1977) point out, the line between domestic and international politics has blurred.

10. The loss of explanatory power by the realist paradigm is not universally accepted. Krasner (1978) and Gilpin (1975) offer dissenting views.
11. It is unreasonable to expect a large and complex government with a large number of often conflicting international interests to function as a coherent entity. One can argue that, at times, government agencies such as the Defense Department, the Department of Agriculture, and certainly the development agencies function as relatively autonomous transnational actors (Huntington, 1973).

UNITED STATES HEGEMONY

From the end of World War II through the latter 1960s, the United States exercised hegemonic control over the international political-economic system (or at least that part of it containing the market-oriented economies). The control was not complete, but the United States was "able and willing to determine and maintain the essential rules by which relations among states were governed" (Bergsten, Keohane, and Nye, 1975:14). Rule-making power involves both compromise and the inability to ensure enforcement. The rules developed under American hegemony were formulated at the 1944 Bretton Woods conference. They set up an international economic system administered by the International Monetary Fund. Currencies were relatively stable, and there was a decided preference for an open international economy without restrictions on the free flow of goods and factors of production across national borders. The system was based on a presumption of the inviolability of private property.

As Krasner (1978:348) notes, the Bretton Woods rules facilitated the operations of multinational corporations: "The United States helped establish a stable international monetary system that made it easy to transfer capital from one country to another. It supported an open trading system that allowed multinationals to move their products around the world. American officials insisted that the treatment of foreign subsidiaries of multinational firms should be nondiscriminatory—that is, the rules governing their activities should be the same as those applied to domestic firms. The United States had the economic, ideological, and military power to maintain these practices over a wide geographic area for some twenty-five years."

The sources of American hegemony were varied. First, the United States was the only major industrial power left unscarred by World War II. In 1945 it dominated the world economy as no other country has done before or since. Second, the outcome of the war helped to "demonstrate" the wisdom of the American political and economic system (Krasner, 1978). To many, a liberal system seemed the best path to development. Third, the idealism of the immediate postwar period was quickly transformed into the realism of a bipolar world. American hegemonic power flowed, in part, from the need for its nuclear protection against a perceived Soviet—or, for a period, a Sino-Soviet—threat.[12]

12. Gilpin (1975:152) argues that the process was reciprocal. Whereas American he-

Although the United States may still be the major Western power, it is clearly no longer a hegemonic power. For many reasons, including the recovery of Europe and Japan, the economic and political development of Third World nations, the easing—at least through 1980—of cold war tensions, internal economic instability, and increased resource scarcity, the United States no longer has the ability to set the rules. One manifestation of the decline in its hegemony is the sharp increase in takeovers or expropriations of the subsidiaries of MNCs in the late 1960s and especially in the early 1970s. I found (Kobrin, 1980) 511 acts of forced divestment involving more than 1,500 firms in 76 LDCs from 1960 to 1976. Only 20 percent occurred before 1967; more than half came in the five-year span 1972–1976. The consequence, especially for American firms, is a more complex and more variable environment and a more pluralist world. In the absence of a clear and dominant set of rules, international relationships are more likely to be issue- or even situation-specific. It is now more difficult to resolve conflicting interests and to predict outcomes.

IMPACTS ON STRATEGY

The changes in the political-economic environment since the end of World War II mean that political factors abroad will have more impact on managerial strategy. In most countries where MNCs operate, particularly in LDCs, their subsidiaries are major economic actors. The increased politicization of economic activity, particularly governmental acceptance of responsibility for socioeconomic welfare, has strengthened the pressure on regimes to exert control over their economies and over important economic actors. The inevitable intervention has been both direct, in terms of competition from, or pressure to join with, public sector enterprise, and indirect, through policies designed to affect the behavior of private firms. As a result, potential constraints, such as local content regulations, price controls, requirements for the indigenization of personnel, and expropriation of assets, have become more of a threat.

---

gemony facilitated the establishment and growth of MNCs, the expansion of MNCs was also a basis of American hegemonic power: "In effect the multinational corporation enabled the United States to resolve, at least in part, the conflict between American economic and security interests. It decreased the cost to American economic interests of rebuilding the European industrial base."

The conflict in objectives between global firms and nation-states suggests that increased nationalism will lead to more intensive pressure for national control. The higher value placed on independent national goals, and the ability to achieve them, have heightened governmental sensitivity to differences between MNCs and host countries. The problem is exacerbated by the reality of economic independence and the political ramifications of MNCs as autonomous transnational actors. And the decline of the hegemonic power of the United States has made American MNCs more vulnerable to political events abroad.

These changes have also increased complexity and variability for international firms, which must deal with a bewildering variety of environmental units. The number of nation-states has doubled and the range of differences between them—in economic, political, and social development, in ideology, and in goals—has expanded exponentially. With more nongovernmental links between states, the line between domestic and international politics has blurred.

Within states, the politicization of economic activity has proliferated governmental and nongovernmental organizations that have a direct impact on a firm's operations. Examples are regulatory agencies, public enterprises, and consumer and special interest groups. The firm may have to deal not with a single coherent government, but with a variety of interest groups with conflicting positions and objectives.

The frequency of change and the degree of difference caused by each change have also increased significantly. Major internal discontinuities, a shift in regime accompanied by a policy shift, are more common. Chile abandoned a mixed economy in favor of socialism when Allende was elected in 1971, and the countercoup in 1973 led to adoption of a laissez-faire philosophy. The dramatic increases in oil prices in 1973–74 and again in 1979 caused a marked redistribution of the world's wealth. Widespread nationalization of the petroleum industry between 1968 and 1976 led to a basic structural change, as equity ownership yielded to contractual arrangements.

The political-economic environment is sometimes a turbulent one. Interactions are complex and results unpredictable in a field that is constantly in motion. Examples abound. The 1973 Arab-Israeli war brought on the Arab oil boycott of 1973–74; beginning as a political action, it ended with a fourfold price increase and a major transformation of the international economic system. The transition from fixed to floating exchange rates took place between August 1971 and the spring of 1973. A sharp increase in LDC external debt, certainly not planned or even fore-seen, has threatened the economic stability of the industrialized world and linked bankers and developing countries in a way that would not have been predictable a decade ago. (See Aronson, 1979, for an analysis of this phenomenon.)

Large multinational firms are clearly major forces contributing to turbulence. Although the "Gnomes of Zurich" may be a myth, the existence of large, integrated, centrally controlled multinational firms was a factor in the final breakdown in the early 1970s of the postwar system of fixed exchanged rates. MNCs are significant nongovernmental trans-national actors. They can and do make foreign policy, which may or may not conflict with that of their governments. As amply documented else-where,[13] both home and host countries have learned how to use the web of multinational corporate relations to extend their extraterritorial reach.

THE EXPANSION OF THE TASK ENVIRONMENT

My basic argument here is that the task environment of most large United States firms has expanded over the past thirty years to include political factors. Political variables not directly related to demand for the firm's products have become relevant to strategic planning and decision making. I have argued that the expansion of the task environment is a function of two postwar trends: the internationalization of production and secular changes in the political-economic environment.

The increased relevance of the political environment to planning and decision making has two main components. First, political factors are more likely to have a direct bearing on decision outcomes, that is, the magnitude of cash flows and returns. Second, heterogeneity, variabil-ity, and turbulence increase business risk by making decision outcomes uncertain.

The increased importance of political factors is a result of the inter-nationalization of the firm and the politicization of economic activity, at both intra- and interstate levels. Factors seen as parameters, and thus as constants, by domestic firms become variables after internationalization. Since the most serious strategic problem of international firms is to avoid suboptimization—that is, to function as a unified global system in a frag-

13. See Vernon (1977) for a discussion and review of the relevant literature.

mented world—these variables must be considered in planning and decision making. It is the differences in environments, market as well as political, which provide the unique set of potential constraints and opportunities facing international firms.

Changes in organization and environment are interactive. The transnational political scope of international firms makes national control over economic policy more difficult. The size of these firms, together with the probability of conflict between their global objectives and the host country's objectives, has focused attention on the question of national (and international) political control of MNCs.

Furthermore, as noted earlier, internationalization of firms and changes in the political-economic environment have raised uncertainty about decision outcomes and thus contributed to business risk. An increase in the heterogeneity, variability, and turbulence of the environment heightens perceptions of uncertainty on the part of decision makers. As the number of environmental elements and the differences between them grow larger, prediction of the future environment (in the sense of specifying causal relationships) and its impact on corporate operations becomes more difficult. Decision makers are hard put, in Shackle's (1969) terms, to "imagine outcomes" and assign probabilities to them. The emergence of the political assessment function reflects managerial perceptions of an increased probability of significant contingencies arising from the political environment.

5

Institutionalization
of the Political
Assessment Function

A basic assumption of open systems theory is that performance of the boundary spanning function, at least in regard to the task environment, is universal. If political factors are perceived as relevant, political assessment is inherent in the management of international operations. Assessment may be intuitive, encompassing no more than a quick judgment that the investment climate is poor and that the country looks shaky, or even an unspoken consensus that a particular market is "not our kind of country." Nevertheless, it is an intrinsic component of foreign direct investment decisions and of international strategic planning.

Institutionalization of a managerial function implies well-established and relatively permanent relationships that are accepted as an integral part of the organization. Institutionalization entails both differentiation or specialization of roles and functions and formalization of explicit expectations about means and ends. More specifically, it entails (1) explicit assignment of responsibilities, (2) formalization of the analytical process, (3) coordination of information flows, and (4) centralization of control.[1]

Institutionalization is a bipolar rather than a binary concept: it is defined in terms of a continuum of practice. Two crucial points should be made. First, although institutionalization has both analytical and operational significance, it is impossible to specify the exact point of transition between firms that have institutionalized the assessment function and

---

1. The concept of institutionalization of the assessment function was initially developed by myself and Dr. Stephen Blank of the Conference Board in conjunction with preparation of materials for the International Social and Political Analysis Program.

those that have not. Second, complete institutionalization has not yet been achieved. The political assessment function is not fully established as an integral part of any of the organizations discussed in this study, or in any firm known to me. The function is only partly institutionalized: structures have been established, but relationships are still being formalized.

INSTITUTIONALIZATION DEFINED

Specialization is differentiation of function, role, or position. Do firms recognize the political assessment function as a separate and specialized task? Do distinct and identifiable positions or organizational units exist? Or, at a minimum, are responsibilities for political assessment assigned as part of the job specification of a given position? Formalization concerns the extent to which expectations about means and ends are complete. If the political assessment function is formalized, such procedures as establishing formats for reports, requiring that political evaluations accompany investment proposals, and standardizing analytical methods are made routine. Institutionalization thus entails differentiation or specification of responsibilities attached to a position and explicit rules for performance of duties associated with those responsibilities.

Katz and Kahn (1978) define an intrinsic function as a direct outcome of an organizational subsystem and an extrinsic function as an outcome whose primary effect is on other subsystems. The immediate and direct objective of the subsystem is intrinsic (e.g., selling the product); less immediate objectives (e.g., providing information about customers' needs and contributing to profit) are extrinsic. To continue the analogy, providing information about customers' needs is an extrinsic function of the sales force and an intrinsic function of a market research department. In essence, the intrinsic-extrinsic dimension is a measure of the degree of specialization. When the political assessment function is completely differentiated or specialized, it becomes intrinsic to the organizational unit responsible for it.

Differentiation of function and role may occur without specialization of organizational position or unit. A differentiated political assessment role may be, and often is, only a part of an individual's assigned activities. Complete specialization, however, requires the existence of a position or an organizational unit whose primary responsibility is political assessment. Differentiation of function and differentiation of role are closely correlated. If the function is a separate task, it entails a differentiated role. The task must be defined in terms of a set of activities or of specific forms of behavior associated with one or more positions. (Boundary spanning may be only one of several roles associated with any given position.) When function, role, and organizational position are all differentiated and formalized, a new management function has clearly emerged and is becoming institutionalized. If the function is not differentiated, it is performed as part of, or in conjunction with, another organizational activity, perhaps strategic planning or investment decision making. It may be implicit in another activity and performed intuitively, or it may be an explicit subtask consciously, if informally, undertaken.

As noted above, institutionalization is conceived of as a bipolar continuum rather than as a discrete or binary classification. The distinction between a firm in which the function is explicit but not differentiated, and a firm in which function and role are differentiated but position is not specialized, may not always be clear. Despite borderline cases, the vast majority of firms can be unambiguously classified.[2]

DETERMINANTS OF INSTITUTIONALIZATION

One of my basic hypotheses is that institutionalization of the political assessment function is an adaptive response by managers to a greater probability that potentially significant contingencies will arise from the political environment. Perceptions of such contingencies depend on (1) the vulnerability of the firm (or project) to the impact of political events and processes, and (2) the potential cost of contingencies should they arise.

Vulnerability to political risk is a function of the interaction between the environment and the firm's strategy and structure. Vulnerability alone, however, does not raise the specter of significant political risk.

2. At this point the typology must be considered static rather than dynamic. Although firms can be classified with a reasonable degree of confidence, a judgment as to whether the continuum represents an "evolutionary path" cannot be made from the available data. Comparing results with previous research (e.g., Root, 1968a) does, however, reveal a marked increase in the tendency to formalize the function. Root reported no evidence of a systematic approach to the assessment of political risk.

That depends also on the potential costs of politically generated contingencies. Cost, in turn, depends on (1) the extent of asset exposure and (2) the firm's evaluation of the effect of a reduction of or interruption in earnings. The former is governed by a number of factors, perhaps the most important being the amount of capital required to establish productive operations. The latter depends on the degree to which any given subsidiary is integrated into the global network (e.g., whether it is a major source of intermediate products), the value of the particular market, the size of the subsidiary, the degree of competition in the industry, and the like.

Vulnerability and cost are often independent of each other, and though there are exceptions to the rule—for example, the size of a subsidiary of a resource-based company may increase its visibility—it is usually difficult to predict the nature of the interaction and thus to determine the significance of any given contingency. For example, let us imagine a two-by-two matrix with relative vulnerability and cost as the rows and columns. The outcome of the cells on the diagonal are clearly determinate. High vulnerability and high cost mean a high probability of significant contingencies, and low vulnerability and low cost mean the opposite. On the other hand, the outcome of the other two cells is clearly indeterminate. As will be obvious shortly, numerous situations fall into those two categories.

I have assumed that, if environmental factors are held constant, pressures for institutionalization of political assessment, including both differentiation and formalization, flow from changes in organizational strategy. Although most of the important determinants of institutionalization fall within the vulnerability-cost framework, one is relatively independent of that context.

SIZE

Organizational size is a major determinant of the decision to differentiate organizational functions and roles, including the boundary spanning function. A large firm has the resources to support a complex organization and, as the limits of informal structure and flexibility are reached, the need to develop one. Since this argument applies to the differentiation and formalization of the political assessment function, institutionalization is to some degree a function of firm size.

INTERNATIONALIZATION

According to Robinson (1978), the evolution of the international firm involves two distinct processes: the geographic dispersion of resources and the pattern of functional and organizational development. While the two are certainly not independent, they are also not perfectly correlated. Both affect the vulnerability to and the cost of potential contingencies generated by the political environment.

Institutionalization is related to the degree of internationalization of the firm, measured by such variables as the number of countries in which the firm operates and the percentage of sales or profits generated by overseas operations. It is reasonable to argue that, if host country differences remain constant, the more widespread the international involvement the stronger the potential impact of the political environment. (See chap. 4 for supporting arguments.) The international dispersion of an enterprise transforms politics from a parameter to a variable, increasing environmental complexity and variability and thus uncertainty. Other things being equal, the higher the percentage of the firm's business generated abroad and the larger the number of countries in which it operates, the more vulnerable the firm is to contingencies arising from foreign political environments, and the greater its propensity to institutionalize the functions.

Such contingencies gain importance as impediments to the achievement of international objectives when a firm sets out to centralize control, unify strategy, and integrate operations across national borders, or, in other words, when it mobilizes and allocates resources on a global basis and pursues system-wide objectives through a common strategy. Any firm pursuing a global strategy is more vulnerable to contingencies arising from fragmented national political environments than is the firm whose international subsidiaries are a more autonomous group of national companies. In Perlmutter's (1969) terms, perceived vulnerability and costs increase as organizational strategy evolves from a polycentric to a geocentric orientation.

The evolution of a firm's international strategy is reflected in organizational structure. Furthermore, despite a degree of firm-to-firm variation in organizational development, a basic evolutionary path that characterizes most firms clearly exists (Robinson, 1978; Stopford and Wells, 1972; Vernon, 1971b).

The initial base for international expansion is export, but pressures quickly develop for more intensive participation in overseas markets through licensing or direct investment. Exporting usually leads to the establishment of manufacturing subsidiaries abroad and the creation of an international division. Most large American firms are organized on the basis of autonomous product divisions, and the international division is simply grafted onto the existing structure. The international division is most frequently organized by geographic area.

Although establishment of an international division is advantageous at early stages of internationalization, it also embodies inherent contradictions that tend to constrain the achievement of objectives as international operations become increasingly important. The structural dichotomy—international division and domestic product divisions—seems more and more artificial and dysfunctional as the firm's strategy achieves a global dimension. The result is often the replacement of the international division with a global form of organization in an effort to eliminate the distinction between international and domestic business and to pursue system-wide objectives through global mobilization and allocation of resources. Global organization may be based on geographic areas, worldwide product divisions, managerial functions, or a matrix combining aspects of each.

There is a direct, if not a unidirectional, relationship between strategy and structure. When a firm adopts a global strategy, it is forced to develop a compatible organizational structure. According to Robinson (1978), that point is reached when international sales account for 40 to 60 percent of the company's total. Stopford and Wells (1972) conclude that pressures for the transition to a global structure becomes intense when the size of the international division approaches that of the largest domestic product division.

Because the emergence of boundary spanning units is a result of perception of environmental contingencies, it would seem that, all else being equal, institutionalization of the political assessment function is closely related to the strategic and organizational evolution of the international firm. The propensity to institutionalize the function is stronger among firms with global strategies and structures than among firms whose domestic and overseas operations are differentiated, that is, firms that maintain separate domestic and international divisions.

EXPERIENCE

It is also likely that the institutionalization of political assessment is positively related to the extent of the firm's international experience. The longer the firm has been operating in the international arena, the stronger the possibility that the manager will be aware of contingencies that may arise from political environments. And indeed there is evidence that the pattern of expansion abroad usually proceeds from the familiar to the unfamiliar. The first subsidiaries are slated for countries that are closest to the home country, both geographically and culturally (e.g., Canada and the United Kingdom for American MNCs); as experience is gained, operations are established in more distant environments (see Richardson, 1971). While gaining experience abroad and venturing into less familiar environments, firms begin to realize that politically generated contingencies may be a problem. Yet experience also is likely to reduce perceptions of risk over time. As management gains more experience in a diversity of countries with disparate political institutions, the very differences should be less persuasive as determinants of perceptions of risk. Uncertainty is positively related to the degree of unfamiliarity.

INDUSTRIAL SECTOR AND TECHNOLOGY

Institutionalization of political assessment also depends on industrial sector and technology, which are closely related. For example, companies in the extractive sector—oil production or the mining of metals— realize that the political environment will have a significant impact on their operations. Extractive investment is heavily politicized in most host countries because of its dominant role in many developing economies and because of the singular history of the industry.[3] By the late 1970s, virtually all developing countries with significant foreign investment in petroleum production had expropriated at least some of the international companies (Kobrin, 1980). In addition, the technology used in extracting raw materials is mature and reasonably available on the open market. In what has been described as an obsolescing bargain (Bergsten, Horst, and Moran, 1978; Vernon, 1971*b*), negotiating power has shifted from the

3. See Bergsten, Horst, and Moran (1978), Moran (1974), and Vernon (1971*b*, 1977), for further discussion of the role of extractive FDI in the LDCs and its politicization over time.

foreign companies to governments of host countries. For these reasons companies engaged in extractive industries are particularly aware of political risk and more likely to respond by institutionalizing the assessment function.

The maturation and intensity of technology also affect perceptions of vulnerability and the tendency to institutionalize the function. Negotiating power and value of the contribution to the local economy are the important intervening variables. Firms in industries whose technology is new, intensive, and contained are perceived as transferring valuable resources to host countries.[4] When the technology is seen as necessary and is unavailable from alternative sources, the firm's bargaining power is strong. Firms in high technology industries, such as computers and industrial chemicals, are less vulnerable to political contingencies than are firms in industries whose technology is mature and widely available. In view of their limited contribution to the local economy in terms of needed resources and of the availability of alternative sources, the latter retain minimal bargaining power.[5]

The relationship between technology and the propensity to institutionalize the assessment function is extremely complex. One important factor is the potential cost of environmental-related contingencies, measured in part by the amount of investment required to establish productive facilities in a given country. Firms producing consumer products like soap, detergents, toilet articles, and packaged foods provide an example. Their production technology is mature and widely available, and the investment required to establish productive facilities is low relative to company size. Furthermore, their foreign direct investment is often defensive, motivated by the need to protect their share of the market in the face of barriers to continued import or local competition. Their investment considerations typically center on marketing rather than financial factors. Although firms making consumer products would seem to be vulnerable on the basis of technology, the assets at risk and the

---

4. Foreign direct investment entails the transfer across national borders of resources such as management, technology, capital, access to markets, and the like. Thus, one would expect that FDI in industries that are technologically innovative would be perceived as making a valuable contribution to the development of the host country.

5. A study of factors that affect vulnerability to expropriation suggests that firms in sectors such as textiles, shoe manufacturing, and food processing, which embody mature technologies, are significantly more vulnerable than those in pharmaceuticals, chemicals, and the like, whose technology is more intensive (see Kobrin, 1980).

nature of the investment decision process minimize the potential cost of any contingencies that may arise. Pressures for institutionalization of the political assessment function are thereby lessened, for potential gains are not justified by the value of assets or returns at risk in any given country.

ANALYSIS OF THE EMPIRICAL DATA

INDICATORS OF INSTITUTIONALIZATION

Two proximate indicators of institutionalization of the environmental assessment function were derived from the data gathered for this study. The first is the existence of a group or unit at corporate headquarters which reviews overseas political and social factors in conjunction with new investment proposals.[6] More than half (54.9 percent) of the respondents reported the existence of such a unit. A second, more restrictive, indicator of institutionalization requires both the existence of such a unit and the use of specific analytical methods. Thirty-five percent of the respondents reported a unit and routine use of one or more of six methods: standardized checklists, investment models, statistical analysis, scenario development, structured qualitative, or delphi.

The first indicator of institutionalization seems to measure differentiation of role and function, but the interview data reveal that it actually encompasses a broader range of experience. In practice, a number of firms wherein political assessment is a conscious activity performed within the organization, but is not differentiated but associated with another task, report the existence of a unit. (See chap. 6 for further discussion of this distinction.)

Although an admittedly imperfect approximation, the second indicator corresponds conceptually to institutionalization because it includes both differentiation of function and role and formalization of methodological approach. It is therefore used here as the primary measure of institutionalization.

Qualitative classification of firms using interview data to make judgments about differentiation of roles and functions (i.e., explicit as-

6. Respondents were asked, in separate questions, about the existence of a unit to review overseas social and political factors in conjunction with new investment and about a unit to monitor existing investment. Because responses to the two were virtually identical and the correlation between them was quite high, only the former is identified.

signment of responsibilities) and formalization of analytical approach is in rough accord with survey results. As noted above, 35 percent of the firms responding to the survey may be said to have institutionalized the political assessment function using the more restrictive indicator. Of 34 firms interviewed from which sufficient data were obtained to permit classification, 13, or 38 percent,[7] were judged to have institutionalized the assessment function.[8] Thus empirical data indicate that somewhat more than a third of the American firms included in this study have taken steps to differentiate and formalize the political assessment function. A marked change has taken place since Root (1968*a*) found no evidence of a systematic approach to political risk analysis in the firms he interviewed. (For an extensive analysis of the interview data, see chap. 6.)

DETERMINANTS OF INSTITUTIONALIZATION

A cross-tabulation of institutionalization (INSTUT) and a number of indicators of the organizational variables discussed above are presented in table 5–1. Again, 35.2 percent of all respondents (N = 193) have institutionalized the political assessment function.

The relationship between the propensity to institutionalize political assessment and firm size measured in terms of global sales is significant. Only 14.5 percent of firms with sales under $750 million have done so, compared with 54.4 percent of those with sales above $2.5 billion. This finding is supported by interview data. Mean global sales for the 13 firms that were judged to have institutionalized the function were $8,096 million, compared with $1,879 million for the 21 firms that had not. The difference is statistically significant.[9]

A significant relationship also exists between the propensity to institutionalize the function and two measures of internationalization. Of

7. The difference between the 35 percent of respondents reporting both a unit and use of a method in the mail survey and the 38 percent classified as institutionalized from the interview response is not statistically significant, even at the .10 level.

8. Comparison of survey and interview results reveals that three firms (9 percent) were misclassified on the basis of survey data. The error was unidirectional. All three firms were classified as institutionalized on the basis of survey data and not in the interviews. None of the firms in which the function was judged to be differentiated on the basis of interviews were classified as noninstitutionalized from survey data. Given the exploratory nature of this study, any attempt to classify the firms interviewed must be considered tentative. As noted previously, classification of firms must be based on ex post facto analysis of interview data that were not always specifically generated for that purpose.

9. T = 3.03 with 32 degrees of freedom; p = .002.

TABLE 5-1

INSTITUTIONALIZATION OF THE ASSESSMENT FUNCTION

Variable	Percentage of respondents	Number of cases	Statistical significance[a]
All cases	35.2	193	
Global sales		187	
(in millions of dollars)			
Less than 750	14.5		
751–2,500	39.7		$X^2 = 21.2$ p = .001
More than 2,500	54.4		
Percentage of sales abroad		178	
0–10	28.9		
11–25	29.2		$X^2 = 5.76$ p = .06
More than 25	46.7		
Number of countries		182	
1–4	20.6		
5–10	21.4		$X^2 = 15.2$ p = .001
11–20	37.8		
More than 20	52.2		
International experience		178	
Pre–World War II	39.4		
1945–1965	36.5		$X^2 = .79$ p = N.S.
After 1965	29.6		
International organization		168	
Preinternational	15.6		
International Division I	28.6		$X^2 = 16.27$ p = .001
International Division II	46.4		
Global	56.0		

[a] The letter p stands for statistical significance; N.S. = no significance.

firms with less than a quarter of their sales generated abroad, 29.0 percent reported institutionalization, as compared with 46.7 percent of those with more than 25 percent. Similarly, the value of INSTUT was 21 percent for firms operating in ten or fewer countries, 37.8 percent for those in 11 to 20 countries, and 52.2 percent for those in 21 or more countries.

Internationalization of strategy could not be determined from the available data, but a clear and significant relationship between INSTUT and the degree of internationalization of organizational structure emerged. The respondent's structure was classified as preinternational, early or mature international division (I or II), or global, based on the presence or absence of an international division and of a number of measures of internationalization (see App. A). Table 5–1 shows that only 15.6 percent of firms with preinternational structures and 28.6 percent of those with early international divisions reported institutionalization. In contrast, 46.4 percent of those with a late international division structure and 56.0 percent of those with true global structures have institutionalized the function.

The relevance of organizational structure—again assumed to reflect strategy—is confirmed by data derived from the interviews. Differences in organizational structure are significant.[10] Seventy-five percent of the institutionalized firms had either mature international division or global structure, compared with 62 percent of the noninstitutionalized firms. In contrast, a third of the noninstitutionalized firms could be characterized as having preinternational structures, whereas none of those in which the function is differentiated fell into that category.

It is noteworthy that the relationship between international experience (calculated from date of establishment of first subsidiary) and institutionalization is not significant. Possibly the nature rather than the extent of international experience is the variable related to the propensity to institutionalize. For example, pre–World War II experience may not have been relevant in terms of the causal texture of the environment encountered and its impact on the organization.

Gross differences in industrial sector are usually not significantly related to institutionalization. The outstanding exception is the raw materials or extractive sector. Fifty-seven percent of resource-based companies have institutionalized the environmental assessment function, as opposed to 35 percent of all respondents. (The difference is significant at the .05 level.) The absence of other significant direct relationships between sector and institutionalization may reflect empirical difficulties encountered in analyzing complex phenomena rather than the lack of a causal relationship.

The relationship between industrial sector and institutionalization

10. Chi-square significant at .05.

reveals the complex interaction between organizational stategy on the one hand, and texture of the environment on the other, as determinants of managerial perceptions of potentially significant politically generated contingencies. As noted above, vulnerability and cost are often independent of each other and often have opposite effects on managers' perceptions. For example, the bargaining power of firms producing consumer goods is limited because their product and process technologies are mature and their rents flow from the promotion of branded products. Their exposure is also limited, however, as relatively small amounts of capital are required[11] to establish and maintain operations. Whereas firms in that sector may be vulnerable to environmental contingencies, their potential cost is comparatively low.

On the other hand, firms with high technology have more bargaining power because their technology is restricted and necessary. Firms in such sectors as industrial machinery, chemicals, plastics must make substantial capital investments and thus face potentially high costs from politically generated contingencies, but their vulnerability is limited because they are technology-intensive. Since low vulnerability partly offsets high potential costs, the percentages of institutionalized firms in chemicals and plastics (41.2), high technology (30.4), primary and processed metals (37.5), and tools and industrial machinery (29.6) cluster around the mean for all firms (35.2).

All petroleum firms are classified as institutionalized. Petroleum is a highly politicized industry in most host countries, most oil firms are large and international, and their technology is mature or at least widely available. Their international investment is motivated by their need for access to reserves of crude oil, which are not always located in countries with positive social and political environments.

On the other hand, none of the consumer goods or drug firms interviewed had institutionalized the assessment function. The reasons are clear. In both industries asset exposure is minimal. For example, a pharmaceutical firm estimated that two-thirds of its investments abroad amounted to less than $12 million and the other third ranged from $15 to $25 million. Low capital investment clearly lessens the potential cost of

---

11. I have been unable to locate an empirical measure of the amount of capital required to establish facilities abroad across industries. As absolute rather than relative amounts of capital are at issue, indicators such as the capital-output ratio are not appropriate. What is needed is an indicator of average plant size in terms of capital investment, controlling for size of market.

contingencies arising from the political environment. It is difficult to justify commitment of substantial corporate resources to political assessment when only minimal capital is at risk.

The complex relationship between industrial sector and the propensity to institutionalize the assessment function may well be overshadowed by other factors, such as internationalization, organizational structure, and firm size. It does seem reasonable, however, to assume that differentiation of the assessment function is less likely when factors associated with industry reduce to a minimum the potential costs of political contingencies. Whereas one might expect to find firms in industrial sectors requiring substantial amounts of capital to operate abroad which have not institutionalized the function, one would not expect to find many firms in sectors where exposure is low which have. In the former case, a number of factors, including size and degree of internationalization, may reduce the probability of costly environmental contingencies, regardless of the amount of assets actually exposed abroad. On the other hand, if exposure is minimal the perceived cost and thus the significance of political contingencies will be low, regardless of other factors involved.[12]

RELATIVE IMPORTANCE OF DETERMINANTS OF INSTITUTIONALIZATION

Four significant organizational determinants of institutionalization have been singled out: firm size (global sales); percentage of sales generated abroad; number of countries in which a firm operates; and organizational structure. These determinants are not necessarily independent of one another, nor are they necessarily of equal importance. Sorting out their relative importance requires more extensive multivariate analysis.

Table 5–2 shows the rank order correlation coefficients (all variables are ordinally scaled) between each of these determinants (and experience) and institutionalization (INSTUT). All coefficients except that for international experience are significant; the relationships between INSTUT and size (SIZE), number of countries with operations (COUNTRIES), and international organization (INTORG) are roughly twice as

12. The point is supported by my experience in obtaining permission to conduct personal interviews in a sample of firms drawn from respondents to the mail survey. I attribute the willingness of the majority of firms to be interviewed to the high degree of interest in the topic combined with the fact that few firms had developed the function to the point where much existed which could be considered proprietary. On the other hand, the reluctance of consumer goods firms to be interviewed has to be taken as an indication of the lower salience of political risk to that sector.

TABLE 5-2

RANK ORDER CORRELATION COEFFICIENTS (KENDALL'S TAU)
BETWEEN DETERMINANTS AND INSTITUTIONALIZATION

Determinant	Correlation coefficient[a]
Global sales	.35
Percentage of sales abroad	.17
Number of countries	.30
International experience	−.06
International organization	.33

[a] All coefficients but experience are significant at .01 or higher.

strong as the relationship between percentage of sales generated abroad
(INTSALES) and INSTUT. Furthermore, the determinants of institutionalization are not independent, instead, they show a relatively high
correlation with one another. (A correlation matrix is presented in table
5–3.) The relative importance of (and the relationships among) the determinants of institutionalization are analyzed through the use of first-order
contingency tables and through multinomial logit analysis.

The first concern is the effect of the two measures of internationalization—global sales and number of countries—on institutionalization. As
expected, the correlation between them (Kendall's tau = .43) is moderately strong. As observed in chapters 2 and 4, the number of countries in
which a firm operates should be a more important determinant of institutionalization than the percentage of sales generated abroad. The former
measures diversity or heterogeneity of the firm's task environment; the
latter measures the relative importance to the firm of international operations. The difference is relevant for several reasons. First, it is heterogeneity that contributes to uncertainty and thus to the perception of
potentially significant political contingencies. Second, as the scope of international activities broadens, effective informal assessment of political
factors becomes more difficult. Problems encountered in attempting simultaneous operations in a large number of environments produce pressures for differentiation and formalization. Third, the more countries in
which the firm operates, the more likely it is to find significant constraints imposed as a result of political factors. As noted above, both
theory and empirical research in international business strongly suggest

TABLE 5-3

CORRELATION BETWEEN INDEPENDENT VARIABLES (KENDALL'S TAU)

Variable	Sales	Percentage of sales abroad	Number of countries	International organization
Sales	—	.229[a]	.431	.454
Percentage of sales abroad	—	—	.503	.533
Number of countries	—	—	—	.592

[a] All coefficients are significant at .001.

that foreign direct investment follows a pattern—expansion first into environments that are culturally and geographically closest to the home market, and only later into those more distant in both senses.[13] Finally, the point is intuitive, at least at the extreme. A firm that generates 50 percent of its sales abroad in a single country has less need for formal and differentiated environmental assessment than a firm 25 percent of whose sales are generated in thirty countries.

One means of testing this hypothesis is through first-order contingency table analysis. The relationship between INSTUT and sales generated abroad, controlling for the number of countries, may be compared with the relationship between INSTUT and number of countries, controlling for sales generated abroad. Table 5–4 reports the results of such a test. To the extent that a relationship between two variables is a function of a third intervening variable, one would expect the relationship to disappear or at least to diminish when controlling for the intervening variable. Comparison between zero-order and first-order (partial) gamma, which is an ordinal measure of association similar to Kendall's tau except that it differs in terms of the handling of ties,[14] may be used to test

13. There is a good deal of evidence in the international business literature supporting the existence of a definite pattern of firm expansion abroad through direct investment and licensing. See Richardson (1971) and Johanson and Vahine (1977).

14. Gamma is a measure of rank order correlation suitable for ordinally scaled data. The formula for computation is $\gamma = C\text{-}D/C\text{+}D$, where C is the number of concordant pairs and D, discordant pairs. As gamma excludes ties from the denominator it cannot be compared directly with Kendall's tau. See Blalock (1972:424).

the hypotheses. As shown by table 5–4, the gamma for INSTUT and INSALES falls to about a third of its zero-order value (.295 versus .093) when controlling for COUNTRIES. On the other hand, the degeneration of the relationship between INSTUT and COUNTRIES is minimal when controlling for INTSALES (.438 versus .395). To a large extent, then, the relationship between INSTUT and INTSALES derives from the fact that firms with a large percentage of sales generated abroad tend to operate in a large number of countries. Of the two measures of internationalization, COUNTRIES is the most important determinant of INSTUT. This conclusion is consistent with the results of the logit analysis presented below.

The relationship among institutionalization, organization of international operations, and number of countries is also germane. INTORG is constructed from data on the presence or absence of an international division, on COUNTRIES, and on INTSALES (see App. A). It is therefore possible that the relationship between INSTUT and INTORG is a function of the internationalization of operations rather than of underlying organizational strategy and structure. The data in table 5–5 do not support that argument. Again, zero- and first-order gammas are compared. The table reveals more deterioration in the relationship between INSTUT and COUNTRIES, controlling for INTORG, than in that between INSTUT and INTORG, controlling for COUNTRIES. Because of the obvious limits of multivariate contingency table analysis, I pursue the question of relative importance of determinants through logit analysis.

LOGIT ANALYSIS

The problem here is to analyze the simultaneous effects of a number of independent variables (firm size, internationalization, structure) on a dependent variable (institutionalization). Although ordinary least squares regression analysis is typically applied to this type of problem, difficulties arise when the dependent variable is discrete rather than continuous. Logit analysis, which is appropriate for evaluation of a model containing a binary dependent variable and categorical independent variables, has been applied to the problem at hand. The results are only summarized here. (For detailed technical discussion, see App. B.)

First, logit analysis confirms the earlier finding with regard to the relationship between institutionalization and internationalization. The

TABLE 5-4

RELATIONSHIPS AMONG INSTUT, INTSALES, AND COUNTRIES

INSTUT and INTSALES controlling for COUNTRIES:	
Zero-order gamma	.295 (100)
First-order gamma	.093 (32)
INSTUT and COUNTRIES controlling for INTSALES:	
Zero-order gamma	.438 (100)
First-order gamma	.395 (90)

significant direct relationship is between INSTUT and COUNTRIES. When an equation containing both INTSALES and COUNTRIES is evaluated, the coefficient for INTSALES does not approach significance but that for COUNTRIES is highly significant: that is, the larger the number of countries the higher the probability of institutionalization. In fact, adding INTSALES to a model containing INSTUT and COUNTRIES produces no significant effect.

Second, logit analysis is used to determine the relative importance of SIZE, COUNTRIES, and INTORG as determinants of INSTUT. On a univariate basis, all three variables produce a highly significant effect on INSTUT. When all three are included in the same equation, however, the coefficient of COUNTRIES is no longer significant. In fact, given the variables available, the model containing indicators of SIZE and INTORG cannot be improved upon as a way of explaining the probability that a firm has institutionalized the political assessment function. SIZE is the most important determinant of INSTUT, a conclusion consistent with the literature on boundary spanning surveyed in chapter 2. It is also noteworthy that the stage of evolution of the organizational structure of the international firm is a significant determinant of the propensity to institutionalize, and that its effects seem to transcend those of the degree of internationalization. Differences in organizational structure, which I assume reflect differences in strategy, have a significant effect on the propensity to differentiate and formalize the political assessment function.

TABLE 5-5

RELATIONSHIPS AMONG INSTUT, INTORG, AND COUNTRIES

INSTUT and INTORG controlling for COUNTRIES:	
Zero-order gamma	.476 (100)
First-order gamma	.275 (58)
INSTUT and COUNTRIES controlling for INTORG:	
Zero-order gamma	.430 (100)
First-order gamma	.191 (44)

CONCLUSIONS

The empirical data presented in this chapter are consistent with the conceptual arguments put forward in chapters 2 through 4. Holding environmental factors constant, institutionalization is related to organizational conditions that would increase the probability of perceptions of significant politically generated contingencies or, in the case of firm size, make it more difficult to deal with them on an informal basis. Large international firms in the latter stages of the evolution of a global strategy are significantly more likely to have assigned explicit responsibilities for political assessment and to begin to systematize its performance.

Factors such as the intensity of technology, politicization of the sector, asset exposure, and the degree of global integration of the firm affect both vulnerability to political events and processes and the potential cost of their impacts upon the firm. If both vulnerability and cost are perceived to be high, pressure for institutionalization is strong. If both are low, the opposite is true. The two intermediate cases are of interest. I hypothesize that when vulnerability is high and cost is low the probability of institutionalization is also low. The potential impacts on the firm do not justify a substantial commitment of resources to political assessment. On the other hand, high cost and low vulnerability imply low probability but potentially high impact, which may well justify a significant commitment of resources to institutionalize the assessment function.

It is important to note that all the arguments made about institutionalization up to this point assume a causal relationship between differentiation and formalization of the function and effectiveness of political assessment. The available data do not allow explicit testing of that hypothesis, and it obviously cannot be taken as an article of faith. The question of effectiveness requires a clearer understanding of patterns of organization of political assessment.

6
Organization of the Political Assessment Function

Wilensky (1967:179) concludes his study of intelligence in a pessimistic vein: "If anything is clear from this book it is that intelligence failures are built into complex organizations. On the one hand, the most readily accomplished revamping of structure turns out to be mere organizational tinkering. . . . On the other hand, even when the reorganization of formal structure is pushed to its limit, the basic sources of distortion remain in some degree."[1] Although it may be impossible to resolve the conflict between organizational complexity and an effective intelligence function, organizational design is without doubt a crucial factor.

Effective political assessment is a managerial problem. Managers must exploit existing organizational resources to scan the external environment, analyze information flows, communicate the results within the organization, and use the acquired data in policymaking. Like all managerial functions, successful political assessment requires the design and implementation of an effective strategy. The link between strategy and structure is well established. Although the notion of an optimal structure uniquely determined by strategy may not be reasonable, choice of structure does make a difference. Structure is contingent on strategy; not all organizational structures are equally effective in implementing a specific strategy (Galbraith and Nathanson, 1978; see also Chandler, 1962).

1. Wilensky concluded that the organizational impediments to the effective gathering and utilization of intelligence require managers to ignore existing organizational structures and go directly to sources: "Thus, the alert executive is everywhere forced to bypass the regular machinery and seek firsthand exposure to intelligence sources in and out of the organization" (1967:179).

The political assessment function is universal among international firms but its location, its links to the environment and to planners and decision makers, and the resources it commands vary considerably from one firm to another. Organization and, more specifically, institutionalization do make a difference. The explicit assignment of responsibilities, the systemization of analytical process, and the coordination of information flows all contribute to more accurate assessments of potential contingencies and to more effective integration of those assessments into planning and decision making.

In this chapter I describe the range of organization and performance of the political assessment function in the firms surveyed and interviewed in this study. To facilitate analysis a typology of institutionalization of political assessment, based on differentiation of function and role and formalization of process, is developed. An understanding of the organization of the function underlies the discussion of its performance (i.e., scanning and utilization) in later chapters and of its effectiveness in the concluding chapter.

A TYPOLOGY

Systematic classification of a phenomenon serves two functions. First, it provides an analytical guide or "road map." Second, by enabling the analyst to factor the phenomenon into its component parts, it permits the analysis of determinants and effects. The typology facilitates better understanding of the process itself and, through classification of the firms interviewed, further exploration of differences among companies at various stages of institutionalization.

The typology of institutionalization, presented below in outline form, makes a basic distinction between firms in which the function has not been differentiated and those in which it has. Since political assessment is universal, firms that have not differentiated the function have made it, either implicitly or explicitly, a part of other responsibilities. It is implicit in planning and decision making even when neither function, role, nor position is differentiated. Managers making foreign direct investment decisions must take politics into account. Assessments may be intuitive, may be expressed in dichotomous terms (i.e., a good or a bad investment climate), may reflect impressions gained from travel, the media, and the like, and need not be formally presented or even explicit. Nonetheless, they are an important determinant of, or deterrent to, investment decision making.

There is a distinction in practice among firms where the function is implicit. In certain industrial sectors, the managerial function itself is so politicized that environmental assessment is an inherent part of it. The best examples are the large international construction firms that deal extensively with governments in less developed countries. The size of the project and the governmental level at which decisions are reached make the relationship between firm and client a political one.[2] In a very real sense a large part of the international manager's job is political analysis, whether or not it is recognized as an explicit function.

Institutionalization of the Political Assessment Function

I. *Noninstitutionalized*: function, role, and position not differentiated
   A. Function implicit
      1. Not inherent in task: intuitive judgment by line and particularly top management
      2. Inherent in nature of task, especially in construction and mineral trading firms
   B. Function explicit: informal responsibility of line management

II. *Institutionalized*
   A. Function and role differentiated, position not differentiated: part-time responsibility attached to staff position
   B. Function, role, and position differentiated: function may be intrinsic
      1. Staff coordinator
      2. Independent units
         a. Political reporting
         b. Systems approach

In the modal category for the noninstitutionalized firm, the function is explicit but not differentiated. The political assessment function

2. The politicization of publicly funded construction contracts is not limited to less developed countries. During my years in Boston, the political nature of the construction business, particularly in the case of the University of Massachusetts, was painfully obvious from headlines in the local papers.

may not appear in any formal job description, but it is an explicit responsibility of international management. Affiliate managers may routinely report on political developments in monthly letters or telephone conversations. Investment proposals will contain a few paragraphs (or perhaps even pages) of analysis of political factors. Nevertheless, the function, though explicit, is informal and unstructured. It is perceived as part of the task of line or, in a few instances, staff management, and it is in no sense differentiated or specialized.

At a minimum, institutionalization requires differentiation or specialization of function and role. Political assessment is recognized as a distinct task, as a specialized set of activities assigned to a given position. In a sense, the function exists independently of a given individual and, in fact, the ability to handle political analysis may be one of the requisites for a position. Typically, in this minimal degree of institutionalization, part-time responsibilities are assigned to a junior-level analyst in a staff group, perhaps a strategic planning unit or the treasurer's office.

In complete specialization of the assessment process, function, role, and position are all differentiated, and in some instances the function is intrinsic. Specialized organizational units whose primary mission is political assessment are created. The two basic types of assessment units differ in degree of independence. In the first, the emphasis is on coordination and facilitation rather than on original assessment and evaluation. The unit is typically an integral part of a staff group, such as a strategic planning group.

The second type of assessment unit is a relatively independent one. It generates political assessments either through a political reporting approach or through a structured and formalized attempt to develop and implement an assessment system.

A breakdown of the number and percentage of the firms interviewed in each category of the typology is presented in table 6–1. Thirteen of the 34 firms (38 percent) for which data are available are classified as institutionalized, that is, as having differentiated the function. Of these, six have fully differentiated function, role, and position. Thus, roughly 18 percent of the firms interviewed have specialized political assessment units. Twenty-one firms (62 percent) are classified as noninstitutionalized; that is, the function is not differentiated. In two-thirds of these political assessment is explicit, and in one-third it is implicit. Therefore, as noted in chapter 5, the qualitative classification of firms using interview data to make judgments about differentiation of the assessment function is in

TABLE 6-1

THE INSTITUTIONALIZATION TYPOLOGY

| | *Noninstitutionalized* | | | |
| | *Function implicit* | | | |
	responsibility	*inherent*	*Function explicit*	*Total*
Number of firms (N = 34)	5	2	14	21
Percent of total	15	6	41	62
Mean sales (in millions of dollars)	1,366	3,520	1,826	1,878

| | *Institutionalized* | | | |
| | *Function but not position differentiated* | *Function and position differentiated* | | |
	(Part-time staff)	*Coordinator*	*Unit*	*Total*
Number of firms (N = 34)	7	3	3	13
Percent of total	21	9	9	38
Mean sales (in millions of dollars)	3,503	7,182	19,638	8,096

rough accord with the quantitative classification based on survey responses to questions about the existence of units and the utilization of formal methods. Thirty-eight percent of the firms interviewed were judged to have institutionalized the function, as opposed to 35 percent of those responding to the survey.

Table 6–1 also gives the mean global sales of firms in each category. With the exception of the two firms classified as noninstitutionalized, implicit, and inherent—a somewhat anomalous category—there is a perfect ordinal correlation between sales and category. The difference between noninstitutionalized and institutionalized firms is striking and statistically significant.[3] The mean sales for the six firms with specialized political assessment positions (or units) are more than seven times the mean sales of the average noninstitutionalized firm.

3. $T = 3.03$ with 32 degrees of freedom; $p = .002$.

TABLE 6-2

LOCATION OF RESPONSIBILITY FOR POLITICAL ASSESSMENT IN
FIRMS NOT REPORTING A GROUP CHARGED WITH THAT FUNCTION
(N = 76)

Location	Percentage
Top management	72.6
Headquarters, international division[a]	76.9
Affiliate managers	28.2
Regional headquarters	28.4
Product line management	21.6
Planning	18.9
Legal	12.2
Economics department	5.4
Government relations	0.0

[a] Includes only firms with an international division.

LOCATION OF THE POLITICAL ASSESSMENT FUNCTION

An overview of the location of the political assessment function is provided by responses to the mail survey. Of the 193 firms that responded, 106 (55 percent) reported the existence of a group (or groups) within corporate headquarters to review social and political factors when new investments are proposed. This proportion encompasses a broader range of firms than does the group that have institutionalized the assessment function (see chap. 5).

Firms that have no unit charged with political assessment tend to locate the function at upper levels of management. In 73 percent of such respondents the responsibility lies with top management; 77 percent of the firms that have an international division place the responsibility there (see table 6–2). Only slightly more than a fourth of the firms not reporting a unit assign the assessment function to lower levels of line management, and only a small minority report the involvement of staff groups. The survey data are thus consistent with the conclusion that political analysis in noninstitutionalized firms is an informal process, with assessment and evaluation handled as part of top management decision making.

TABLE 6-3
LOCATION OF GROUPS TO REVIEW OVERSEAS POLITICAL
ENVIRONMENTS
(N = 115)

Location	Percentage
International division[a]	88.1
Planning	66.1
Treasurer/finance	67.0
Legal department	57.5
Product lines	41.7
Corporate economist	25.2
Public affairs	20.8

[a]Includes only firms with an international division.

The location of political assessment groups in firms reporting the existence of one or more such groups is shown in table 6–3. The vast majority (88.1 percent) of firms with an international division locate groups there. About two-thirds of respondents with such units locate them within two major staff groups: planning and the treasurer/finance function. It is not surprising to find that the legal department is involved in more than half (57.5 percent) of these firms, for many political factors of concern are inextricably bound up with legal issues.

The corporate economist's office and the public affairs section are only moderately involved in political analysis. A fourth of firms with groups have located them in the corporate economist's office; about a fifth, in public affairs.[4] That the assessment function is not frequently located in public or governmental affairs groups may reflect their fairly recent emergence.

ORGANIZATION OF THE ASSESSMENT FUNCTION

Using the typology as a guide, organization and performance of the political assessment function are explored through examples selected from

4. The petroleum industry is an exception; 42.9 percent of respondents in that sector reported assessment units located in corporate economics sections. This situation may re-

the interview data. Whereas the cases represent actual firms, the need to maintain absolute confidentiality is paramount. Hence certain data, such as the industrial sector, may be presented at a higher level of aggregation than would be optimal from the point of view of analysis alone.

FUNCTION NOT DIFFERENTIATED BUT IMPLICIT

In two firms the political assessment function is neither differentiated nor explicit. The first is a medium-size producer of fabricated metal and plastic products with approximately 12 percent of its sales generated by international operations in more than twenty countries. International operations are decentralized and the financial reporting system is the vehicle through which the small headquarters organization excercises its limited control over affiliates. There is no planning department, and forward planning is described as a "bottom-up" process based on the efforts of subsidiary management. The polycentric organizational structure clearly developed from the historical process of internationalization. When the firm went abroad to service its major customer (the oil industry), its FDI was basically defensive. The result was a network of joint ventures that were given considerable autonomy. Despite the survival of only a few joint ventures, and despite extensive diversification of the product line produced abroad, the legacy of the initial pattern of internationalization remains.

The company relies on affiliate management for assessments of political environments, a situation that is not unusual, since most of the firms surveyed depend mainly on local management for political information. In this firm, however, headquarters management was only peripherally involved; the managers interviewed did not even mention their own role in the process through travel, discussions with outside sources, and the like. In fact, they did not suggest the use of any outside sources in the assessment process and, when probed, mentioned only other firms. As one of the managers reported, "What happens in Rome, until it affects our business directly, doesn't really concern us" (Italian communism was the subject under discussion).

Political assessment seems to be completely informal. No routine reporting or analysis in the context of investment decision making or

---

flect the historical politicization of the industry and the resulting difficulty of separating politics from economics.

strategic planning was noted. Rather, assessment takes the form of a continuing discussion focused on specific problems.

The second company is a medium-size chemical manufacturer with about 35 percent of its sales generated abroad, two-thirds of them in Europe. International operations are regional, with one group responsible for Europe, one for the western hemisphere (excluding the United States), and the third for Asia. All the European manufacturing affiliates are wholly owned; in the Americas and Asia they are exclusively joint ventures.

The primary responsibility for political assessment, which is quite informal, rests with the affiliates, especially those outside Europe. No routine reporting requirements were mentioned by any of the managers interviewed, nor was it ever suggested that staff groups were called upon. In outlining an assessment of Brazil, for example, the manager in charge of that region described the local affiliate as a joint venture and claimed that host country employees had good contacts with the government at the "highest levels."

When this firm is compared with the first firm, a major difference is seen: regional managers are actively engaged in the process. They form assessments of political environments based on travel and on discussions with sources such as bankers, lawyers, accountants, and sometimes government agencies. One regional manager said that he maintained close relationships with the State Department at the country desk level.

In summary, the political assessment function in these two firms may be characterized as informal, nonroutine, and reactive. The basic responsibility for tracking political factors, though not clearly defined, lies with subsidiaries. Headquarters management takes part in some situations. With the almost complete absence of written assessments, evaluation, when necessary, is achieved through informal discussion. In fact, even in the context of new investment decisions, political factors may be ignored unless the environment is obviously a risky one. The European regional manager for one of the firms interviewed found that, to his later regret, "so-called environmental factors played no role in new investment decisions."

FUNCTION IMPLICIT BUT INHERENT

In a number of firms the political assessment function is inherent in the structure of corporate activities, even though it is neither differentiated nor explicit. Basic strategic activities include political assessment, in varying degrees. A large mineral trading firm is an excellent example.

The key individuals in the firm are traders who are responsible for a specific commodity. To function, they need a great deal of information about everything that can affect the commodity they trade internationally. Political factors are obviously included. The assessment function, though not even minimally formalized, is an inherent part of the trader's job. In fact, in this instance it may not be reasonable to attempt to distinguish between market and political factors. Intra- and interstate politics are a basic determinant, for example, of the demand for precious metals.

The traders travel widely and enjoy a broad range of personal contacts. It is noteworthy that the firm regards the interchange of information as a basic and crucial function. Meetings are frequent and are deemed important, and the company's telex system is said to rival that of the State Department.[5]

FUNCTION NOT DIFFERENTIATED BUT EXPLICIT

In firms in this category the political assessment function is explicit in that it is a recognized and routinized aspect of managerial responsibilities. It is, however, not differentiated; it is considered an integral part of a manager's job, and little in the way of specialization is evident. In the majority of such firms political assessment is an exclusive responsibility of line management. If staff members are involved, it is usually on an informal and unspecialized basis. Thus the function is explicit but it is neither differentiated nor formalized.

The potential impact of politically generated environmental contingencies on the fourteen firms in this classification is limited by a number of factors. First, half are either pharmaceutical firms or consumer goods producers (in one instance, both) whose investment in any given country is rather low and is defensively motivated. For three of the remaining firms, international operations are limited. Two are suppliers to another industry, drawn abroad primarily by the need to service major customers. Of the remaining two firms, one is concerned with offshore

5. There is an obvious parallel with the intelligence systems in large Japanese trading firms (see Yoshino, 1976; Vogel, 1979). Vogel claims that Japanese trading companies have better international networks than do other firms, either Japanese or foreign. In fact, he believes that these firms have at times outdone the Japanese Foreign Ministry, even in the area of political information.

rather than market-oriented production. That is, its international investment is motivated by the need to find relatively low labor cost facilities to produce components for the world market and thus its vulnerability is limited to supply side considerations. Although the fourteenth firm is very international, its level of asset exposure in each host country is low.

Four firms may be selected as examples. The first is a pharmaceutical company with global sales of somewhat over $1 billion and manufacturing operations in almost forty countries. The organizational structure may be described as a limited area-product matrix dominated by geographic regions. Political assessment is basically a line responsibility. The head of international operations stressed his opinion that political assessment does not require specialized expertise, either within or outside the company. The director of international planning confirmed this view, noting that it would take too long to bring outside consultants "up to speed in our area."

Top international management, regional managers, and affiliate general managers are all deeply and directly involved. The affiliate general manager was described as the chief political officer of the local company. The assessment process, though it may be dominated by affiliate and area managers, certainly does not account for a major part of their activities, except in highly unusual circumstances. We are explicitly told, in fact, that general managers focus first on the product, where "95 percent of their thinking is concentrated."

Political assessment is routinized in two contexts: the affiliate manager's reports and the planning process. Each affiliate manager writes to his or her area manager once a month. The report is structured, based on an extensive checklist of financial and business factors. At the end is a single overall question about the political environment. Answers to this question vary from a simple notation, "No change," to a number of pages in times of crisis. One report from the manager of a fairly stable country devoted three lines to political factors.

The annual and five-year plans prepared by the affiliates require formal comment on the economic and political climate and outlook in each country. General managers are responsible for outlining key environmental issues that could have either a negative or a positive effect on operations. The planning department produces an executive summary of affiliate plans, including an analysis of the social and political environment facing the company, but the summary is based on assessments provided by line management.

The second example is a pharmaceutical and consumer goods producer with global sales of almost \$2 billion and extensive operations abroad. International operations are organized through an area-structured international division. Again, the primary responsibility for political assessment lies with affiliate general managers and area vice-presidents. Evaluations of the political environment are required both for capital appropriation requests and for strategic planning. Only to that extent, however, is the process formal. The format, substance, and breadth of the assessment are left almost entirely to affiliate and regional management. The contribution of staff members is limited; individuals in financial groups have, at times, provided some analyses of social and political environments. It was emphasized however, that no one within the firm can be considered a specialist in this area. One example of a long-range plan (for a major Latin American country) contained a rather extensive discussion of the economic environment, but only one paragraph was devoted to political matters.

The third firm, though relatively small, is a widespread international producer of tools and appliances. It is organized in area-based international divisions. The company relies almost entirely on overseas managers for political information. The assessment process is less formal than in the first two firms discussed, but it is nonetheless explicit. Investment and reinvestment proposals all include environmental background information, perhaps a review of the government's economic and political performance or an assessment of the general investment climate. In addition, affiliate and regional managers are responsible for informing corporate management of any political factors that may affect operations, "at the earliest possible stage." Prime emphasis is to be placed on the manager's development and maintenance of appropriate local contacts.

The fourth firm is of interest in that it uses an informal but explicit approach to political assessment. It is a small manufacturer of machine tools whose international operations are both recent and limited. In fact, the responsibility for international business had been centralized under one individual only four months before the interview, and it was apparent that the operating divisions continued to exert substantial power within the firm. The managerial style is unstructured, depending largely on personal decision making and on informal interpersonal relationships.

As expected, the political assessment process is also very unstructured, but it is clearly explicit. It is the responsibility of top management: the chief executive officer (CEO), the international vice-president, and the treasurer. The objective of the process is to provide a collective understanding of the impact of political factors on the business. Consultants are used routinely as needed. Top management puts together possible scenarios of social, political, and economic environments using information gained from banks, other companies, conversations, and interviews, sometimes with cabinet-level officials or local counsel. The seeming exclusion of affiliate managers from the process may reflect jurisdictional problems caused by the recent attempt to establish independent responsibility for international operations.

In summary, the political assessment function of firms in this category is explicit but not specialized. It is explicit in two senses. First, it is a recognized responsibility of management, typically of country and regional management. Second, in varying degrees it is routinized in that certain internal actions or events, such as an investment proposal or the strategic planning process, require the preparation of a written political assessment. The function, however, is not differentiated or specialized. It is a responsibility that, in other than extraordinary circumstances, accounts for only a minor portion of the manager's time. Assessment, far from being the manager's prime focus, is merely a marginal factor in recruitment and reward, unless circumstances happen to be exceptional. Finally, the function is not specialized in the sense that formalization is minimal. Assessment may be required, but its form and substance are discretionary.

FUNCTION DIFFERENTIATED BUT NOT POSITION

Political assessment may be said to be institutionalized in firms where the function is differentiated but the position is not. Differentiation is based on specialization. The seven firms in this classification all employ at least one individual, always in a staff group, who has specialized political assessment expertise and is formally assigned assessment responsibilities on a part-time basis. That, however, is not the same as employing a political assessment specialist; no member of the organization is exclusively concerned with political environments. Still, environmental assessment is a significant responsibility for the individual assigned to it, and presumably competence and performance affect recruitment and reward. The difference between firms in this category and in the one discussed previously is a matter of degree, of the extent of formalization and specialization.

There are, however, clear-cut distinctions between the attributes of firms in this category and those of firms in which the function is explicit but not differentiated. The potential impact of political contingencies on all the firms in this category seems to be stronger, owing either to exposure or to the characteristics of the industrial sector. Two firms are in the oil industry and three are in sectors that require substantial capital investment to establish manufacturing facilities. The sixth is a major international construction firm engaged in large-scale public projects. Only the last is potentially ambiguous, as it produces high-technology products that seemingly give it considerable bargaining power.

From the perspective of the firm as a whole, the assessment function in companies in this category resembles that in companies where the function is not differentiated but explicit. The primary source of assessments is likely to be line managers, and assessments are motivated by much the same kind of internal stimuli. The difference, which has conceptual importance, is that through evolution or design an individual or a unit within the firm has been given part-time environmental assessment responsibilities which are not part of a more general managerial function.

An oil company and a producer of paper products have been chosen as examples. Staff responsibility for political assessment in the petroleum company is lodged in the office of the corporate economist, where junior analysts prepare two types of reports with political content. The first, a monthly report giving a thumbnail sketch of developments in markets of interest to the company, is primarily concerned with economic developments and only in a limited way with politics. Reports of the second kind, concerned with politics as well as with the economy, are produced on an on-demand basis, usually when a new investment is being considered or when something "of interest" happens in an important country. The corporate economist's office, though not the primary source of political information, was mentioned as an important source by all the line managers interviewed. In comparison, line managers in companies where the function is explicit but not differentiated rarely mentioned staff groups as sources of political information. The firm also maintains a Washington office staffed by a former intelligence officer who apparently spends 10 to 15 percent of his time in political assessment. His duties are unstructured and his relationship with the corporate economist is informal.

The assessment function is more formalized and structured in the paper company. An analyst in the international treasurer's office has formal responsibility for analysis of investment environments, including political and social aspects. Assessments are undertaken independently whenever new capital investment abroad is under consideration. They follow a detailed outline or checklist for a "country study." Considerable emphasis is placed on political factors. If the report is satisfactory, the next step is to assemble a field task force composed of representatives from the international treasurer's office, an international staff group, and the operating group whose members visit the country and meet with individuals there. The formalized function is restricted to new investments. No attempt is made routinely to monitor environments in which the firm has established operations.

Thus the organizational structure of the political assessment function in firms in this category represents a first stage of institutionalization. Whereas no one individual can accurately be described as a political assessment specialist, specialized expertise and responsibility clearly exist. The function, but not the position, is differentiated.

In all seven firms responsibility for political assessment has been explicitly assigned to a staff group on a part-time basis. In the two firms singled out for detailed consideration, the function resides in the economist's and the international treasurer's offices. In the others it is located in groups such as corporate marketing services, corporate product services (a planning and development function), public affairs, the legal department, new business development, and a divisional manufacturing staff concerned with international plant location. In no instance is the group in question either primarily occupied with or solely responsible for political assessment; however, it plays a nontrivial and recognized role in the process. The political assessment function is differentiated in the sense that it exists independently of business unit managerial responsibilities.

FUNCTION AND POSITION BOTH DIFFERENTIATED

In six of the firms interviewed both function and position are differentiated. A specialized individual or unit exists whose primary responsibility is the assessment and evaluation of political factors abroad. Institutionalization, however, is a matter of degree. In virtually every firm interviewed or surveyed, line management—that is, affiliate and regional or product managers—were the primary source of information about political environments. In some firms assessment units seem to be an integral part of the process, with power to influence outcomes. In others they are no more than an additional source of information about political factors, for consideration by decision makers. (For the utilization of assessments, see chap. 9.)

The six firms where function, role, and position are differentiated all face potentially significant contingencies resulting from political environments. One is a major international oil company and another is a large international construction firm in direct contact with numerous governments. The other four are major American industrial firms whose investment in manufacturing facilities abroad requires a substantial amount of capital. They fall into the heavy industry category. The firms may be divided into two subclassifications: (1) those whose political assessment specialist functions primarily as a coordinator or a facilitator, and (2) those where the primary task of an individual or a unit is to produce original, often independent, analyses.

THE STAFF COORDINATOR

When interviewed, the largest of the three construction firms had just established an assessment unit charged with a coordinating function. The company is heavily international and does a large percentage of its business directly with host governments. Each operating division is responsible for worldwide operations and has its own business development department.

The newly appointed head of the corporate assessment unit, a senior vice-president, said that his primary mission was to centralize information gathering and assessment with regard to external business environments. He specified two immediate objectives: first, the development of an intracompany information system; second, the establishment of relationships with the operating divisons. The second is perceived to be as important as the first, if not more so. These relationships are completely informal and, in fact, participation is on a voluntary basis. The motivation for establishing the unit was the need for centralization and coordination when the company was confronted by problems associated with multiple decision points vis-à-vis the environment. In response, a senior vice-president who was near retirement was charged with the development of such a function. Partly in jest, the new unit manager said he was given the job because he was the only person in the company with no enemies and because, being close to retirement, he did not pose a threat to anyone. A second position will be filled from within the firm.

In this firm, political assessment is an inherent part of the primary business activity. Business development and marketing personnel in the operating divisions are still the main source of political assessments, but the need for coordination has led to the establishment of a unit responsible for better utilization of intrafirm resources through development of a more effective internal information system.

A second example of coordination and facilitation is a large chemical firm with extensive international operations; about a third of its sales are generated abroad. Organizational structure is based on a product-area matrix. The firm's six operating companies have worldwide responsibilities, although to a varying degree. The international division, which shares profit responsibilities, comprises three self-contained regional groups. Each has its own planning staff. The matrix has evolved over time from almost entirely product-dominated to what is now described as a 70 percent/30 percent product area mix. The political assessment unit is part of the planning department of the international division. A manager for international economic and political analysis reports to the planning director. The former is clearly a specialist, with a degree in international relations and experience with a major oil company in the same capacity.

The chief function of the unit is coordination, as most of the environmental assessments are made by the regional groups. It was in fact the need to have assessments pulled together which led to establishment of the unit, which acts as an intermediary between line management and the planning departments in the regional groups. It parcels out requests for studies and follows up on the reports to ensure that the information provided is realistic. For example, the head of the international division wanted to know what impact French elections might have on the company's operations. The unit forwarded the request for a study to the European regional group, suggesting a possible outline to the area planning director. The coordinating unit is now developing checklists for the use of regional planning departments in preparing country studies.[6]

Political assessments are made in monthly reports, capital appropriation requests, and strategic planning. In each instance, the basic source of information is host country affiliate management and the regional groups. As in firms where the function is not differentiated, operating management supplies the needed data. In this firm, however, the func-

6. The unit also works on developing a complex priority ranking of countries in which the company operates, based on macro- and microeconomic and political factors.

tion is differentiated and more formalized, both at regional headquarters and at corporate levels. The corporate international political assessment unit seeks to coordinate performance across regions and operating companies. The objective is a more systematic approach to environmental assessment, increased comparability of reports, and more effective use of existing intrafirm resources.

The third firm in which coordination is the primary role of the political assessment unit is a large, diversified industrial firm. Although the organization structure is complex, with both international and product divisions, it is not a matrix in the true sense. Rather, the international division, which has profit responsibility, is linked to the product divisions through internal agreements.

The manager of environmental analysis, an economist with a strong interest in noneconomic factors, is associated with the international planning department. The unit's primary duty is to coordinate and facilitate political analysis, but its relationships with operating affiliates are more formal than in the other two companies with similar structures. The assessment unit provides political-environmental information for strategic business units' plans and for their investment proposals. It has some control over outcomes, as it must formally sign off completed documents. The manager of environmental analysis puts together environmental assumptions for planning in a large number of countries. Although he does some of the analysis himself, most of it is handled by a worldwide network of consultants. The unit also compiles an international environmental summary, whose sections deal with trends in the international environment at large, and a more detailed summary for somewhat less than thirty major countries. Again, since extensive use is made of consultants, the role of the environmental analysis manager is primarily to edit and organize the information. The unit has developed a basic outline for the use of consultants, and it also conducts in-depth studies as need dictates.

The primary responsibility for political analysis rests with the strategic business units. The assessment unit coordinates company-wide efforts, provides a consistent set of assumptions for planning, and acts as a resource for the rest of the company.

POLITICAL ANALYSIS UNITS

Three of the firms interviewed had differentiated and specialized political assessments units, staffed by specialists responsible for generating independent political analyses. The firms are large: the smallest had annual sales of more than $5 billion, and the other two, of more than $25 billion each. The first firm to be discussed produces consumer durables, which require investment of extremely large amounts of capital to establish manufacturing facilities abroad. The company is the most widespread internationally of all American firms in the industry.

International operations are organized on a geographic basis. The political assessment unit, which consists of two full-time professionals who have foreign service backgrounds, is located in the international governmental affairs department. It was created in the mid-1970s in response to the chief executive officer's perception of a need for a source of political information independent of operating management.

The unit provides analysis of specific countries on a regular basis and responds to requests for political analysis to support strategic planning and investment proposals. There are no standard operating procedures to define its relationships with other staff groups or with line management. The unit operates entirely on an informal, ad hoc basis. In fact, other staff and line managers interviewed did not consider international governmental affairs to be the primary source of political analysis. Whereas the assessment function is clearly differentiated and formalized, it is only minimally institutionalized within the context of the company as a whole. (Postinterview contacts with company officials, however, reveal that a gradual process of institutionalization is taking place over time.)

The analysts rely on secondary sources, on outside contacts such as banks and other companies, and heavily, as expected from their background, on the Washington foreign policy establishment. Output takes the form of reports and memoranda.

The primary source of political analysis in the company at large is clearly affiliate and regional managers. The comptroller responsible for a major portion of international operations admitted that the firm has no systematic or logical system for the evaluation of political environments. The individuals concerned "look carefully" at the country in question, prepare detailed analyses of political and social systems, assess such factors as the country's attitude toward foreign investors, and use the resulting evaluations as background for strategic planning and decision making.

All planning documents begin with an evaluation of the external environment, including the competitive situation as well as social, political, and regulatory conditions. The extent and the source of analyses vary from country to country. In Europe, use is made of consultants and of whatever in-house capacity for governmental and political analysis exists in the region. In other areas local operating management is relied on almost exclusively. Also, top management officials, both staff and line, travel extensively and maintain numerous in-country contacts. The vice-president responsible for Latin American operations reported that on a recent trip he had spent less than 50 percent of his "in-country" time with his own people. He recalled extensive conversations with dealers, with both local and expatriate business people, and with government officials at policymaking levels.

The company's performance of the political assessment function is not unlike the typical firm where the function is explicit but not differentiated. Affiliate and regional managers are the primary source of political information, and political assessment is basically reactive, triggered by investment proposals, the strategic planning cycle, and the like. There is, however, a major difference. Management at the highest level, recognizing the need for an independent source of environmental information, differentiated the function by establishing a specialized political analysis unit. The unit is still at the periphery of the organization, but it will probably become more integrated over time. The vice-president for Latin American operations pointed out that the firm was placing increased reliance on external sources through the development of staff people who have good judgment and are familiar with the information already available. The reference was clearly to the international governmental affairs department.

The second example is a major oil company in which the assessment function is differentiated through the employment of three specialists who engage in traditional political analysis. All have foreign service or international relations backgrounds.

Although a political analysis capacity has existed in the company since the end of World War II, the function was first formally established in 1965, when the chief executive officer set up a unit to furnish "unbiased and unfiltered reports that did not emerge through any division." In the words of one of the respondents, he wanted his own "mini-intelligence unit." The unit, lodged in the international governmental affairs department at the corporate level, reported directly to the chief executive officer. Some years later, when a change in management led to reorganization, the unit was merged with the international public affairs department and "pushed down" from the corporate to the international division level. By the mid-1970s, however, the difficulty of combining public relations and environmental analysis became apparent, and in a third reorganization the political analysis unit was transferred to the international division's planning department. Later, two other major divisions of the company were given political analysis capability. At present, then, there are three political analysis units within the company: one in the international division, one in exploration and production, and one in the Middle Eastern division.

The responsibilities of the analyst in the international division, who has a staff of three, are the most general. Primarily, he assesses political factors in conjunction with new investment proposals, at times in cooperation with the exploration and production division. The analyses are qualitative and unstructured, relying on traditional secondary and governmental sources. The international division's unit is also formally involved in the planning process, although its function seems to be one of coordination and facilitation. Each affiliate is responsible for political assessment, and an assumptions report (for planning purposes) is forwarded to the regional headquarters annually. The section of this report dealing with the political environment is reviewed by the division's assessment unit. The unit also responds to special requests from management for studies of specific problems.

The duties of the analysts in the other two divisions are more specialized. The analysts in the exploration and production division have sole responsibility for a few countries, and they also analyze the political environment in new countries that seem promising from a geological standpoint. If a preliminary analysis indicates that the environment is at least minimally acceptable, an in-depth study of factors that could affect the company's relationship with the host country is undertaken. That study then becomes part of a larger recommendation which, not surprisingly, is dominated by geological factors.

The role of the political analyst in the Mideastern division differs from that of his colleagues in the other analysis units. He is concerned, almost exclusively, with ongoing operations, and his responsibilities are more anticipatory and, in a real sense, more routinized than are those of the other two. Since the company is involved only in joint ventures in the Middle East, the planning process differs from its counterpart in other regions. The analyst, who is basically a desk officer, reports orally once a week and less regularly in written memoranda. When interviewed, he described his job as not merely following events, but giving them a context and drawing out important issues.

The assessment function in this company is differentiated, specialized, and formalized, if somewhat decentralized. The three political affairs analysts are all specialists by virtue of education and background rather than managers "rotating through" the function. Their approach to political assessment is similar, despite obvious differences, to their earlier work in the Foreign Service, and it may be characterized as political reporting.

The third firm in this category is a large, diversified manufacturer of heavy industrial and defense products. At the time of the interview it could be characterized as implementing a systems approach to environmental assessment. In a subsequent reorganization the assessment function, though still clearly differentiated and specialized, was converted to the political reporting approach of the other firms in this category.

At the time of the interview, the assessment function was located in the international business analysis department within the corporate international staff. As requests for information from the operating divisions increased, professionals in the department created a risk assessment vehicle based on the systematic collection and processing of expert opinion coming from intra- as well as extracompany sources. The main element is a 96-part questionnaire covering three major environmental categories. The objective of the system, which was designed to focus on new investment opportunities, was to provide better subjective assessments that could be efficiently and effectively summarized and communicated to management.

Respondents noted the need to "sell" the system, created independently by the international business analysis department, to the operating divisions. Shortly after the interview, a professional political scientist was hired to develop the system further and to manage it. Within a year, however, a major reorganization led to dissolution of the international division. Since then the risk assessment system is apparently "dormant," and the function is performed through unstructured political analyses provided on request.

The systems approach to environmental assessment is not an empty cell in the typology or a theoretical construct. A small number of United

States international firms have professionally staffed assessment units that have developed methods of assessing noneconomic environments and are implementing them on a regular basis. The best known of these units work with systematically collected and carefully analyzed expert-generated opinion.[7]

In six of the firms interviewed for this study, the political assessment function is fully differentiated and specialized and at least partly institutionalized. The last description must, however, be qualified. In virtually all the companies, the primary sources of political assessments are operating management, the affiliates, and regional headquarters. The integration of specialized political analysts into actual decision-making and planning processes varies widely and is still less than complete in most firms (see chap. 9). It would thus be more correct to say that in such firms the function is only partly institutionalized. Still, the need to institutionalize the political assessment function has been recognized in all six firms and, at the least, a first substantial step has been taken.

It is worthwhile to compare the three firms whose assessment units are primarily concerned with coordination and facilitation with firms whose units provide independent analysis. In two of the three companies in the latter category, the explicit motivation for establishment of the unit was a perceived need on the part of top management for an independent source of political assessment. Again in the latter category, the three independent assessment units are staffed by specialists whose education and occupational backgrounds have given them expertise in political analysis. With one exception, the coordinating units are staffed by managers who are not specialists.

An interesting hypothesis emerges from the foregoing analysis. There may well be a trade-off between independence and expertise, on the one hand, and integration into planning and investment decision making on the other. Two of the three firms with independent units experienced difficulty in completing the process of institutionalization of the function. Whereas individual analysts have valuable experience and expertise, their relationships with other staff groups and operating personnel are tenuous.

On the other hand, in two of the three firms whose assessment

---

7. One example of a systems approach is the ASPRO-SPAIR system developed by the Shell Oil Company (see Gebelein, Pearson, and Silbergh, 1978).

units' role was primarily coordination, they appeared to be reasonably well integrated, at least vis-à-vis the planning process. They were, after all, located in international planning groups. Still, they lacked the expertise and the assessment capability of independent units. One of the companies solved the problem by using a network of external consultants. While their independence from the operating units cannot be evaluated, it is probably compromised by the necessity to rely on affiliates and regional headquarters for the actual environmental assessments.

7
Managerial Perceptions of Political Risk

The task environment is inherently subjective. Environments are perceived by individuals through the interaction of objective events with individual or organizational factors, such as background, position, experience, and strategy. The concept is particularly true of political environments abroad. Virtually all research efforts, including this study, have found similar managerial perceptions of political risk. Most managers are concerned with "macro" risk, that is, with the general investment climate rather than with specific contingencies. Such concerns are typically expressed in terms of characteristics of the political environment— instability or conflict, for example— rather than as specific potential impacts on firms.

I believe that this generalized concern with the macro environment stems from a lack of widespread managerial experience with politically general contingencies abroad. The attention focused on political instability and conflict, and to a large extent on expropriation, reflects considerable uncertainty about the nature of political environments abroad and about potential impacts upon firms.[1]

PREVIOUS STUDIES

After interviewing thirty-eight companies in the early 1960s, Aharoni (1966) concluded that the assessment of political risk associated with investment in an unfamiliar country is strongly influenced by a priori as-

1. It has consistently been shown that managers of American firms consider political instability or political risk to be a major factor, if not the chief factor, in the foreign direct

sumptions. These assumptions are subjective and general; they "are based on a general image of a specific country, of a whole continent, of less developed countries as a whole, or even of foreign countries in general. . . . [Risk] is . . . described in general terms and stems from ignorance, generalizations, projection of U.S. culture and standards to other countries and an unqualified deduction from some general indicator to a specific investment" (1966:94). Political risks are seldom specified directly; when they are enumerated, observers tend to describe them in terms of the environment (e.g., instability) rather than in terms of their potential impact on business decisions.

The National Industrial Conference Board (1969) surveyed firms in twelve nations to elicit information about obstacles and incentives to investment in 1967–68. Although "political uncertainty" and "political instability" were cited as major factors in foreign investment decisions, the Board found that assessments of political environments were not related to specific constraints on operations: "A great many investors from capital exporting countries report that they have eliminated countries— and even whole geographic regions—from their investment considerations for political reasons." The Board concluded that environmental assessments are subjective and that "obstacles to investment exist in the mind of the investor" (1969:2).

The findings of studies undertaken in the 1970s are consistent with those reported above. La Palombara and Blank (1977) concluded that top levels of management view the political environment as unpredictable and that managers develop a "feeling" about the politics of a country. Political instability and attitudes toward foreign investment were regarded as the most important environmental attributes. Van Agtmael (1976), drawing on his experience as vice-president of a large international bank, found managers focusing on political risks in general rather than on specific impacts on business operations. When there is concern about political risk, he notes, it is often exaggerated, emotional, and ideological.

Root's (1968*a*) survey of top international executives in 331 large American firms in 1966 suggests that concepts such as instability stand as proxies for underlying uncertainty about political risk.[2] Clustering atti-

---

investment decision process. For example, see Aharoni (1966), Basi (1963), Keegan (1974), National Industrial Conference Board (1969), Piper (1971), Root (1968*a*), Stobaugh (1969), and Zink (1973).

2. A seven-point semantic differential scale was used to solicit manager's attitudes toward factors associated with the government and with investment opportunities in a

tudes revealed that managers associated political stability with honesty and with a safe and profitable investment opportunity. On the other hand, an unstable government was linked with corruption, with a risky and an unprofitable investment environment. An anti-American attitude was associated with government obstructionism and restricted investment opportunities. Root concludes that executives' attitudes about instability are important determinants of their attitudes toward the safety and profitability of investment.

In 1970 Swansbrough (1972) surveyed 213 firms, which accounted for more than 80 percent of United States FDI in Latin America, about obstacles to American investment in that area. The study is of particular relevance as it deals specifically with the relative importance of problems confronting United States investors. Respondents were asked to rate six potential problems from high to low on a six-point scale. Unfortunately, the problems were stated too generally: restrictive economic policies, political instability, hostility to private enterprise, inflation, expropriation, and discriminatory tax rates.

One hundred usable responses were received. The first two factors, restrictive economic policies and political instability, were given a high rating by a majority of the respondents—54 percent and 53 percent, respectively. Thirty-one percent evidenced similar concern about hostility to private enterprise, and only 18 percent so rated expropriation.[3] (Thirty-three percent of extractive firms, however, did consider expropriation to be a matter of concern.)

The findings of surveys of managerial opinion on foreign political environments have been consistent over the past two decades. Political factors, usually expressed as political instability or political risk, are considered important determinants of foreign direct investments and are perceived in diffuse, subjective, and impressionistic terms. Managers' attention seems to be focused on the general environment rather than on potentially significant impacts on specific projects. The linkage between the two is loosely defined and intuitive. (See Kobrin, 1979, for a complete review of the literature.)

---

number of countries. Examples of the former are stable-unstable, pro–United States–anti–United States, dynamic-static, and honest-corrupt. The latter was scaled in terms of safe-risky, profitable–not profitable, broad-limited, and so on.

3. The lack of concern about expropriation may be attributed to the fact that expropriations, especially of manufacturing firms, were limited until the early 1970s (see Kobrin, 1980).

MANAGERIAL CONCERNS

Respondents to the mail survey were presented with a list of nine aspects of the political environment and asked to select the four they considered the most important (see table 7–1). Two factors, political instability and the investment climate, were selected by an overwhelming majority of respondents (79.5 percent in each instance). Except for two financial variables, remittance restrictions (69.4 percent) and taxation (51.1 percent), none of the specific potential constraints were selected as important by even a third of the respondents. About 28 percent selected expropriation, 24.2 percent, political party attitudes, and 21.1 percent, labor disruptions. That more than half the respondents chose remittance restrictions and taxation reflects, in part, respondents' function, as a fair number of them were in finance.

Categorizing respondents by size, internationalization, or even institutionalization of the assessment function did not significantly change the results. Sector, however, does make a notable difference. Fifty-four percent of extractive firms selected expropriation, compared with 28.4 percent of the total sample (the difference is significant at the .05 level).

When managers in the firms interviewed were asked what it was about the political environment which concerned them, many of them had difficulty in responding. Their concerns were obviously so general and intuitive that they could not be expressed in terms of specific political factors that might impose constraints upon, or provide opportunities for, their operations.

Nevertheless, forty-two managers in 26 firms (out of a total of 115 respondents in 34 firms interviewed) provided reasonably specific information about political environmental factors. As respondents were not asked to rank-order the factors, the relevant measure is simply the number of times any given aspect was mentioned. As seen in table 7–2, results are consistent with previous research. Political instability, heading the list, was noted by almost twice as many respondents (32) as the second factor, restrictions on remittances and payments, mentioned by 17 respondents. The third-ranking factor includes hostility to private enterprise, to business in general, or to foreign investment in particular. Reflecting a generalized notion of opposition to business or to foreign investment, it was selected by 16 of the managers interviewed. All other aspects received less than 10 mentions each. Those chosen by more than

TABLE 7-1
SELECTION OF ASPECTS OF THE POLITICAL ENVIRONMENT
AS ONE OF THE FOUR MOST IMPORTANT
(N = 190)

Aspect	Percentage
Political instability	79.5
Investment climate	79.5
Remittance restrictions	69.4
Taxation	51.1
Expropriation	28.4
Attitudes of political parties	24.2
Labor disruptions	21.1
Administrative restrictions	15.8
Public sector competition	13.2

five managers include expropriation, industry-specific problems, government regulation, currency restrictions, and labor problems.

With the exception of restrictions on remittances and payments, widely held concerns about the political environment are related to stability and the investment climate. Only minor differences marked the rankings of factors by managers from firms that have institutionalized the assessment function and from those that have not. The high level of concern with restrictions on remittances reveals the importance of the problem to the international firm and the proportion of financial and economic specialists among the managers interviewed. Twenty-eight percent of the respondents who provided specific information about environmental factors were in this field, and they accounted for 41 percent of the mentions of remittance restrictions.

Results are consistent with earlier findings, for general indicators of the political environment were selected by the highest percentage of respondents and, except for financially oriented constraints, aspects related more specifically to operations were selected by a much lower proportion. When, however, respondents are asked about both general and specific aspects of the environment (e.g., the investment climate and labor disruptions), one would expect, all else being equal, an aspect at a higher level of aggregation to be selected by a larger number of respondents. This problem was remedied in a second mail survey conducted approximately one year after the first. The results suggest that concern with generalized aspects of the environment may reflect unfamiliarity and thus uncertainty.

UNFAMILIARITY AND UNCERTAINTY

The sampling frame was made up of United States–based, Fortune 500, industrial firms with operations in four or more countries.[4] Questionnaires were sent to senior international managers in 301 companies. By January 1980, when responses were tabulated, replies had been received from 80 firms (26.6 percent of the total). Comparing the profile of respondents with the population indicates that the returns are biased: they are skewed toward large firms in industrial sectors that are more likely to face politically generated contingencies.[5]

Respondents were asked to select from a list of thirteen political-environmental events the nine most important and to rank them according to their potential impact on overseas operations. The process was undertaken separately for less developed and for developed countries.

The thirteen events were civil disorder, external war, labor disruptions, price controls, expropriation, contract cancellation, fiscal changes, remittance restrictions, indigenization of personnel, partial expropriation, import restrictions, forced export commitments, and withdrawal of investment incentives. All are defined in terms of specific impacts on operations, that is, external war as potential damage to company facilities or destruction of the national economy. Findings are reported in table 7–3. As the data are ordinal, medians are compared. (As respondents were

4. The population was obtained from a list in Bavishi (1978). The study was conducted in conjunction with "Outlook," which was then a service of the Chase World Information Corporation. Conrad Pearson was an active coparticipant.

5. See chapter 5 for a complete discussion of firm-related factors that increase sensitivity to political environments. The survey was originally sent to two managers in each firm, one with international line responsibilities and the other in the international planning section. Multiple responses were received from only seven of the eighty firms responding. As analysis revealed no significant differences by managerial function, and as the vast majority of responses were from planners rather than line managers, data were analyzed on a firm rather than on an individual basis. In the seven instances of two responses, the one from staff planning was selected for analysis. I will supply further information on request.

TABLE 7-2
MENTIONS OF ASPECTS OF THE POLITICAL ENVIRONMENT
(N = 42)

Aspect	Number of mentions
Political instability	32
Restrictions on remittances and payments	17
Hostility to private enterprise, foreign investment, or business in general	16
Expropriation	9
Industry-specific problems	8
Government regulation	7
Currency restrictions	6
Labor problems	6
Price controls	5
Partial divestment	4
Contract problems	4
Import restrictions	3
Forced exports	3
Corruption	3
Taxation	2
Problems with expatriates	2

asked to select 9 of the 13 events they considered important, missing data indicate a ranking of 10 or higher. Medians are thus computed on the basis of all 80 respondents.)

In interpreting results, it should be noted that the respondents had already established the threshold at which an event becomes an extraordinary business risk and were evaluating relative importance in that context. In less developed countries, the only events with median rankings of less than four were the two indicators of conflict—civil disorder and external war—and expropriation. Seemingly respondents are most deeply concerned with aspects of the environment which suggest political instability or major discontinuities. Differences among the other six events with a median ranking of less than 9 are not so clear-cut. However, labor disruptions (5.5), price controls (6.0), remittance restrictions

TABLE 7-3

RELATIVE IMPORTANCE OF RISKS BY MEDIAN RANKINGS

Risk	Overall	Sales		Number of Countries		Percentage of sales abroad	
		Less than $2 million	$2 million or more	10 or less	11 or more	20 or less	21 or more
LESS DEVELOPED COUNTRIES							
Civil disorder	1.8	2.4	3.9	1.6	2.1	2.7	2.0
War	3.6	4.4	5.3	4.7	4.5	3.0	4.7
Labor disruptions	5.5	6.3	6.8	6.1	6.6	6.7	6.5
Price controls	6.0	7.3	6.4	6.6	7.2	5.5	7.5
Expropriation	2.4	3.2	3.5	3.4	3.4	4.3	3.1
Contract cancellation	7.6	8.2	7.1	7.1	8.1	7.7	8.9
Fiscal changes	7.3	8.6	7.6	7.4	7.3	8.3	8.3
Remittance restrictions	5.3	6.8	5.9	6.8	6.1	6.8	6.4
Partial expropriation	5.7	6.5	7.8	7.1	5.9	8.5	5.9
INDUSTRIALIZED COUNTRIES							
Civil disorder	5.5	3.9	8.2	4.5	6.9	4.0	6.7
War	8.4	8.5	—	8.5	8.8	—	8.9
Labor disruptions	3.7	4.8	4.6	4.8	4.7	3.0	4.8
Price controls	3.2	5.1	3.5	5.2	3.2	3.0	4.0
Expropriation	6.0	5.9	9.7	5.5	8.6	9.0	7.5
Contract cancellation	7.2	7.9	9.5	7.4	3.9	8.0	8.0
Fiscal changes	5.5	6.1	6.3	6.3	6.4	7.0	6.1
Remittance restrictions	4.4	5.6	5.6	6.5	5.3	6.5	5.4
Partial expropriation	6.9	7.8	8.2	7.1	8.8	7.8	8.1

(5.3), and partial expropriation (5.7) do appear to be of more concern than contract cancellation (or renegotiation) or fiscal changes.

As expected, the rank order of events differs markedly in industrialized countries. Respondents are less concerned about civil disorder, war, and expropriation than about specific managerial contingencies. Of most concern are price controls (3.2) and labor disruptions (3.7), followed by remittance restrictions (4.4). Fiscal changes, civil disorder, and expropriation follow with median rankings between 5.5 and 6.0.

Differences in managerial concerns between developed and developing countries appear to reflect substantive differences in the respective political environments. Civil disorder, war, and expropriation are not commonplace events in advanced industrial countries. Managers' apprehensions about the political environment therefore shift to specific policy outcomes like price controls and remittance restrictions and to events like labor disputes. If results are disaggregated by firm characteristics, however, another explanation is possible. The ranking of events in less developed countries is, with minor exceptions, not sensitive to such characteristics as firm size, internationalization, and sector. In every instance, civil disorder, war, and expropriation were chosen as the three most important contingencies. Extractive firms differed in regarding contract negotiations and partial expropriation as more important than did the other respondents, a finding that seems to be consistent with the history of the industry.

The characteristics of respondents do have some bearing on the rankings of potential risks in developed countries. Specifically, the importance of civil disorder seems to depend on the size and the international experience of the respondent. Whereas larger, more widespread firms do not consider civil disorder a threat in developed countries, small firms and those maintaining operations in less than ten countries rank it first. So, even in developed countries, firms that are inexperienced internationally and thus unfamiliar with the environment are most concerned about political instability.

To some extent, the differences between developing and developed countries may reflect differences in familiarity with the environment. Investors know more about the political environment in developed countries because they have had more contact with them—the vast majority of American FDI is in industrialized countries—and because such countries are more like the United States than any of the LDCs. Familiarity reduces overall uncertainty and arouses investors' concern about the effect of the political environment on specific operations, rather than about a generalized notion of the investment climate. The argument is supported by the fact that perceptions of the relative importance of general indicators of instability in developed countries reflect international experience, extent of internationalization, and firm size.

Managers' concern with political instability and political risk in LDCs reflects inexperience and unfamiliarity with political environments and the constraints they may impose on operations. Uncertainty in terms of business risk or of subjective perceptions of the impact on cash flows or returns is increased, and articulation of specific concerns about the impact of the political environment on a particular project is more difficult. Uncertainty or anxiety about LDC environments is therefore expressed in terms of general indicators, such as political instability or conflict, which are aspects of the environment most different from those of the home country.

Some firms and some individual managers have had extensive experience in LDCs, but by and large widespread investment in those markets is fairly new. In the manufacturing sector, for example, serious investment in developing countries did not begin until the mid-1960s (see chap. 4). And it is not simply experience, but relevant experience, that matters. Even in LDCs the expansion of the task environment to include political factors is a recent development.

UNCERTAINTY AND PERCEPTIONS OF POLITICAL RISK

Many of the managers interviewed found it hard to explain exactly what it was about political instability which troubled them. They simply could not be very specific. For example, the vice-president in charge of Latin America for a large pharmaceutical firm volunteered instability as a political factor of concern, but he then went on to say that it is not easy to determine when political instability exists because we really do not know how to define it. A strategic planner, pressed to explain what instability meant to his firm, a large industrial company, mentioned economic upheaval, expropriation, problems of employee safety, difficulty in recruiting expatriate managers, and a shift from a capitalist to a more regulated environment, in a sort of stream-of-consciousness reply.

Some managers, however, directly related political instability to uncertainty. A planner in a pharmaceutical firm said that the basis of political risk is stability or instability of government: "What is terribly important is predictability. The company does not mind if a country is difficult as long as it is predictable." The director of international business planning in an industrial firm replied that the reliability of the government was crucial: "We can live with all kinds of government economic policy as long as we know that it is coming. . . . In uncertainty we don't move." And the president of the international division of a pharmaceutical firm put it directly and succinctly: "We are willing to cope with harsh rules or even bad regulations, so long as we know what the rules are and that they won't be changed. But give us uncertainty and then we flee." The tendency to express perceptions of political environments in terms of general notions such as instability or the investment climate reflects unfamiliarity with political processes abroad and their implications for business operations and therefore a high level of uncertainty. It is uncertainty that intervenes between managerial perceptions of political environments and responses in terms of investment decision making and strategic planning.

The rather high level of perceived uncertainty may be attributed to several factors. First, difficulties in understanding the existing environment result from many American managers' lack of familiarity with foreign political processes and their potential impacts on operations. Second, it is much harder to forecast political processes than economic phenomena or specific business risks, such as the success of a new product or the supply of an input, because the art of political forecasting is not fully developed and because the underlying phenomena are extremely complex.

Even though numerous managers of United States–based international firms have had experience abroad in a wide range of developed and less developed countries, expansion of the task environment to include political factors is fairly recent. Few managers have had to strive for a thorough understanding of the political process and few have experienced a substantial number of impacts of political environments on business operations. For example, a number of respondents, when asked why they were concerned about instability, replied that they were worried about expropriation. Yet most of them admitted that their firms had had only limited experience with expropriation. In fact, one manager said that the only time his company, which manufactures transportation products, had come close to expropriation it was actually seen as a desirable outcome; the government backed off when it realized the company would be more than happy to leave with some compensation. While expropriation certainly occurs, it may also serve as a proxy for undefined concerns about the investment climate. Given the low frequency of expropriation outside the extractive sector, the latter appears likely.

Uncertainty, broadly defined, includes lack of knowledge about current environmental processes and their relationship to the firm and about outcomes of future events (see chap. 3). The two are related in that an understanding of current environments is necessary if predictions are to be made about the future. Based on the research findings, I would conclude that many managers of American international firms possess only limited understanding of political processes abroad. Concern is usually focused on dramatic and irregular events rather than on precise sources of potential impacts on operations. Because instability and civil disorder represent a potential for discontinuous change, managers' concern with these aspects of the general environment may reflect a high degree of uncertainty about current relationships. The link to the forecasting problem is direct. The managers interviewed found it hard to specify possible outcomes of events.

There were, of course, exceptions. Some managers did express concern about the political environment in terms of potential constraints on operations. Most of these concentrated on the effect of government policies or regulations. A senior vice-president of an oil company was not worried about the stability or instability of governments; he really did not care how frequently a government changed hands. In his view the major problem was government policy vis-à-vis foreign investors in general and oil companies in particular. Were policies transparent and would they be altered when a change in government, expected or unexpected, took place? A regional vice-president of a food products company echoed the same idea in acknowledging that what is of concern is government regulations that might adversely affect his business. Other respondents spoke of specific issues, such as remittance restrictions and labor problems. Only a minority, however, explicitly said that their major concern with political environments centered on potential policy changes caused by political events. And they were not a random sample of all who responded to this question; rather, they were usually in sectors with wide experience in LDCs. Furthermore, the character of these industries makes managers more sensitive to project-specific impacts. For example, two of them worked for construction firms whose projects' relatively brief duration limits potential impacts. A construction company may indeed operate in a given country over a long period, but specific projects, and the risks associated with them, are usually short-term.

Two other firms concerned about specific policy are in the pharmaceutical industry, which is heavily regulated and publicly administered in most countries, regardless of their socioeconomic ideology. Such companies are of necessity alert to the possible impact of governmental policy and regulation on their operations, either at home or abroad. Several managers in oil firms also gave specific rather than general answers; the petroleum industry is highly politicized and has been dominated for some time by the question of relationships with governments. The wave of petroleum expropriations since the late 1960s has in fact changed the very basis of international involvement from equity-owned concessions to contractual relationships with governments, either directly or through state-owned companies.

MULTIPLE TASK ENVIRONMENTS

A review of managerial perceptions of the political environment provides some evidence, albeit anecdotal, that multiple and segmented task environments exist within the same firm. In a number of instances, evaluations of the importance of a given environmental factor varied dramatically among managers in the same company. For example, a senior regional manager said that his firm definitely preferred market-oriented democracies because they tended to be the most stable over time. A more junior director of strategic planning, on the contrary, played down the company's reaction to the political or economic orientation of a given country and claimed the firm made no moral judgments about the form of government or the social system so long as the government was reliable. The difference in perceptions probably stems from disparities in background, age, and socialization process. A construction firm manager admitted varying perceptions of a country among the company's operating units, perhaps owing to differences in strategy.

The most clear-cut example of multiple task environments was encountered in a petroleum company with a large chemical products division. Managers involved primarily with petroleum operations cited expropriation as an important environmental concern, the treasurer and the chief economist both defining political instability in terms of the threat of expropriation. On the other hand, the vice-president in charge of chemical operations denied that expropriation was a major issue for companies such as his. Both, of course, are right. Petroleum companies are vulnerable to expropriation, whereas manufacturing firms, especially in industries that are technologically intensive, are much less so.[6] The difference in definition of the respective task environments is a direct function of organizational strategy.

CONCLUSIONS

The findings presented in this chapter are among the most tentative of any in this study. Both the mailed survey and the personal interviews focused on the nature and organizational structure of the political assessment function. Although considerable information about managerial perceptions is available, it was not obtained in a form that permits a rigorous evaluation of attitudinal data. The findings of this study, however, are consistent with those given in the existing literature. Managers of international firms perceive the political environment in diffuse terms and express their perceptions as anxieties about political instability or deterioration of the climate for foreign investment or for private enterprise in general. These perceptions reflect a high degree of underlying uncertainty about political environments and their relation to business operations. The uncertainty reflects unfamiliarity. Except for remittance restrictions, the vast majority of managers interviewed did not relate their concerns to potential constraints on operations. They focused on changes in the structure of the environment rather than on impacts on their firm.

Managerial perceptions of political environments abroad should change over time, as the international experience of United States firms, particularly in LDCs, becomes more extensive. Indeed, in the relatively short period of time between the fieldwork and the writing of this chapter, the number of managers aware of specific impacts of LDC political environments on their firms, rather than simply instability and conflict, has noticeably increased. The extensive discussions of political risk following upon the overthrow of the shah in 1979, as well as additional experience, have no doubt influenced this shift in perspective.

6. See Kobrin (1980) for an analysis of firm and industry factors affecting vulnerability to expropriation.

8

Scanning the Political Environment

The spanning of organizational boundaries to scan external environments is the operational core of the political assessment process. There are two basic aspects of scanning: (1) the stimuli that precipitate it and (2) international firms' sources of information about political environments abroad.

In an open system, strategic planning requires that assumptions be made about political and economic as well as competitive and technological environments. This process demands extensive and reliable environmental information. One result of the attention given to strategic planning over the past decade and the implementation of sophisticated long-range planning systems has been an increased emphasis on environmental scanning (Khalas, 1978; Montgomery and Weinberg, 1979; Preble, 1978). Although the literature is still rather limited, especially on the scanning of political environments by international firms, a number of studies are relevant to this research.

MOTIVATIONS FOR SCANNING

There seems to be general agreement that scanning, at least at this point, is reactive and crisis-oriented rather than proactive and continuous. Using a limited number of case studies, Segev (1977) finds that a "trigger," that is, a specific event that motivates requests for environmental information, is an important element in the scanning process. Triggers may be internal events, such as the annual planning cycle, or they may be in the external environment, such as a political coup or a major change in economic conditions. Segev concludes that the reactions to most triggers are requests for new environmental information.

Fahey and King (1977), interviewing twelve large firms, found only two that could be characterized as having scanning systems in place which maintained continuous, organizationally structured, and systems-oriented monitoring of environments. Both firms were capital-intensive: one produced heavy industrial equipment and the other petroleum. In nine of the firms interviewed, environmental analysis was clearly ad hoc in nature, motivated by unexpected events.

Three studies dealing specifically with international companies likewise show that environmental scanning tends to be reactive. Behrman, Boddewyn, and Kapoor (1975:45) conclude that "business executives tend to react to their environment as developments come to their attention, rather than to anticipate them through systematic forecasting." Keegan (1974), interviewing managers in the headquarters of multinational firms, found scanning to be very unsystematic. Only 35 percent of large multinational corporations responding to a survey by Zink (1973) attempted continuous political forecasting. Furthermore, from follow-up interviews Zink concluded that the survey "somewhat overstates the case."

The findings of this study are consistent with those of earlier studies. Respondents to the mail survey were asked how often they carried out political analyses with respect to a given country. As seen in table 8–1, a large majority of respondents (79.3 percent) assess political environments on demand, that is, in response to a pending investment proposal, an important event in the country, or a like stimulant. In contrast, only 33.7 report routine annual environmental monitoring. (The responses are not mutually exclusive, as the two possibilities can total more than 100 percent.)[1]

Table 8–1 also shows significant differences in routine monitoring of political environments by characteristics of respondents. About 59 percent of firms that have institutionalized the function report routine environmental monitoring, compared with only 19.2 percent of those that have not. Both are significantly different from the average for all respondents (33.7 percent) at the .01 level. The difference is hardly surprising, since routinization is an aspect of formalization and institutionalization.

---

1. A third possible response to the question is "cyclically, every 2, 3, or more years." Since it was selected by only a small minority of respondents (3 percent), it was not included in the tabulation.

TABLE 8-1

FREQUENCY OF POLITICAL ANALYSES
(IN PERCENTAGES OF RESPONDENTS)

Variable	Number of respondents	On demand	Routinely each year
All	193	79.3	33.7
Function institutionalized			
No	120	84.2	19.2[a]
Yes	68	70.6	58.8[a]
Global sales			
(in millions of dollars)			
Less than 750	63	84.1	22.2[b]
751–2,500	70	82.9	40.0
more than 2,500	59	69.5	37.3
Percentage of sales abroad			
0–10	38	94.7[c]	15.8[c]
11–25	68	75.0	29.4
26 or more	77	76.6	48.1[c]
Number of countries			
1–4	34	91.2[a]	23.5
5–10	42	85.7	19.0[b]
11–20	39	69.2	43.6
more than 20	72	75.0	44.4
International organization			
Preinternational	46	91.3[a]	23.9
International Division I	42	83.3	16.7[c]
International Division II	58	77.6	50.0[a]
Global	26	61.5[c]	50.0[b]

[a]Difference in proportions versus all respondents significant at .01.
[b]Difference in proportions versus all respondents significant at .10.
[c]Difference in proportions versus all respondents significant at .05.

Small firms are significantly less likely to monitor environments routinely than larger firms, whose propensity to do so does not differ significantly from the average. On the other hand, routine environmental scanning is clearly related to internationalization in terms of sales generated abroad, the number of countries in which the firm operates, and the organizational structure of international operations. Forty-eight percent of firms with 26 percent or more of their sales generated abroad, 44.4 percent of those with operations in more than twenty countries, and exactly half of those with global organizational structures report that environments are routinely scanned each year. As noted in chapter 5, however, institutionalization of the environmental assessment function is far from complete. More than 40 percent of firms where the function is institutionalized, and about 50 percent of the most widespread international firms, report no routine environmental scanning. Even in these firms assessments are undertaken only when triggered by a specific event within the firm or in the external environment.

The interview data corroborate the findings of the mail survey. Few of the managers interviewed provided evidence of routine or systematic monitoring of political environments abroad. Most assessments are stimulated by a specific need or unusual event. Furthermore, the stimulus motivating a political assessment is more likely to be found inside the firm than in the external environment. Although such outstanding events as the election of Allende in Chile, the overthrow of the shah of Iran, and the triumph of the French Socialists in 1981 undoubtedly precipitate reviews by a number of firms, more often the "trigger" is the need to support an investment proposal or the development of a strategic plan.

A number of firms do scan external political environments, especially in high priority countries, on a regular basis. Even those engaged in systematic monitoring, however, are most likely to do so in the context of the strategic planning cycle. The fact that most political assessments are reactive and are rarely independent of a pending proposal of one sort or another is significant. (I return to this point later in the chapter.)

SOURCES OF INFORMATION

A number of studies have focused on sources of environmental information. In one of the earliest and most extensive, Aguilar (1967) interviewed 137 managers in 41 United States and 6 European firms. In computing relative usage of sources of external information, Aguilar found that personal sources dominated impersonal ones (71 vs. 29 percent). His conclusion is directly relevant here: ". . . the scanning process for important external information appears to rely heavily on the manager's personal network of communications (including both private and organizational contacts)" (1967:68).

Although outside sources were used more frequently than inside sources (55 to 45 percent), the single most important source of information about external environments was other managers within the firm (32 percent of responses). Aguilar found some interesting differences in the relative significance of outside sources among respondents and organizations. Outside sources tend to be more important at lower levels of management (46 percent of responses for first-level general managers vs. 60 percent of second- and third-level managers), and for staff (63 percent) as compared with line (51 percent) managers. Outside sources are also relied upon more heavily in small and medium firms (68 and 65 percent, respectively) than in large companies (36 percent of responses).

Several studies deal with the scanning of external environments by international firms. Zink (1973) was concerned with assessment of political risk by large United States–based international firms. Of 187 questionnaires sent to companies with manufacturing operations outside the United States and Canada, 91 usable responses were received. Respondents rated a number of sources of information as important, occasionally important, or unimportant. A large majority of managers (79 percent) considered reports from employees in the host country important. General news sources (61 percent) and financial institutions (56 percent) were ranked second and third. American government agencies (43 percent), other companies (32 percent), and industry associations (31 percent) were also ranked as important by more than a fourth of the respondents.

Keegan (1974) interviewed 50 executives in the headquarters of

13 United States international corporations. Respondents were asked to recall up to four instances over the past six months in which they had received information relating to external international environments. Again, human sources were dominant, accounting for 66 percent of all those mentioned. Keegan concluded that businessmen, to be effective, "must have . . . a network of human or personal information sources" (1974:413). The single most important source of external information was the company's executives located abroad (15 percent of all mentions): "The general view of headquarters executives was that company executives overseas were the people who knew best what was going on in their areas" (1974:414).

Information sources tend to be higher-level managers in the local affiliate: the general manager or heads of sections. Keegan noted that little or no information was obtained from lower-level employees, even though they were in closer daily touch with the environment. The second-most important source of external information is characterized as service organization staff, including bankers, lawyers, public accountants, and the like. In their analysis of relations of international business with governments, Behrman, Boddewyn, and Kapoor (1975:45) also concluded that managers of United States international firms "prefer personal sources of information based on networks of oral communication." And Bauer, de Sola Pool, and Dexter (1972), in a classic study of trade politics, discovered that the managers they interviewed gained their most vivid impressions of foreign economic affairs, not from reading, but from correspondence and personal experience.

Two salient points emerge from the literature. First, the most important source of information about external environments abroad in international firms is affiliate management. Second, managers rely on a personal network of human sources for information about those environments. Both the mail survey and the personal interviews conducted in conjunction with this study are consistent with the existing literature. Response to the former provides an overview of information sources considered important by American firms.

AN OVERVIEW

Respondents to the mail survey were asked to rate seventeen potential sources of information about overseas political environments on a scale of 1 (most important) to 5 (least important). Table 8–2 reports the

TABLE 8-2

IMPORTANCE OF INFORMATION SOURCES
(IN PERCENTAGES OF RESPONDENTS RATING 1 OR 2)
(N = 193)

Information source	Percentage
Subsidiary managers	74.6
Regional managers	68.9
Corporate headquarters personnel	64.8
Banking community	44.6
External consultants	28.0
Business periodicals	24.9
Other firms	22.8
Agents and outside counsel	22.3
United States embassies	17.6
United States government domestic agencies	16.6
Professional journals	14.5
Trade associations	13.0
International organizations	10.9
Newspapers, radio, television	10.4
Academics	9.3
American Chamber of Commerce	8.3
Journalists	8.3

percentages of respondents rating each source as at least relatively important (1 or 2); only sources internal to the firm are so rated by more than a minority of respondents. Rank-ordering in terms of the percentage rating 1 or 2, subsidiary managers (74.6 percent) come first, regional managers, second (68.9 percent), and corporate headquarters personnel, third (64.8 percent). The only external source of environmental information rated as relatively important by any number approaching a majority of respondents is the banking community (44.6 percent). A sizable gap separates banks and the fifth-most important source, external consultants (28.0 percent). Business periodicals (24.9 percent) constitute the only non-human source rated 1 or 2 by more than a fifth of respondents. Other firms are so rated by 22.8 percent of respondents, and agents and outside counsel, by 22.3 percent.

Four other sources of information that received rather low ratings are of particular interest. American embassies abroad (17.6 percent) and government agencies within the United States (16.6 percent) are both considered unimportant sources of information about political factors. The point is reinforced by the responses to a second question, which requested that interviews with the departments of State, Treasury, and Commerce, and with United States embassies be rated on a scale of 1 (important) to 3 (unimportant) as sources of information about political matters. Interviews with the State Department and with embassies abroad were rated as important by only 27 percent and 28 percent, respectively; neither Treasury nor Commerce was so rated by even 20 percent of the firms. It is clear that the United States government is not considered an important source of information about overseas political environments. Two other potentially useful sources, academics and journalists, are considered relatively important by only a small minority of respondents (9.3 and 8.3 percent, respectively).

Disaggregating by institutionalization, internationalization, or firm size does not significantly alter the results. Subsidiary, regional, and headquarters managers are the most important sources of external information in each category, by a fairly wide margin, and banks are universally the single most important external source. No significant differences were tabulated in the rankings of agencies of the United States government, journalists, or academics.

Again the survey findings are consistent with those reported by other researchers. The only sources rated as important or relatively important by a majority of respondents are subsidiary, regional, and headquarters managers. The major external source of information about environments is banks. Human sources clearly dominate over nonhuman agencies, as of the eight information sources rated as relatively important by more than a fifth of the respondents, only one—business periodicals—was inanimate.

This finding is in accord with the conclusions reached by Aguilar (1967) and Keegan (1974), who reported that human or personal sources accounted for 71 percent and 67 percent, respectively, of all information sources. Although these data do not lend themselves to a direct comparison, the interviews strongly suggest a larger degree of reliance on human sources when the object of scanning is political environments abroad. The distinction becomes sharper as one moves up the managerial hierarchy to the decision-making level. Senior managers with line responsibilities for international operations—corporate chief executive officer, vice-chairman, head of international operations, or vice-presidents responsible for major regions—were interviewed in 21 of the 34 companies. Only a small minority volunteered nonhuman sources when asked where they obtained information about political environments. To be sure, further discussion revealed that most of them read widely and that all were exposed to the general and business press. They seemed, however, to view the media as supplying background rather than as a major source of information about political factors abroad. (As seen in chapter 9, however, the background gained from exposure to the print and broadcast media may exert a strong influence on investment decisions.)

A number of the managers interviewed were explicit about their reliance on interpersonal networks of communication and on human sources. The president of the international division of a large pharmaceutical firm put it succinctly: "I bet on people every time." Numerous respondents said they had to be in touch with someone who knows his or her way directly, that they needed someone on the ground whom they could trust. In this regard, the comment of a senior vice-president and director of a large international construction firm is worth quoting in full: "The best method is to get someone on the site. . . . You need someone like _____ in _____ . He knows the right people, he knows how to meet them, has their confidence, and so on. . . . The point is that you must know individuals, especially in the developing countries. You must really rely on personal relationships." It is obvious that many managers at the decision-making level have a network of trusted colleagues, both within and outside their firms, whom they know well and with whom they regularly keep in touch. As the chairman of a large industrial firm said, "There are two dozen people that I have great respect for. This is my best source of overseas information. I have learned to ask them the best questions."

INTERPERSONAL INFORMATION SOURCES AND UNCERTAINTY

As uncertainty increases, individuals tend to place stronger reliance on human information sources and to make more use of social referent networks. Interpersonal relationships thus play a major role in the assessment of the impact of political factors on a firm's operations, for that is an area where uncertainty is quite high.

The preference for interpersonal or social sources of information when uncertainty prevails has often been commented on in the literature. Festinger (1954:118) hypothesizes: "To the extent that objective, nonsocial means are not available, people evaluate their opinions and abilities by comparison respectively with the opinions and abilities of others." Pfeffer, Solanick, and Leblebici (1976) studied grants awarded by the National Science Foundation and concluded that the use of particularistic criteria derived from social familiarity and social influence is more frequent under conditions of uncertainty. They argue that social influence, in the absence of shared criteria and in the presence of uncertainty, accounts for much of the variance in decision outcomes.

Similarly, Duncan (1973) claims that individuals lacking preestablished rules and procedures for decision making place heavy reliance on an informal network of relationships. They utilize such networks for two reasons. First, social comparison processes (the term is Festinger's) establish and validate a priori beliefs about states of nature. They develop and reinforce the decision maker's simplified model of the external environment. Second, social referent networks, as sources of environmental intelligence, help to confirm the decision maker's own information and operate as mechanisms through which raw intelligence can be evaluated. (See Aldrich, 1979, and March and Olsen, 1976.)

Logically, then, this phenomenon should be characteristic of managerial evaluation of foreign political environments because (1) levels of uncertainty and ambiguity are high and (2) the assessment function is fairly new. It arose in response to the internationalization of American firms and to changes in national and international political–economic environments, and rules and standard operating procedures are almost nonexistent. Hence the marked tendency to rely on interpersonal networks, on colleagues, internal and external to the firm, whom the manager knows and trusts. Information is generated and opinions are validated through the use of social referents.

The importance of human sources was made clear in the interviews. Affiliate general managers are the most important source of information about political environments in countries where operations have been established. In all but two of the firms interviewed, affiliate general managers or personnel on site (in construction firms) were mentioned as an important source. In the two exceptions, interviews were restricted to staff specialists who emphasized their own sources. The importance of subsidiary personnel is obvious from interviews with top management at the decision-making level. In all of the twenty-one firms whose senior managers were interviewed, affiliate or local management was noted as a significant source of information about political environments abroad. Twelve of the respondents at this level went even further, however, stating explicitly that local management was the source of information in this area. On this specific point, no differences by degree of institutionalization were observed. Respondents repeatedly stated that it is hard to keep ahead of people on the scene, that it is the local people who really count. The words of an international vice-president are pertinent: "We put a hell of a lot of stake in our local managers. That's where we get our basic advice."

The second-most important information source, also internal, is the decision makers themselves, including the chief international executive, regional managers, and sometimes product managers with global responsibilities. Their knowledge of political environments comes primarily from direct contact. They travel widely, and in host countries they talk with government ministers and officials, often at the highest levels, with customers and suppliers, with members of the local and expatriate business communities, and with local and foreign banks. While many managers have made an impressive effort to broaden their base of information, there are still real limits to the range of opinion solicited.

GENERAL EXTERNAL SOURCES

A third major source of information, which seems to have been understated in responses to the mailed questionnaire, is other firms. Managers at all levels concerned with political assessment reported having frequent contacts with colleagues in other American firms operating in the country of interest. Preexisting relationships are often exploited. Tire companies entering a market to serve the needs of automobile manufacturers naturally turn to them for help in evaluating nonmarket factors. Similarly, automobile firms keep in constant touch with a network of suppliers who may already be maintaining operations in the country in question.

The interview data confirmed survey findings that banks are the major external source of information about political environments. Although managers sometimes asked banks to prepare written environmental reports or followed written publications put out by banking institutions, for the most part the contact is informal and unstructured. A telephone call is made; a bank's subsidiary is visited; or a bank representative is called upon for advice when visiting the United States. In fact, a number of respondents reported that contacts were purposefully kept informal owing to the sensitive nature of the subject.

Other sources of information included local lawyers and counsel, large international public accounting firms, and a variety of "old hands" —former ambassadors, former government officials, and the like.

SPECIALIZED EXTERNAL SOURCES

It is clear from table 8–2 that specialized information sources such as United States government agencies, consultants, and academics are considered relatively useful by only a minority of respondents. As these groups are potentially valuable sources of information about political environments abroad which are not widely utilized, it is worthwhile to examine them in some depth.

Government agencies.—American embassies and government agencies in the United States were mentioned as information sources by twenty-one of the firms interviewed. More than half of the respondents volunteering the government as a potential source were explicitly, and often strongly, negative. Respondents in only four firms expressed a positive point of view, and in those firms the assessment function is differentiated and specialized. Two of the four are in the petroleum sector. A number of respondents, however, did mention embassies and other government agencies as an information source, but made little comment.

Most of the negative appraisals were related to experience with embassies abroad. A number of respondents noted in a general way, often in colorful and vehement terms, that embassies were unhelpful and unreceptive and that the information derived was too varied to be of much use. Some simply reflected the adversary relationship with the government which many managers in the private sector consider endemic. One respondent, for example, said that Washington was the last place to go for information about political environments; another, asked about embassies, replied, "They give good parties."

Several respondents, whose replies were more specific and considered, got to the heart of the matter. A vice-president of a large construction firm found that State Department information was not commercially oriented and hence was of little value. Although granting that the department provides good general information and overall surveys, he went on to say that there is no such thing as general business activity. Several other managers complained that both the State Department and its embassies lacked even a rudimentary understanding of important business considerations. In fact, a number of firms claimed that the foreign services of some European countries were much better attuned and more responsive to the needs of American firms, and it was those services that the firms routinely approached through their subsidiaries.

The appropriate role of the State Department in advising individual firms about specific political environments is a subject enmeshed in controversy. Some foreign service officers may strike managers as incompetent, uninterested, or even overtly antibusiness, but in reality an embassy's primary mission is to represent the interests of the United States as a whole. The relationship of embassy officials with individual firms looking for either advice or assistance has never been clearly defined. Yet some firms do make effective use of the State Department and other American agencies of international scope, and so it is worthwhile to look at their characteristics.

The four firms that mentioned the State Department and other government agencies as important sources of political information had all taken steps to institutionalize the assessment function. Perhaps more important, each of the four has a degree of specialized in-house expertise which facilitates effective utilization of government sources. In some instances the expertise has been developed through experience, as in an international oil company that has had a long history of interaction with the State Department. Other firms hired former foreign services officers or international relations specialists to staff political assessment positions, thus gaining expertise directly.

Consultants.—Respondents were also asked how frequently they used outside consultants for environmental assessment. Table 8–3 shows that only 20.2 percent reported frequent use (i.e., several times a year). About thirty-seven percent indicated infrequent use (i.e., once every two or three years), and 38.3 percent reported no use at all. When firms are categorized, some interesting differences emerge. Thirty-four percent of firms in which the function is institutionalized, 38.5 percent with operations in 20 or more countries, and 38.9 percent with sales of $2,501 million or more use consultants regularly. The differences versus the average

TABLE 8-3

FREQUENCY OF USE OF CONSULTANTS

(N = 193)

Frequency	*Percentage of respondents*
Never	38.3
Once every 2 or 3 years	37.3
Several times a year	20.2

for respondents as a whole (20.2 percent) are significant at the .05 level. It is apparent that external consultants are more likely to be called upon frequently by larger, more widespread international firms and by those that have institutionalized the assessment function. In a very real sense, these firms have most compelling need for, and the best qualifications to make effective use of, outside expertise. They must simultaneously conduct operations in a large number of different environments, and their very specialization and differentiation facilitate communication with outside specialists.

Some respondents admitted their desire to make more extensive use of academics, but said they were inhibited by their lack of knowledge of the "academic market" or of contacts with the appropriate people. A regional manager of a pharmaceutical firm did not call upon academics because he did not know how to judge their quality. Concerns vis-à-vis consultants tended to center on their lack of specific knowledge of industry or firm. Although academics and other consultants might be well informed about a country, such knowledge did not necessarily qualify them to give advice in particular situations faced by firms in that country.

The interviews suggested two reasons for the underutilization of specialized information sources about external political environments. First, it is often difficult for an outsider to locate appropriate sources of information about specific countries in the government, in universities, and even in consulting firms or, once they have been found, to judge their competence. Managers simply lack information about these specialized experts.

The second reason, by far the more important, flows directly from the nature of political risk assessment, which poses a complex forecasting problem (see chap. 3). It requires, first, a forecast of a future political environment, no mean task in itself, and, second, application of that forecast to determine likely impacts on a project. In a real sense the political forecast is merely input that is necessary but is not sufficient to predict probable impacts on the project. The two phases of the assessment process require two very different bodies of knowledge and experience. Political forecasting is grounded in knowledge of the political process and extensive country-specific expertise, whereas the prediction of impacts upon the firm is impossible without specific knowledge of both industry and project. It necessitates an understanding of technology, of industrial organization, and of the managerial process. It is unlikely that these two bodies of knowledge will exist in the same individual.

The two problems—knowledge of the market and what I call the need for a "translation"—are best illustrated in the context of the use of government sources by international firms. Both problems, however, are also of concern to firms that rely upon other specialized sources of political information.

When dealing with government sources, a firm must first locate individuals within the system who possess specific knowledge. Although desk officers or embassy officials may be easy to contact and may seem the obvious choice, they are not necessarily the most competent source of information. Because the State Department is given to frequent transfers and short-term assignments, the desk officer or the political officer in an embassy may be too inexperienced to be helpful. [2] An excellent source of information may be an individual in an unrelated assignment. Furthermore, as in any organization, government officials cover a wide range of competence and interest. The net result is that to use the system effectively a manager needs to have insight into the informal organization.

Second, as several respondents noted, few international agencies of the United States government are commercially oriented. Foreign service officers can provide potentially valuable information about political environments, but they have much more difficulty in evaluating investment environments or the probability of constraints being imposed on specific firms. A translation function is thus needed. Either the political assessment provided by government sources must be filtered and used in developing a specific appraisal of potential constraints, or questions must

2. The arguments for frequent transfers of foreign service personnel are the breadth of experience gained from a variety of assignments and the avoidance of overidentification with any given host country. Arguments for the frequent transfers of personnel by American international firms are virtually identical.

be framed in such a way as to elicit information that is directly useful. Specialized expertise within the firm is required to bridge the gap resulting from government officials' lack of specific knowledge about industry or firm and to facilitate the use of specialized sources of information about political environments abroad. In-house political specialists are likely to be reasonably well informed about gaining access to government agencies and they can serve as translators and thus facilitate project-specific forecasts of political risk.

The point also applies to academics and other consultants. Use of all these sources requires knowledge both of the market and the translation function. It is predicated on the ability to locate individuals with appropriate expertise and to evaluate their competence. It requires the ability to draw implications relevant to a specific problem from a body of general knowledge. It also requires the ability to compensate for the fact that the outside expert often does not know a great deal about the industry or the firm in question.

As with government sources, there is a relationship between effective use of academics and consultants as sources of information about political environments and institutionalization of the assessment function. Respondents who voluntarily named academics and consultants as useful sources tended to be in firms where the function is differentiated. In fact, they were often directly responsible for the assessment function and often were specialists themselves. This line of reasoning has important implications for the nature of the environment scanning process.

This point emerged clearly in an interview. A large industrial firm had recently sought to differentiate the assessment function by hiring several former foreign service officers. Although managers at all levels said that the most important sources were affiliate and regional managers, they all reported that the company was increasingly soliciting the help of outside sources, such as the State Department and private consultants. The interviews did not reveal an explicit linkage, but apparently management recognized that having in-house expertise enabled the firm to use specialized external sources more effectively.

PROBLEMS IN RELYING ON INTERNAL SOURCES

The scanning of political environments abroad is thus a boundary spanning process dominated by three groups of managers who are most likely to come into direct or indirect contact with relevant external environments. They are the managers of affiliates, higher-level managers with international responsibilities, and, in firms where the function is institutionalized, individuals in differentiated political assessment roles. Other international staff, such as planners and those serving in a financial capacity, may also come into contact with external sources of information. In most firms, however, they cross organizational boundaries to scan political environments much less frequently than do the first three groups.

One would expect a multinational corporation to take full advantage of its global network of affiliates in scanning political environments abroad. The very fact of its transnationality, of its direct access to a large number of political systems, is its major advantage. Having a person "on the spot" in Bogota, Tokyo, Lagos, Paris, or in any number of other places who is simultaneously integrated into both the domestic political-economic system and the multinational corporate system is a valuable asset. For precisely this reason, affiliate and regional managers constitute the most important source of information about political environments abroad. Certain problems must be resolved, however, if full advantage is to be taken of this valuable resource.

SOURCES OF BIAS

Affiliate and regional managers, though a potentially valuable information source, are unlikely to be disinterested. Sources of bias are inherent in a manager's position and in his or her relationship with economic and political environments. They are structural in that they arise from the processes of uncertainty absorption and filtering. There are three potential sources. First, managers typically have "an oar in the water," a vested interest in the outcomes on which evaluations of political factors will bear. Second, managers of host country affiliates are not neutral observers reporting dispassionately on the local scene; rather, they are part of the local elite whose viewpoint is directly influenced by their positions. Third, when local or regional managers are host country nationals, as is happening with increasing regularity,[3] the situation is even more complex. On

3. There is substantial evidence of a reduction in the number of expatriate managers maintained abroad by American firms and of their replacement by host country (or to a lesser extent, by third-country) nationals. The reasons include the increasing development of managerial and technical competence abroad, legislation and regulation in host countries,

the one hand, their dual role as full-fledged members of local society and polity and of the international firm gives them unique capabilities to judge the impact of the environment on business operations. On the other hand, dual roles may produce conflict, especially when the question at hand concerns a difference between a foreign firm and the manager's government. The dual loyalty of local nationals is thus a third potential source of bias.

As noted earlier, assessments of political environments abroad are usually reactive rather than proactive; they are most often motivated by an internal need like an investment proposal or the strategic planning process. Rarely are they independent of an action being recommended by someone within the firm. The source of both the recommendation, whether for additional investment or a five-year plan, and the environmental assessment is likely to be affiliate management. An obvious conflict is thus set up: Why would anyone recommend that the company spend $50 million for plant expansion in an unfavorable investment environment?

The problem is exacerbated by the fact that line managers, and especially managers of international affiliates, are typically selected for their ability to run the business aggressively. They tend to see the world in terms of obstacles, including political environments, which must and can be overcome. As one respondent noted, it is difficult for someone who is "business-oriented" to oppose a project based on political factors; a recommendation against such a project is considered an example of "negative thinking." Another commented that local managers are attempting to "promote their business" and that their environmental reporting may reflect "other objectives." Although the possibility of overt manipulation of environmental reporting by affiliate management does not stretch credence to the breaking point, the problem is structural. Bias is inherent in situations where environmental assessments and business recommendations are not independent of each other and where the same business unit, or even the same individual, is the primary source of both. It reflects the potential conflict between the affiliate manager's role as a boundary spanner and his or her broader responsibilities.

---

the advantages accruing to nationals from operating in the home environment, and—an important point—the increased cost of maintaining United States managers abroad. Robinson (1978) argues that, despite the decline in the number of expatriate managers, there is some evidence that multinational corporations actually plan on maintaining between 5 and 10 percent expatriates or third-country nationals in subsidiary managements.

The second source of bias is the relationship between a manager and the host society. Affiliates of large international firms are often important industrial enterprises in their host countries, especially in less developed countries which are of major concern in this study. Affiliate managers, whether nationals or expatriates, are usually in the upper strata of socio-economic hierarchies. As members of the local elite, they may belong to the same clubs and move in the same social circles as government ministers, military leaders, and local industrialists. (Whether traditional elites are included or not varies from country to country.) The chairman of a major firm producing heavy industrial products put it well: "It is not that they like the establishment, but that they are the establishment."

Membership in the local elite brings certain advantages to representatives of international firms. Managers have excellent access to government, often at the highest level. They may be kept well informed as to future policy vis-à-vis foreign firms, and they may even be able to exert influence on the shape of that policy. The costs, however, must not be overlooked. Affiliate managers are likely to see the world from the point of view of the current regime. They may feel no inclination to seek out and understand opposition groups and other sources of opinion, though in some countries such contacts may not be feasible for political reasons or for reasons of personal safety.

Because affiliate managers are biased by their standing in local society, they may see the world through the eyes of the current regime and discount the possibility of a major discontinuity such as the overthrow of Batista in Cuba, of Salazar in Portugal, of Somoza in Nicaragua, and, perhaps the best example, of the shah in Iran.[4] More important, as the number of revolutionary changes in a regime is limited, they may underestimate the opposition's ability to influence the policy of the current regime regarding foreign investment in general or their industry, or even firm, in particular. They may assume a continuity of the status quo when such an assumption is unwarranted.

The tendency toward an elite bias is intensified when firms rely on top management of the affiliates for political assessments. Interviewees came up with comments such as, "It is his job that is on the line," sug-

---

4. As reported in the press, the failure of the United States government fully to anticipate the overthrow of the shah is an example of a similar phenomenon in government agencies. Official identification with the shah's regime, and severe restrictions on contact with the Iranian opposition by government personnel, clearly affected the objectivity of political reporting and forecasting. There was definitely an elite bias.

gesting that is the case. Dependence on top management for assessments has two drawbacks. First, as noted above, elite bias is likely to be intensified. Second, the firm may be losing a potentially valuable source of environmental information by not consulting managers in the lower echelons. They are, after all, closer to academics and perhaps more technically oriented and thus may have better contacts and more empathy with a wider range of social groups, including students, the political opposition, and middle-level government bureaucrats (or "technocrats"), who often influence political-economic policy.

The third source of bias in environmental reporting by affiliate management is dual loyalty. A number of respondents expressed doubts about the objectivity of host nationals, especially in countries regarded as overtly nationalistic. A regional vice-president put it directly and colorfully: "When you have an indigene in a large nationalistic country they are never completely corporate. There is a trade-off; they will also be concerned about their country. . . . My experience is that a Frenchman is French first, a father second, a husband third, and corporate fourth. That is the way it is. That is where corporate comes." Another respondent commented: "I think their reports are colored by their interests as nationals." It is difficult to reach a conclusion on this subject given the data at hand. Host country nationals are a singularly valuable source of information about local environments and about their potential impact on business operations. They span the boundary, not only between organization and environment, but between cultures. Their unique position, however, tends to exacerbate the role conflict experienced by boundary spanners (see chap. 2) and to heighten the distrust between individuals at the organizational core and those at the periphery who are much closer to the environment. Dual loyalty affects every member of an organization who feels the pressure of multiple roles. Frenchmen are not the only fathers and husbands.[5] It is particularly divisive, however, when a host country national serves as a manager of an international firm in a developing country.

The managers interviewed were well aware of the problem. While relying primarily on internal sources of political information, they realized that a possible lack of objectivity exists. Their concern reflects the common distrust of boundary spanners, but it also, more particularly, is

5. See Smetanka (1977) for an analysis of dual loyalty and a thorough review of the literature. Smetanka's study has to do with Canadian management of American subsidiaries.

based on recognition of the difficult role of an affiliate manager, who must balance a position in the organization with a relationship to the host country.

INFORMAL AND FORMAL SEARCH

The interview data point to a significant difference between the approach of general management (either line or staff) and that of environmental assessment specialists to the scanning process. Aguilar (1967) suggests four modes of scanning, two of which are of interest here.[6] He distinguishes between informal and formal search (1967:19). The former is defined as "a relatively limited and unstructured effort to obtain specific information for a specific purpose"; the latter, as "a deliberate effort— usually following a preestablished plan, procedure or methodology—to secure specific information or information relating to a specific issue." Although the fit is far from perfect, I suggest that general management tends to engage in informal search and that political assessment specialists prefer formal search. There is a major difference in sources of information, questions asked, and search or scanning procedures.

Given the limitations of the data, findings as to differences in the scanning process are speculative; they are hypotheses rather than conclusions. Because affiliate managers were not interviewed, only secondhand data about their sources of information are available. The responses of managers who were interviewed, however, strongly suggest that systematic differences in environmental scanning patterns exist.

Managers, whether at the affiliate, regional, or headquarters level, are likely to avoid specialized sources of information. They talk with a range of people and, as noted above, tend to prefer interpersonal contact. Their sources are often specific, but they are not specialized. They are likely to include managers in other firms operating in the same country, bankers, host government officials and "old hands," but not academic specialists, United States government sources, and local experts.

The environmental assessment specialists interviewed utilized a broader range of more specialized sources. All made extensive use of United States government agencies concerned with foreign policy. They routinely contacted academic specialists and made use of country or re-

6. Aguilar's other two modes of scanning are undirected and conditioned viewing.

gional associations (e.g., the Japan Society), foundations, and lower-level bureaucrats and technocrats in the host government. Specialists reported occasional reliance on international organizations such as the World Bank, and they keep up with the specialized country and regional literature.

Environmental scanning by management may be characterized as embracing rather informal attempts to "get a feel" for the situation facing a firm. Managers are usually concerned with general aspects of the environment, as reflected in their assessments of political instability or the business or investment climate. Specialists concentrate on separate aspects of the political process and tend to pursue specialized sources of specific information. As contrasted with managerial search procedures, those of specialists are, in Aguilar's terms, more formal and systematic.

In the firm whose assessment function is institutionalized, informal scanning by line managers and formalized scanning by specialized personnel occur simultaneously. Organizational boundaries are crossed as environmental assessments are undertaken by all three groups of organizational representatives—affiliate managers, corporate international management, and political specialists.

9

Evaluation and
Utilization of
Political Assessments

Institutionalization is incomplete if the political assessment function is not fully integrated into the firm. Although functions, roles, and positions have been differentiated, relationships are often informal and variable, particularly at the point where the process is linked to other managerial activities. Virtually all firms, regardless of the degree of institutionalization, find it difficult to use political assessments in strategic planning and investment decision making.

The external environment is one of the major determinants of organizational strategy. In his classic work on strategy and structure, based on a historical analysis of the emergence of the modern corporation in the United States, Chandler (1962) concludes that changes in strategy are the managerial response to new opportunities and needs created by changes in the external environment. The proposition is inherent in an open systems view of organizations and is frequently discussed in the planning literature (see, for example, Fahey and King, 1977; Neubauer and Solomon, 1977; and Montgomery and Weinberg, 1979). Once one goes beyond the notion that the environment is a major determinant of strategy, however, the literature has little to say about the integration of environmental information into planning and decision making.

What is available is primarily normative and prescriptive. Several authors discuss such methods as directional policy matrices and cross-impact analysis which purport to facilitate the integration of environmental information into strategic planning (see Robinson, Hichens, and Wade, 1978; Hussey, 1978).[1] A few articles on international financial

1. There have been a number of attempts in the international business literature

management deal with the integration of political risk into capital budgeting (Shapiro, 1978; Stonehill and Nathanson, 1968; and Stobaugh, 1969).

Little has been written, however, on actual managerial practice. Aharoni (1966) found that managers do not formally integrate risk assessments into investment decision making; rather, they subjectively determine the degree of "risk" associated with a given country or area of the world and then avoid investments with other than normal business risks. Stobaugh (1969) concludes that most companies make foreign investment decisions on a "go or no-go" basis, subjectively integrating a general impression of the environment into the process. According to Fahey and King (1977), firms have not yet succeeded in integrating environmental scanning into strategic planning. Similarly, Segev (1977), surveying a limited number of firms, found no companies that directly translated environmental analyses into strategy changes; he concludes that environmental perceptions, responses to triggers, and the impact of analyses were subjective. In short, the utilization of environmental information in strategic planning and decision making is not formalized or institutionalized. My findings do not alter that conclusion.

USE OF POLITICAL ASSESSMENTS

Political assessments are used most frequently in investment decision making and strategic planning (see table 9–1). Of respondents to the mail survey, 78.8 percent reported systematic utilization of political analyses in making decisions on initial investments abroad; 69.9 percent, in strategic planning. Less than half (42 percent) use environmental analyses in international exchange and currency management; only 25.4 percent, in day-to-day operations. Firms that have institutionalized the function are more likely to use assessments in decision making and planning, but they are not significantly more inclined to use them in day-to-day operations (29.4 percent as opposed to 25.4 percent).

---

to use impact matrices to analyze systematically the potential effects of environmental constraints on aspects of management. In perhaps the best known, Farmer and Richman evaluate relationships between critical managerial elements (e.g., planning and innovation, control, organization) and external constraints arising from educational, sociological, political-legal, and economic environments (see Richman and Copen, 1972, for an elaboration).

TABLE 9-1
SYSTEMATIC UTILIZATION OF POLITICAL ANALYSES
(IN PERCENTAGES OF RESPONDENTS)

Objective	All respondents (N = 193)	Respondents from institutionalized firms (N = 68)
Initial investment	78.8	91.2[a]
Strategic planning	69.9	83.8[a]
Reinvestment	65.8	77.9[b]
Divestment	47.2	67.6[c]
International exchange and currency management	42.0	63.2[c]
Day-to-day operations	25.4	29.4

[a] Difference versus all respondents significant at .05.
[b] Difference versus all respondents significant at .10.
[c] Difference versus all respondents significant at .01.

Despite the regular use of political assessments in investment decision making and planning, managers are far from satisfied with current practice. Fifty-eight percent of all respondents and 70.6 percent of those in institutionalized firms felt that better integration of political analysis into planning and investment decision making is essential if the function is to be improved. Relating environmental analysis to operations was deemed essential by 30.6 percent of all respondents and by 41.2 percent of those in firms that have institutionalized the function.[2] Respondents are aware that institutionalization of the political assessment function is still incomplete (see table 9–2).

EVALUATION AND ANALYSIS

Because the managerial process is my primary interest, the mailed questionnaire asked for only basic data on use of information about ana-

2. The questionnaire suggested other steps to improve the quality of the function, such as modifying recruitment patterns and establishing better guidelines for the provision of relevant information. None of these was selected as essential by even 10 percent of the respondents.

TABLE 9-2
STEPS TO IMPROVE POLITICAL ANALYSIS
(IN PERCENTAGES OF RESPONDENTS)

Population	Number	Integrate analysis into planning and investment	Relate analysis to operations
All	193	58.0	30.6
Institutionalized firms	68	70.6	41.2
Large firms	59	67.8	37.3

lytical methods. (For a more general discussion of methods of political risk assessment, see App. C.) Respondents were requested to indicate their use of and their relative reliance on six methods of analysis. As response to the latter was minimal, only the data on use are reported in table 9–3. Qualitative methods are dominant. Almost half the respondents (46.1 percent) reported using one or more qualitative methods. Standardized checklists were used by 30.1 percent; scenario development, by 26.4 percent; delphi techniques, by 9.8 percent; and other structured qualitative formats, by 16.1 percent. In contrast, only 19.2 percent reported using any quantitative method.

The proportion of institutionalized firms reporting use of specific methods is higher. (Use of a specific method is an element of the definition of institutionalization.) Almost all of them (94.1 percent) use a qualitative method, and 42.6 percent, a quantitative method. The follow-up interviews, however, suggest that the latter figure is somewhat overstated, perhaps reflecting experimentation rather than actual utilization.

Table 9–4 shows the use of any qualitative or quantitative method cross-tabulated by characteristics of respondents. Two groups of firms—those that have institutionalized the function and those that are larger and more widespread internationally—indicate a significantly greater propensity to use a specific qualitative method than did all respondents. Except for firms where the function is institutionalized, differences by size of firm, international organization, or extent of internationalization do not significantly affect the use of quantitative methods.

The personal interview data confirm the findings of the mail survey. When a specific analytical method is used, it is likely to be a loosely structured qualitative approach such as a checklist or an outline of factors

TABLE 9-3

USE OF ANALYTICAL METHODS
(IN PERCENTAGES OF RESPONDENTS)

Method	All respondents (N = 193)	Respondents from institutionalized firms (N = 68)
Standardized checklist	30.1	60.3
Scenario development	26.4	54.4
Structured qualitative format	16.1	36.8
Statistical analysis	13.5	29.4
Computerized investment model	10.9	26.5
Delphi techniques	9.8	10.3
Any qualitative method	46.1	94.1
Any quantitative method	19.2	42.6

to be covered in a country study. Furthermore, in the light of the interview data, I suggest that such terms as "scenario development" and "delphi method" be broadly interpreted, reflecting more often than not an unstructured and informal use of those techniques.

PATTERNS OF COMMUNICATION

Boundary spanners are linked to the ultimate users of environmental information—planners and decision makers—in at least two ways: (1) through the transmission of reports, analyses, and the like; (2) perhaps more important, through formal and informal channels of communication. For the political assessment function, the findings of this study indicate that these channels are often limited and unidirectional. Direct contacts between assessment specialists and decision makers are the exception rather than the rule; and communication is often the transmission of information upward in the hierarchy without corresponding feedback.

Communication patterns within the firm were identified in terms of the transmission of political assessments and evaluations. Respondents to the mail survey, given a list of eight managerial positions, were asked whether they received political reports frequently, occasionally, rarely, or

TABLE 9-4

USE OF ANY QUALITATIVE OR QUANTITATIVE METHOD
(IN PERCENTAGES OF RESPONDENTS)

Population	Number	Qualitative method	Quantitative method
All firms	193	46.1	19.2
Institutionalized	68	94.1[a]	42.6[a]
Mature international division or global structure	82	61.0[b]	13.4
Large firms	59	59.3[c]	22.0
Firms operating in twenty-one or more countries	72	61.1[b]	15.2
Firms with foreign sales of 26 percent of total sales or more	77	58.4[c]	14.3

[a] Difference versus all respondents significant at .01.
[b] Difference versus all respondents significant at .05.
[c] Difference versus all respondents significant at .10.

never. Results tabulated for frequent receipt are presented in table 9–5. Exactly three-fourths of the firms having an international division replied that the general manager of that division receives environmental reports on a regular basis.[3] Slightly less than a third of the respondents (31.1 percent) said that the chief executive officer receives such reports, and the same percentage named the chief financial officer. The director of planning receives reports on political environments abroad in 26.4 percent of these firms; the legal counsel, in 21.8 percent. Only a small minority of firms routinely send assessments to the corporate economist (14.0 percent), the director of public affairs (10.9 percent), or the director of governmental affairs (7.3 percent).

Patterns of communication are quite different in firms where the function is institutionalized. The director of planning, the chief financial officer, and the legal counsel all receive environmental assessment reports more often than the chief executive officer. Those receiving reports most

3. An obvious source of bias in the selection of firms in this category is the weak but significant relationship between the presence of an international division and internationalization in terms of the number of countries in which a firm operates. (Kendall's tau of .16 significant at .02.)

TABLE 9-5

FREQUENT RECEIPT OF REPORTS ON OVERSEAS POLITICAL
ENVIRONMENT
(IN PERCENTAGES OF RESPONDENTS)

Position	All firms (N = 193)	Firms with function institutionalized (N = 68)	Large firms (N = 59)
Chief executive officer	31.1	33.8	27.1
Chief financial officer	31.1	42.6[a]	28.8
Director of planning	26.4	44.1[b]	37.3
Legal counsel	21.8	35.3[c]	28.8
Corporate economist	14.0	27.9	32.2[b]
Director of public affairs	10.9	17.6	23.7[b]
Director of governmental affairs	7.3	11.8	15.3[c]
General manager of international division[d]	75.0		

[a] Difference versus all respondents significant at .10.
[b] Difference versus all respondents significant at .01.
[c] Difference versus all respondents significant at .05.
[d] Includes only firms reporting an international division.

frequently are the director of planning (44.1 percent) and the chief financial officer (42.6 percent). Both proportions are significantly different from those for all firms. Institutionalization also affects the absolute proportion of respondents reporting frequent reception of environmental reports by various company officials. Differentiation of role and function and more formalization of the process are likely to increase the number of assessments and hence the frequency of reception. Institutionalization and formalization also affect the rankings, markedly increasing staff involvement in the assessment process.

Table 9–5 also gives data for large firms with sales of more than $2.5 billion. The differences versus all firms and versus institutionalized firms are instructive. Large firms show statistically significant differences from all firms for the corporate economist (32.2 versus 14.0 percent), the director of public affairs (23.7 versus 10.9 percent), and the director of governmental affairs (15.3 versus 7.3 percent). The differences reflect the tendency of large organizations to differentiate functions.

Communication between political assessors and management at the policymaking level seems to be unidirectional. When individuals in political assessment units were asked how their output was used in decision making, the usual response was one of uncertainty; often they simply did not know. Downward communication from managers at the decision-making level to political assessors is limited in many firms. The response of an environmental assessor in a large chemical firm was far from atypical: "Remember that we are asked to do these studies and that they do fill special need. But we rarely learn whether the information provided is useful or whether it has a real impact on decisions being taken." The international treasurer of a large firm whose staff prepares extensive country analyses in conjunction with new investment proposals has never been present when the ultimate decision is taken. He does not know how, or if, the information is used or how important it is compared with the analyses and opinions of line managers. It is wholly reasonable to assume, then, that assessors are also unsure of the precise needs of decision makers for political information, except when they receive direct requests.

Another kind of communications gap exists between top management and assessment personnel. A number of respondents were afraid that top management considered their reports superfluous, in view of extensive travel, frequent contacts with high-level government personnel, and the like by senior decision makers. Top management, it was felt, has access to viewpoints and sources of information not available to the "people in the trenches." To junior and middle-level staff personnel, it seems that senior managers value immediate and personal contact more than the expertise of specialized political assessors.

Interviews with managers at the decision-making level indicated that such fears are far from groundless. Two responses are illustrative. A vice-president in charge of chemical operations in a petroleum company, though acknowledging the value of the firm's assessment unit as a source of political information, said that, when it comes to a country with which he is directly concerned, "I tell them to keep out. I know more about . . . the country than they do and get better information from my people there than they can supply." The chairman of a major subsidiary of a large diversified industrial firm said: "I am not sure that they [political assessors] are more than a useful tool for the education of the board. . . . They are great for the education of the people on the ground. It forces them to think more about certain factors." He then went on to emphasize the value of informal judgment and interpersonal contact at the expense of written reports.

Third, the impact of personnel responsible for environmental assessment on the decision-making process seems often to be a function of personal relationships between assessment staff and top management. Units that feel they bring influence to bear on investment decision making, or that know how their output is used, are usually those whose chiefs enjoy direct, personal relationships with high-level managers. According to a senior vice-president of a large construction firm, an environmental assessor, to be effective, "has to have access to senior management. . . . He has to be heard, especially by the top. . . . He has to have the confidence of top management." As noted earlier, management prefers direct, personal contact in this area of high uncertainty.

INTEGRATION INTO DECISION MAKING AND PLANNING

The primary end uses of political assessments are strategic planning and investment decision making. Although few firms are satisfied with the manner in which assessments are integrated into either one, decision making, for a number of reasons, presents more difficult problems than planning.

First, political assessments are more relevant to strategic plans than to capital investment proposals. Much of strategic planning is quantifiable, but basically it is still a deductive logical process of setting objectives and determining strategies to achieve them. On the other hand, the capital budgeting process is inherently quantitative; the decision rests on the expected value and the variance or risk of a distribution of cash flows. Despite a wide difference between the ideal and the actual in capital budgeting, the objective is to express all factors that might affect the project as adjustments to cash flows over time.[4]

Although progress is being made in the quantification of political forecasting, at this point both process and output tend to be verbal and

4. There are a number of surveys of capital budgeting practice in the literature. See, for example, Gitman and Forrester (1977), and Schall, Sundem, and Geysbec (1978). For surveys that deal specifically with international investment, see Baker and Beardsley (1975), Bavishi (1978), and Stonehill and Nathanson (1968).

qualitative.[5] Social and political forecasting is qualitatively different from other types of forecasting. As Ascher (1979:204) notes, "Any observer of social and political forecasting is immediately struck not by the lack of predictions, but rather by the impossibility of appraising the record. Predictions abound, but are rarely expressed in a form that permits evaluation."

Capital budgeting, regardless of the procedure used, requires that political assessments be expressed as impacts on cash flows. Political events are among the most difficult to express in these terms, because of limited experience with actual constraints and the current state of development of political forecasting. The link between political assessments and investment analyses is thus most often intuitive and subjective. It is difficult to formally integrate assessments into the investment decision-making process.

The situation is different vis-à-vis strategic planning, since the nature of political forecasting does not severely constrain the integration of assessments into the planning process. The development of environmental assumptions as the basis for a strategic plan is a qualitative exercise that is both feasible and consistent with the open systems theory. Some of the difference in the degree of formal integration is also due to the fact that strategic planning is a relatively new field which developed, at least in part, with the recognition that organizations are open systems and that strategy must reflect an optimal fit with the environment. The strategic planner may be better attuned to and more deeply concerned with political environments than are the financial economists responsible for recent developments in capital budgeting theory and practice.

INVESTMENT DECISION MAKING

In most firms that have explicit assessment functions and virtually all of those that have differentiated the function, a written evaluation of

5. Although progress is being made in quantification of political and social assessments, the techniques are still of only limited use to international firms. The basic problem is that quantitative forecasts of political factors rather than forecasts of constraints on firms, or "political risk," are being made. For a discussion of attempts at quantitative political forecasting see Choucri and Robinson (1978), Gurr (1978), and Huer (1978). For attempts to quantitatively model aspects of the problem, most notably expropriation, see Jodice (1980) and Kobrin (1980).

the political environment is included in any recommendation to invest abroad. The evaluation may be included in the appropriation request, or it may be a separate memorandum; sometimes it entails a formal presentation to the decision-making body.

The main difference between firms that have differentiated the function and those that have not involves the extent and the formality of the political analysis associated with the capital appropriation recommendation. In a minority of firms where the function is not differentiated the process is completely informal; an investment proposal does not contain a written analysis of political environments. For example, the international treasurer of a large rubber products company said that the investment committee might table discussion on a proposal pending receipt of a political report, but usually there was no formal analysis of environmental factors: "The regional guys know pretty much right off whether we want to invest someplace."

Most of the companies with the function undifferentiated do, however, prefer to see a brief written environmental analysis included with an appropriation request. Typical analyses, ranging from a paragraph to a page, contain general descriptions of the investment climate. The president of the international division of a transportation products company perceptively characterized the evaluation of political risk as a subconscious, before-the-fact process in which managers sort out high- and low-risk environments in advance of investment decision making. Once they reach the point of formal analysis, then, they have decided that a certain opportunity is worth exploiting because the risks are low enough to provide a reasonable environment for investment.

Political analysis as a prelude to investment decision making is more formal and more extensive in firms that have differentiated the function. It is more formal in that the investment proposal package is expected to contain political analysis. It is more extensive in that the analyses are likely to include, for major investments, detailed country studies. For example, the international treasurer of a firm that has differentiated the function, but not the position, has an assistant prepare a country study, using an outline or a checklist, whenever a new international investment is proposed. The international comptroller of a transportation products company reported that thorough country studies were drawn up when major new investments abroad were under investigation.

Differences between types of firms tend to break down at the point where political assessments are integrated into investment decision making. A manager directly concerned in both responsibilities in a company that has differentiated the function pointed out that the findings of country studies, even when reflected in qualitative form in appropriation proposals, are taken into account only informally and subjectively. No structured means of integrating assessments into decision making and no coherent process for weighing political factors exist. None of the firms interviewed gave evidence of a functional relationship between political analysis and investment decision making; country studies and other analyses, including those conducted specifically for investment purposes, serve as a background, or a context. According to a director of business planning, such studies may confirm or deny preconceived ideas held by corporate management. Political assessments, though useful, are not formally integrated into the process of decision making.

Political analyses affect the capital budgeting process in various ways. Most firms look upon them as background. Political factors do not enter directly into the calculations of rates of return, net present value, or the like. A minority of companies, however, do try either to adjust discount or "hurdle" rates for the incremental risk stemming from political factors or to adjust cash flows directly for potential contingencies. In this connection, two points should be made. First, the link between political assessment and an investment proposal is almost always judgmental. Even in the few companies that attempt to add risk premiums, the process is qualitative and subjective. Few, if any, firms integrate assessments into investment decision making mechanically, that is, through rigid quantification. In fact, a number of firms have, after due consideration, flatly rejected this approach. Second, adjustment of cash flows to reflect the potential impact of political factors is more a theory than a practice. Although some firms have experimented with such techniques as sensitivity analysis, none included in this survey or encountered thereafter actually attempt this theoretically preferred approach to integration of political assessments into capital budgeting decisions. As indicated earlier, at this point such integration remains judgmental. Yet there is enough ground between rigid mechanical quantification and completely intuitive "seat of the pants" judgment to permit improvement in the objectivity and effectiveness of the process and thus to generate better-informed judgmental decision making.

PLANNING

Within limits, formal integration of political assessments into strategic planning is more common than formal integration into investment decision making. In addition, the differences between firms that have institutionalized the function and those that have not are more apparent. As with capital budgeting, there is wide variation in practice among firms where the function is explicit but not differentiated, ranging from informal (i.e., nonwritten) integration to an assumptions section of the plan that includes political analysis. Typically, the analysis is a short statement that summarizes major environmental factors. In a number of noninstitutionalized companies using political analysis to develop planning assumptions, respondents belittled its importance by saying, for example, "The operating companies are not bound by the formal assumptions section," or "The affiliates regard it as a duty statement."

As a rule, firms where the function is differentiated, and especially those where function, role, and position are all differentiated, integrate assessments into the planning process more formally. Five of the six firms that employ environmental assessment specialists use political analysis to develop the basic assumptions that underlie strategic planning. (The sixth is a construction firm in which strategic planning is not so fully developed as in industrial firms in the group.) In at least three of these firms, the process is formalized and institutionalized, with the development of environmental assumptions being the first step in the annual planning cycle.

In a large diversified industrial firm, the political assessment coordinator (who is affiliated with the international planning department) works with operating units to develop annual environmental assessments. Outside consultants are employed to work up many of the country studies. The development of environmental assumptions comes early in the planning cycle, with the coordinator continuing to participate in planning. The operating units develop the plans, but the international department signs off the final product, thus sharing in the responsibility.

At least some institutionalized firms, therefore, integrate political assessments into planning more formally than they do into investment decision making. By using assessments to develop an assumptions base, firms are able to functionally relate the political assessment process to its end use. It is impossible, however, to determine from this study—even in relatively institutionalized firms—whether the development of assumptions appears at the beginning of a plan because it is required, or whether it really is a base on which the plan is built. It is not unreasonable to assume that in at least some instances practice is stood on its head and assumptions are developed after the fact to support the plan being recommended. Further research into the utilization of assessments in planning is clearly needed.

One further use of political analysis should be mentioned. Assessment units in some firms develop summaries in the form of books intended to be used as background material by management. Such summaries may report significant issues likely to arise on a global or a regional basis in the future. Or they may discuss demographic and environmental trends that could affect the firm, regulatory pressures, and trade and investment issues. Alternatively, some firms develop summaries of social, political, and economic environments in various countries for use as background in planning, visits, and the like. In several of the firms visited considerable effort and resources are devoted to this activity.

GENERAL CONCLUSIONS

When attempts are made to integrate political assessments into the larger managerial process, differences between firms that have insitutionalized the function and those that have not begin to break down. Whereas the six relatively institutionalized firms where function, role, and position are all differentiated (i.e., firms employing political assessment specialists) prepare formal political analyses in conjunction with new investment decisions abroad, integration into decision making is clearly subjective and intuitive in all of them. Political assessments are communicated to management but they are simply one more item of information considered with impressions derived from travel; meetings with managers in other firms, government officials, and bankers; informal discussions with host country management; the media; and many other sources. It is far from clear that they are the most important input (vis-à-vis political environments), and it is uncertain how their importance is weighted versus other information sources.

A respondent responsible for formal risk assessment said that, at the top level of management, "the bogie of risk rears itself in a very undefined way. . . . The problem is that top management's evaluations are

subjective and more subjective than they have to be, given the information available in the company. Top management is not taking advantage
of the information that is available." Even in institutionalized firms the
output of assessment units seems to serve as background for investment
decisions or as a context in which they are made. A number of respondents noted that a response to their efforts is expected only if top-level
managers disagree markedly with a given assessment. In other instances,
assessments are simply additional background data.

The actual integration of political assessments into decision making
is subjective and implicit in the sense that it is the result of an intuitive
mental process. The director of business planning of a large industrial
firm caught the essence of the problem when remarking that everybody
has a different definition of risk. In the end each individual has to make a
judgment as to whether the risk justifies the return. At least in this industrial firm, a sophisticated multinational that emphasizes both financial
management and strategic planning, there is no precise method of bal-
ancing risk and return.

To characterize integration into decision making as subjective or intuitive is quite different from claiming that the assessment process is itself
based on "gut feelings" or on a "seat of the pants" judgment. Although a
number of companies interviewed could be characterized, and indeed
characterized themselves, as such, virtually all of those in which the function is institutionalized devoted considerable resources to formalizing the
process. Numerous examples of sensitive and reasoned assessments were
made by line managers on the basis of reading, travel, and personal experience which could in no way be called "seat of the pants." When the decision-making point is reached, however, the process by which assessments are translated into estimates of impacts on returns and risks is
clearly intuitive and subjective.

Describing the integration of assessments into decision making as
subjective rather than objective does not refer to the nature of the data,
the extent of formal analysis, or the complexity of the process. As Armstrong (1978) notes, in an analogous although slightly different context,
the critical difference is that subjective processes entail translating inputs
into forecasts in the researcher's head, whereas objective processes involve explicit and clearly specified methods that can be replicated by others. The integration of political assessments into investment decision
making is subjective in the sense that the translation of qualitative sum-

maries of environments into impacts on operations, into forecasts of risk and return, takes place intuitively through mental processes that are difficult if not impossible to make explicit, much less to replicate.

Decision makers must use evaluations of the political environment, which often deal with the investment climate, to calculate intuitively and implicitly, impacts on risk and return. The application of a political assessment to a specific investment often occurs entirely within the mind of the decision maker. It is difficult to determine the importance or even the specific meaning of political events and processes and perceptions of their relationship to the firm's operations. The relative lack of experience in this area and the inherent subjectivity of the task environment provide ample reason to raise concerns about comparability. Two managers on an investment decision-making committee may well see the same event (e.g., a coup) in a very different light and each may have a very different idea of its potential impact on operations.

To conclude that political assessments serve as a context in which investment decisions are made or that integration is subjective does not imply that the assessments do not affect outcomes. Ascher (1979) suggests that the impact of forecasts (or other technical inputs) on policymaking has three dimensions: (1) the attention received from policymakers; (2) the explicitness of use; and (3) "the decisiveness of the forecast in the choice of decision outcomes." Ascher describes explicitness in terms of a continuum, ranging from total disregard of the input by policymakers, through mere inclusion in the information base, to the extreme where policy choices resulting from optimization procedures are regarded as binding. He concludes that, although explicit use may "enhance the decisiveness of forecasts, a forecast may be decisive even if it is not explicitly used in decision making deliberations." According to Ascher, forecasts that are "merely informational can still strongly alter the decision maker's perspective, and hence structure his choices" (1979:17).

Hence, to conclude that institutionalization is incomplete in the sense that integration into decision making and, to a lesser extent, into strategic planning is implicit rather than explicit does not imply that political assessments do not affect strategic outcomes. It does suggest, however, that the link between assessments and decision making is subjective and intuitive, that it depends on judgmental processes. It is markedly affected by individual perceptions of environmental factors and of their relationship to operations. The variations in managerial perceptions will cause substantial variation in individual interpretations of political assessments and in their implications for project risk and return.

BETTER-INFORMED JUDGMENT

There is considerable room for choice between a "seat of the pants" judgment and rigid and mechanical integration of assessments into investment decisions or strategic planning. With the art of political risk assessment not fully developed, the judgmental link between environmental evaluations and an investment decision or a strategic plan is of crucial importance. Its objectivity and effectiveness, however, can be considerably improved.

Two impediments to more effective use of political assessments are the very nature of the assessments and the organizational structures that produce them. Assessments are seldom functionally related to their ultimate use. They vary in quality, in extent of coverage, and in specificity, but rarely do they directly reflect the information needs of capital budgeting or strategic planning. The problem is easiest to see in the context of investment decision making.

Capital budgeting analysis requires that factors with potential impacts on an investment be expressed in terms of their effects on the magnitude and distribution of cash flows. Although precise quantification of such impacts is impossible at this point, it is possible to express political assessments in these terms. To the extent that assessments include forecasts of specific impacts rather than general evaluations of the macro political situation or the investment climate, they can more easily be taken into account in investment decision making. Similarly, the estimating of potential impacts on a year-by-year basis increases correspondence between the political assessment and the input needs of capital budgeting.

Functionally relating political assessments to the capital budgeting process reduces the necessary scope of judgment. It also facilitates more objective judgment as assumptions about the meaning of events and their impact on operations are made explicit. Precise impacts on risk and return may still have to be estimated rather than calculated, but the estimating can be direct, thus minimizing the role of intuition.

Existing organizational relationships reflect, and are indeed partly responsible for, the incomplete institutionalization of the political assessment process. Even in firms in which function, role, and position are fully differentiated, the impact of assessment units on planning and decision making often depends on interpersonal relationships that are not formalized. The extent to which assessments are used may well be a function of relationships between individuals occupying given roles at any point in time, rather than either the potential impact of environmental contingencies or the formal organizational structure for political evaluation.

General organizational problems often affect this function. Political assessment units are constrained by traditional line-staff conflicts. Operating management may see staff groups and/or assessment units as obstacles rather than as assets. In what was described by one respondent as the "not created here" syndrome, affiliate management views the headquarters-based assessment unit as a threat, making judgments on political environments from a distance which might be obstacles to approval of recommendations and business plans. In one extreme instance, presumably atypical, a political analyst in a large industrial firm said he was detained by the general manager of a Latin American affiliate until his report was complete and could be signed off by the individual in question.

MULTIPLE SOURCES OF INFORMATION

The political assessment process involves a large number of flows of information about political factors from a variety of sources that do not converge until the decision-making phase of the process is reached. As I have noted frequently, boundary scanning of political environments takes place at many points throughout the organization. Information is obtained from affiliate management, from travel and personal contact by senior management, from conversations with bankers, from discussions with colleagues in other firms, from the media, and, in institutionalized firms, from formal investigations by assessment units.

Political assessment in all the firms interviewed may thus be characterized by pluralistic boundary scanning and multiple sources. It may also be characterized in terms of independent flows of information that do not converge until they reach the decision maker. The various sources and scattered bits of intelligence are rarely compared and reconciled formally before that point. Rather, many data, ranging from raw unprocessed intelligence to formal evaluations of impacts on investments, converge at the decision point and provide a context for the decision making. There is no official point of uncertainty absorption (see chap. 2). In conditions of uncertainty and ambiguity, multiple sources of data are a decided advantage, but much of that potential advantage is lost if divergent and often contradictory pieces of information are not formally compared and reconciled before they are integrated into decision making.

It is easy to lose perspective when conducting research focusing on a single aspect of a complex phenomenon. Politics, though undoubtedly a factor in investment decision making and strategic planning, is only one of a large number of factors, and in many situations its impact is marginal. With some obvious exceptions—including countries and regions that companies refuse to consider for political reasons—most investment decisions are not based on political factors.[6] For resource-based firms, especially oil companies, geology clearly dominates. Such a company cannot consider a country without oil, even though the political climate may be very attractive. For manufacturing firms the most important factor is market size and potential.[7] It is clear, then, that the political environment may have a major impact on an investment decision but is rarely the basis for it.

6. An example that came up a number of times in the interviews was the "redlining" of Vietnam by several oil companies after bad experiences in the early 1970s.

7. Empirical analysis of the determinants of foreign direct investment clearly demonstrates that the primary determinant of manufacturing FDI is market size and potential. See Green (1972) and Kobrin (1976b). Kobrin (1979) provides a review.

10
Conclusions

Two closely related themes interwoven throughout this book—the emergence and institutionalization of the political assessment function and the effect of uncertainty and ambiguity on its nature and performance—provide the organizational framework for this chapter. First I review and integrate the major findings of this study. Then I apply the findings to managerial practice, arguing that institutionalization results in more effective political assessment by facilitating better utilization of existing resources. I also discuss the organizational implications of the findings, briefly touching on such questions as location and staffing of the political assessment function. I conclude by suggesting that the problems of environmental assessment discussed in this book are found in organizations other than business firms and that in all cases environmental assessment is a problem of managerial process.

INSTITUTIONALIZATION

Assuming that political assessment is inherent in the management of international operations, I have been concerned with the manner in which the function is performed. I have focused specifically on institutionalization, including (1) differentiation of the function through formal assignment of responsibilities and establishment of specialized organizational positions and (2) formalization of the process through use of more explicit methods, centralization of control, and coordination of information flows. Institutionalization, taking concrete form in changes in managerial strategy and organizational structure, is a response of management to perceptions of potentially significant contingencies arising from political events and processes.

Significant impacts are those that can affect the setting and the achievement of organizational objectives. Specifically, they affect returns and/or risks to the extent that project viability is threatened.[1] The probability that significant contingencies will arise depends on the firm's vulnerability to political factors and the potential cost of such contingencies. Vulnerability stems from the nature of the political environment and from the strategy and organizational structure of the firm. The potential cost of contingencies varies with asset exposure abroad (relative to firm size and internationalization) and with the cost to the firm of disruption of the activities of a subsidiary.

Pressures for institutionalization arise from the factors responsible for the expansion of the task environment (see chap. 4), which include politicization of economic activity, the surge of nationalism, the complexity of the international political system, and internationalization of the firm. Pressures for institutionalization are a manifestation of the transnational reality of the global firm. They reflect strategic problems encountered in attempting to operate as a unified system in a world of fragmented and independent nation-states.

My first conclusion, then, is that external political environments are likely to become even more important in determining the strategy of international firms. Managerial concern with politics is not a temporary aberration reflecting short-term environmental fluctuations. Although the form of international business transactions may vary in the future,[2] the global firm reflects the worldwide integration of production through the internalization of market processes. Barring a major discontinuity,

---

1. The formula for discounting cash flows to arrive at their net present values is

$$\text{N.P.V.} = \Sigma \ \frac{cf_i}{(1+r)^i}$$

where i is the period under consideration and r is the cost of capital which includes a premium for risk. Assuming no funding constraint exists, any project whose net present value is positive would be approved. Significant impacts of the political environment on a project may be defined in terms of effects on either the magnitude of cash flows in any period or periods (cf_i) or on their distribution so as to affect the riskiness of the project and ultimately the discount rate chosen. Significant impacts would render the net present value negative when it would have been positive in their absence. It is a rather strict definition in terms of project viability and, given funding constraints, impacts that reduced returns without threatening viability itself could alter the relative attractiveness of a project and thus be significant.

2. Most international firms in the period since World War II have been linked together via equity ownership of assets in the subsidiary by the headquarters, by foreign direct investment. Equity investment is only one of a number of ways to link firms internationally. For example, in most of the large petroleum firms contractual arrangements have

that underlying trend is unlikely to be reversed in the foreseeable future. On the other hand, global political integration is much less advanced. Nation-states will remain the primary unit of social organization. Trends in both environment and organization suggest that firm-state conflict and thus political risk will be a major preoccupation of managers for some time to come.

The expansion of the task environment to include political factors has resulted in the emergence of political assessment as a formal or institutionalized managerial function. More than half of the firms responding to the mail survey have taken at least minimal steps to systematize political assessment, and 35 to 38 percent seem to have begun the institutionalization of the assessment function through the assignment of responsibilities and the formalization of process. There has been a marked change from a decade ago, when similar studies (e.g., Root, 1968*a*) found little if any evidence of systematic response to external political environments.[3]

Institutionalization results from perception of vulnerability to politically generated contingencies and their potential cost to the firm. Companies pursuing global integration are strategically more vulnerable to the fragmenting influences of diverse political environments and are more likely to institutionalize the assessment function than those whose development abroad is at an earlier stage. Companies operating in many countries and thus finding their political environment more heterogeneous and variable than before respond by formalizing political assessment. Larger organizations have more reason to differentiate the function than their smaller counterparts and are better able to do so.

Certain sectors, such as petroleum, are heavily politicized in most host countries, and that fact alone motivates institutionalization. In other instances, however, industrial sector and technology affect vulnerability to, and the potential cost of, politically generated contingencies in partly

---

replaced equity at the production stage. A number of observers have suggested that contractual arrangements such as licensing, management contracts, and contractual joint ventures, which are common in eastern European organizations, may be more prevalent in the future. A move from equity to contract will change the nature of the international firm, but it will not change the need for assessment and evaluation of external political environments.

3. In the period since the survey was conducted (1978–79) and this writing the tendency to institutionalize the assessment function has strengthened. A sizable number of firms, including some of those surveyed and interviewed, have hired political specialists, often with foreign service or intelligence backgrounds.

offsetting ways. For example, firms in the consumer products sector are particularly vulnerable to political contingencies because of their mature technology, but the offsetting factor is that the potential cost is low because the establishment of operations does not require large amounts of capital. The situation of firms in sectors such as chemicals and industrial machinery is less clear-cut. Whereas their high levels of technology may lessen vulnerability, the large capital commitments required to establish operations make political contingencies potentially costly.

Institutionalization of the assessment function is incomplete at present. Almost half (45 percent) of the largest, most international firms have not institutionalized the function. Even though some of these are in sectors where the potential cost of political contingencies is low, the percentage is still striking. Moreover, assessment of political environments is basically reactive. Only a third of the respondents reported routine environmental monitoring. Many firms assess political environments abroad only on demand, as when an investment proposal is pending or a major event takes place in an important country. Of firms that have institutionalized the assessment function, 59 percent reported routine environmental monitoring; thus 41 percent, a substantial proportion, do not.

Most important, institutionalization is incomplete in that the assessment function is not fully integrated into planning or decision making in any of the firms interviewed. Institutionalization breaks down at the point where assessments are used in the managerial process. Although the needed structures have been established, relationships are highly variable and depend on the person rather than on the position. Regardless of the degree of institutionalization, political evaluations most often serve as a context in which investment decisions are made. Because political evaluations are usually not functionally related to the investment decision process, they are rarely incorporated into the decision algorithm in an objective and explicit way. Rather, they seem to be merely an additional item of information for decision makers, along with personal observations, conversations with subordinates, reports from the media, and the like. Data from all these sources are subjectively integrated into decisions. Integration of political assessments into strategic planning is often more explicit because qualitative assessments are more germane to planning than they are to the quantitative capital budgeting process.

Other manifestations of incomplete institutionalization are limited communication between assessment units and management—assessors often do not know how or even if their output is used—the credibility problems of staff assessment units, and the influence of both factors on personal relationships. I suggest that incomplete institutionalization, and especially the unstable relationships and the subjective integration of data into decision making, reflect the high degree of uncertainty associated with political environments abroad and their potential impact on firms.

UNCERTAINTY AND AMBIGUITY

Uncertainty is a major factor affecting the performance of the political assessment function, for three reasons. First, managers are uncertain about existing political environments because their understanding of political processes abroad is limited. The problem is compounded by the necessity of dealing simultaneously with a large number of different political environments.

Second, relationships between political events or processes and the firm's operations are unclear. Managers may realize that constraints have been imposed on their firms, but they cannot as easily trace the underlying environmental determinants. Furthermore, few historical data have been gathered on the relationship between political environments abroad and managerial contingencies. As potential political contingencies are markedly affected by the characteristics of a particular project, it is difficult to generalize. The problem is manifest in attempts at causal explanation couched in terms such as "economic nationalism" and "corrupt politics."

Third, the problem of forecasting the impact of politics on a firm is in itself complex and difficult. Political assessment requires a compound prediction of, first, probable environmental scenarios and, second, the probable impact of each on a specific project. Difficulties encountered in social and political forecasting, and the variance in ultimate effects by project, also contribute to the problem. As a result, it is hard for managers to envision potential outcomes or impacts on firms and therefore to estimate probabilities or to imagine possible futures. They reveal their uncertainty by expressing concern about political environments abroad in diffuse and subjective terms. Although managers worry more about political instability than any other factor, most respondents interviewed were unable either to define instability or to predict how it might affect business operations. Instability is used to articulate managerial uncertainty about political environments.

Three factors account for the high level of uncertainty about political environments abroad and their relationship to the firm's operations: (1) the comparative nature of the political assessment problem in the international firm; (2) the newness of the political assessment function for most firms; (3) the project-specific nature of impacts.

Uncertainty about environmental events may be inherent in the events themselves or it may result from difficulties that individuals and organizations have in observing them. The comparative nature of the political assessment problem exacerbates both of these aspects. Political events do not have universal meaning; they are irregular and destabilizing only to the extent that they violate the established role expectations in a specific political system (Ake, 1974). Whether violent activity or unscheduled changes in regime are irregular depends, to a large extent, on the context in which they occur. To take the most common example, the implications of a coup d'etat vary widely from country to country. A coup in Washington, London, or Tokyo would clearly be destabilizing; indeed, it would be a major discontinuity. In political systems with less fully developed institutions, a coup may simply represent a change in elites and may be neither destabilizing nor discontinuous. In other contexts, or at other times, it is both.

If the implications of political events are specific to a given situation, operating simultaneously in a large number of different environments increases their inherent uncertainty. It decreases a manager's confidence that the correct meaning is being assigned to any given event. The comparative nature of the problem increases managers' difficulties in observing political events. There are few truly "multinational" managers. Most human beings are basically ethnocentric; they tend to interpret stimuli in terms of their own culture and within their own range of experience. The problem is acute in international firms, where decisions must be made in one society based on signals arising in another. Transcultural judgments markedly increase the difficulty of interpreting political events. Thus the comparative nature of the assessment problem increases the ambiguity inherent in environmental events and the difficulties of observing them, and uncertainty is thereby heightened.

The link between models of reality used by individuals or organizations and reality itself is experience (see chap. 2). The implication is that adjustments to an organization's model of an external environment result from interaction with the environment at its boundaries. Political assessment is unique among managerial functions, as it must be newly created when a firm expands internationally rather than merely adapted from the company's domestic experience. Most business functions, such as marketing, finance, and production, have always been basic managerial responsibilities. While they must be adapted to conditions abroad, a firm can draw on its base of domestic experience to do so. Political assessment is quite another matter; it has not been a requisite of effective managerial performance on the home ground. There is no corpus of domestic experience, no "organizational wisdom," on which to draw when a more formal approach to the problem is needed.

There are two problems. Most American managers lack a formal understanding of the political process. International relations is not commonly taught to students in graduate business schools nor is it a significant component of most MBA programs.[4] Furthermore, managers have not had enough experience with political environments abroad to "learn by doing." The same point applies to constraints imposed on firms as a result of politics. Most managers have not had sufficient experience with impacts on operations to understand clearly the relationships between environment and firm. Experiential learning has been limited and modifications to models of reality problematic. In more formal terms, a sufficient body of experience does not exist at either the individual or the organizational level to inductively model either the political environment or its impacts on the firm.[5]

It is particularly hard to achieve understanding of environments and their impacts on firms because such impacts are specific to an industry, a firm, or even a project. It is almost impossible to generalize about the political environment in any given country, or about different projects of a single firm. The experience of other firms is not necessarily relevant, and to build up a body of experience through which models of reality can be modified is difficult.

Uncertainty about political environments and their relationship to the firm's operations affects the political assessment process in a number of ways. The lack of a formal understanding of politics by managers and

4. For example, only 10 of 268 candidates for the master's degree at the Sloan School at MIT in 1980–81 had undergraduate backgrounds in government, politics, international relations, or public affairs. Although the Sloan School may be an extreme case owing to its technical environment, differences among other business schools are those of degree rather than kind.

5. Survey research supports a hypothesis that general, subjective, and intuitive assessments of political environments abroad are, at least in part, attributable to a lack of experience.

of a body of individual or organizational experience means that most observers have no framework within which to interpret environmental information. The result is that there will be wide variation in the interpretation of conversations with host government officials and in impressions gained from travel, media reports, formal political assessments, and so on. Perceptions of political environments and of potential impacts on firms will also vary, especially among individuals in different managerial functions and at different levels in the hierarchy. Perceptions vary considerably between assessment specialists and both affiliate managers and ultimate decision makers. Perceptions of environments and of their relationship to the firm may vary even among members of the same decision-making body.

Uncertainty about political environments and their impacts on firms also means that models of reality tend to be implicit, general, and subjective. Inability to imagine future outcomes leads to difficulty in articulating them and in clearly explaining assessments of either current or future environments. It is difficult to express uncertainty about the environment and its potential impacts except in terms such as a "poor investment climate" or an "unstable situation."

The inability to communicate explicitly means that managers talk to individuals who can be reached on the implicit and intuitive level. This interchange requires a strong commonality in background, experience, and world view. It helps to explain the central role played by line management in the assessment process. Line managers are likely to have the most in common with top management, the ultimate consumer of environmental information. They are likely to be the group with whom, and among whom, implicit and intuitive communication is most feasible and the inability to express environmental assessments formally causes the least difficulty.

Aside from concerns about bias (see chap. 8), the only major reservation about affiliate managers as sources of political information has to do with host country nationals. In part, respondents' doubts about the loyalty of these nationals may reflect cultural distance as a barrier to implicit communication. In short, managers prefer to discuss political environments abroad with people whose thinking they understand.

The same argument extends to bankers, the primary external source of information. In addition to the objective factors that make their assessments valuable, such as knowledge of their clients' business, they have much in common, in background and experience, with the managers with whom they deal. Thus communication about concepts that are difficult to express formally is facilitated.

High levels of uncertainty and difficulties in explicit expression help explain two aspects of the assessment process: (1) the failure of information flows to converge before the decision point is reached, and (2) the lack of communication between assessment specialists and top management. The filtering of organizational communication (see chap. 2) includes uncertainty absorption, an editing process in which the inferences drawn from direct environmental perceptions, rather than direct evidence, are communicated internally. Recipients of transmissions, unable to judge the quality of the evidence, must have confidence in the source of communications. March and Simon (1958) posit that, the more complex the data and the less adequate the organization's language, the closer to the source of information uncertainty absorption is likely to take place and the stronger the tendency to summarize at each step in the process. (See chap. 2 for a discussion of organizational communication, coding, and uncertainty absorption.)

The implication that uncertainty absorption takes place closer to organizational boundaries applies to the political assessment process in an involuted form. I suggest that there is a tendency for the ultimate consumer of political information—decision makers in top management— to span the organizational boundary directly and obtain information through personal experience. As it is difficult to express assessments formally, decision makers prefer firsthand experience to filtered information. They want flows of raw data, particularly in the form of direct communication with individuals they know and trust. They minimize filtering and uncertainty absorption by placing themselves at the boundary of the organization. There is then no formal point of uncertainty absorption, no point at which the varied flows of information about political environments are formally compared and reconciled.

Barriers to communication between political assessment specialists and top management, as described in this study, take two explicit forms. Communication is limited because assessment units often do not know how, or even if, their output is actually used. Such units also find their credibility suspect, as top management distrusts formal assessments and prefers direct input from personal experience or from colleagues. These communication and credibility problems arise from the high levels of uncertainty associated with political environments abroad and the difficulties experienced in formally and explicitly expressing models of reality. It is not easy for top management to communicate intuitively with environmental specialists whose orientation and background are often different, or to evaluate the latter's output.

Finally, difficulties in articulating explicit models of reality detract from the usability of assessments for planning and decision making. Typically no functional relationship exists between assessments and plans or investment decision analyses; political information serves only as a context or background for decision making. Again, the problem stems from the difficulty of expressing political environmental assessments formally. High levels of uncertainty about environments and their relationship to operations are barriers to more explicit integration into capital budgeting analyses and planning.

I am not arguing, however, that uncertainty explains all the variance. There are other important determinants of the tendency to rely on internal and personal sources of information, of barriers to communication between assessors and decision makers, and of the failure to integrate political assessments into investment decisions. Yet uncertainty, and particularly uncertainty about current political environments and their relationship to operations, is a major determinant of the nature of political assessment function in international firms.

ARGUMENT FOR INSTITUTIONALIZATION

Does institutionalization really make a difference? Does it make political assessment more effective? The findings of this study, which did not measure performance, do not provide a definitive answer, but they do suggest an affirmative one.

Institutionalization means the specific assignment of responsibility for political assessment and the formalization of procedures, which usually involves the employment or development of assessment specialists within a firm. Institutionalization makes for better use of existing resources by (1) making scanning more efficient and effective through better utilization of a wider range of information sources; (2) improving patterns of communication within a firm and coordination and control of information flows by providing a focal point for the assessment function; (3) enabling assessment specialists to fill a number of important educational roles within a firm. The third point may well be the strongest argument for institutionalization.

MORE EFFECTIVE SCANNING

A political assessment unit can increase the effectiveness of scanning in a number of ways. Specialists are likely to have access to a wider variety of sources than line management. They approach scanning in a more formal way, contact a broader range of more highly specialized sources, and are more likely to search within an overall intellectual framework, at least regarding the nature of political environments (see chap. 8). They are more inclined and better able to make use of specialized sources for two reasons. First, through education and experience they know more about these sources than do managers in general. They understand the organization of government agencies, such as the State Department, and know how to locate and evaluate academic experts. Perhaps more important, specialists act as translators. They serve as a bridge between a source of country-specific information and the need to assess potential impacts on the firm's operations. Their knowledge of firm-specific factors such as industry structure and technology, combined with their ability to engage country experts, gives access to a broader range of expertise than would otherwise have been available. Translators can apply country expertise to estimates of project-specific political risks.

A further advantage is that the assessment units' estimates of potential contingencies arising from political environments are at least partly insulated from an active interest in an investment proposal or a strategic plan. Institutionalization should help the firm to deal with sources of bias (see chap. 8). Independence, however, is a two-edged sword. Too often assessors are on the periphery of the organization, outside the pale of the managerial process. Since they may not fully understand investment decision making or strategic planning, their actual influence on outcomes may be limited.

Institutionalization may improve scanning through formalization of assessment procedures. As noted above, inherent subjectivity and a rather high degree of uncertainty make comparability a major problem. One can never be sure that different individuals attach the same meaning to environmental events or view their impact on operations in the same way. Conceptual models are lacking. Such problems are exacerbated by the handling of the assessment process in most firms. Country managers, who constitute the primary source of information, typically decide what to report and how to report it on a "bottom up" basis.

Even limited systematization of assessment procedures can therefore make a major contribution to increased comparability. Sophisticated or elegant techniques are not necessarily required, but rather an effort to ensure consistency among individuals spanning organizational boundaries. Some degree of structure, some rough or simple model of the character of the political environment and its relationship to the firm, should be available to individuals who scan political environments. Perhaps nothing more than a checklist or an outline may be required, or a more complex procedure may be desirable (see App. C). In any event, some effort to make procedures more systematic will mean that assessments can be compared across countries and across time (or managers) within the same country.

PATTERNS OF COMMUNICATION

Institutionalization provides a focal point for political assessment within a firm and a means for improving communication flows between those scanning environments and those using their output. Institutionalization should increase coordination and centralization of information flows. In the words of March and Simon (1958:166), "When it is important that all parts of the organization act on the same premises, and where different individuals may draw different conclusions from the raw evidence, a formal uncertainty absorption point will be established, and the inferences drawn at that point will have official status in the organization as 'legitimate estimates.'" The findings of this study suggest that no official uncertainty absorption point exists for political information, even in many of the firms that have institutionalized the function. Multiple sources of information about the political environment which are not coordinated are the rule rather than the exception.

Important information is thus lost. Because of subjectivity and uncertainty, multiple sources of information are clearly an advantage. The way a situation is seen is influenced by the observer's background and position. A local industrialist, a host country government official, a student leader, and the firm's general manager may see the political environment and its potential impacts in different ways, with none of them being entirely wrong. The value of a diversity of opinions, of multiple sources of information and pluralistic scanning, will be lost if divergent views are not reconciled.

Consensus must not be forced, lest the forthcoming average be meaningless, but analyses should be compared and an effort should be made to understand the reasons for differences. That process is facilitated by the existence of a focal point for political assessment within an organization. An assessment unit is just that kind of focal point, providing both the opportunity and the capability to compare and reconcile differences. It provides the potential for a formal point of uncertainty absorption.

Institutionalization, especially the formal assignment of responsibility, also provides the potential for improving communication flows between assessors and users of political analyses. In chapter 9, I suggest that few firms are satisfied with their prevailing method of integrating political evaluations into planning and decision making. A large part of the problem is a breakdown in communications between political assessors and top management. It is likely that many assessment specialists simply do not understand the information needs of strategic planners, and especially of those responsible for foreign investment decisions. The obverse is also true: top management does not realize the capabilities or appreciate the potential contribution of assessors. Difficulties in effectively using political assessments result in part, from a lack of correspondence between the output of assessment units and the input needed by planners and decision makers. Improving the fit requires the establishment of effective communication.

Whereas institutionalization does make possible efficient use of multiple sources of information and the improvement of communication, it does not inherently do so. As noted throughout this book, situations where the assessment unit is not well integrated into the organization, where institutionalization is incomplete, are more common than not. Institutionalization is therefore a necessary but not a sufficient condition for improving communications and coordinating information flows. Whether or not it can be successful depends to a large degree on the way the assessment function is organized.

ORGANIZATIONAL LEARNING

Perhaps the most important benefit of political assessment units is their serving as a catalyst for improving the assessment capabilities of general management. Country and regional managers are the most valuable source of information about political environments abroad. The multinational's network of managers, many of whom are local nationals, operate both within the host environment and in the organization and are in a unique position to scan political environments and assess probable impacts on operations. Line managers will continue to be the most important source of political information in the future; indeed, I argue that political risk assessment is basically a line management function.

Political assessment units can make line managers more effective assessors in at least two ways. First, they can improve the quality of line management's judgment about political risk, both formally and informally. Assessment specialists can increase managers' understanding of the political process, of differences between polities, and of host government interests vis-à-vis foreign firms. I am not suggesting that line managers become experts in political science, but rather that they strive for a better understanding of the underlying environment and its relationship to the firm. Second, the specialists can enhance organizational knowledge of political risk. As pointed out earlier, a major hindrance to accurate assessment of political risk is the lack of historical data, especially regarding specific impacts on projects. To a large extent, the problem can be solved only on a firm-by-firm basis. Each firm must review its own historical experience by asking: When have contingencies arisen from the interplay of political factors? What were their underlying environmental determinants? How did they become apparent to the firm? A systematic attempt to answer such questions is undoubtedly the single most important step that a firm can take to improve the effectiveness of its political risk assessment.

Institutionalization enables a firm to make better use of existing resources, both within the organization and in the external environment. The most valuable contribution of political assessment units is to improve the assessment capabilities of management at large.

ORGANIZATIONAL ISSUES

Despite the capacity of institutionalization to make political assessment more effective, the actual experience of firms has been mixed. Many assessment units are so isolated from the center of the organization that they wield only limited influence on decision making. The method of organizing the assessment function is thus crucial. Because this study does not directly compare alternative organizational schemes as to effectiveness, what follows is a speculative hypothesis rather than a conclusion supported by data.

That caveat notwithstanding, a clear trade-off enters into the organization of the assessment function. Two basic organizational arrangements for specialized assessment units exist. In a number of firms interviewed, quasi-independent units comprising political specialists, often former foreign service officers or trained political scientists, have been set up at either the corporate or the divisional level. In other firms individuals or units charged with political assessment coordinate analyses prepared by other units within the company. (Most coordinators do some of their own analysis; some firms use outside consultants extensively.) These units are usually part of international strategic planning sections.

Each of the two modes of organization has its advantage. A unit composed of specialists usually has available more political expertise than does a unit serving in a coordinating role, and it is more likely to produce environmental assessments independent of other managerial concerns. On the other hand, the coordinating unit is more closely integrated into the organization and is more likely to have an impact on operations. The coordinator, however, may have less specialized expertise available and its assessments are less independent of other managerial concerns.

The trade-off is between independence and expertise on the one hand and integration into the organization on the other. I would opt for the latter, although the situation is not a zero-sum game. That is, a political assessment unit performing a coordinating function can do much to improve the quality of assessments and to offset existing biases (see chap. 8). Nevertheless, integration into the organization as a whole is of overriding importance. Independent units run a substantial risk that assessments will not be directly related to their ultimate use and therefore will not be fully integrated into the decision-making process. If the assessment unit is to be a true focal point, and if it is to establish useful communications with management, it must be fully integrated into the firm. It must not suffer isolation at the periphery. A coordinating assessment unit joined to an established staff group will stand a better chance of achieving those ends than a unit that does its own independent analyses because it can better use existing resources to improve the quality both of political risk assessment and of planning and decision making. Furthermore, the choice is not all or nothing; a political assessment unit that plays a primarily coordinating role can employ specialists for scanning, translating, and educational functions.

In summary, institutionalization facilitates more effective use of existing resources. It allows a firm to take advantage of its network of affiliate managers whose unique position at the boundary of firm and environment makes them the primary source of political information. Through institutionalization a firm enjoys the advantages of more systematic collection of data, of better managerial understanding of the political process, of accumulating organizational experience, and of providing for validation of line managers' assessments.

POLITICS AND THE MANAGERIAL PROCESS

Wilensky (1967:179), whose study focuses on the public sector, writes: "If anything is clear from this book, it is that intelligence failures are built into complex organizations."[6] There is no reason to believe that United States–based international firms are unique. As I learned when I presented preliminary findings of this study to the Department of State,[7] other organizations concerned with the assessment of external political environments have had similar experiences. Foreign service officers who were present perceived close parallels between the reactions of political assessment specialists in firms and their own responses to situations. An example was the tendency of top-level personnel at State to place more value on their own impressions gained from a quick visit to a country than on reports prepared by lower-level personnel in embassies abroad or at country desks in Washington.

Wohlstetter's (1962) classic study of the intelligence failure at Pearl Harbor also provides interesting parallels. Her major conclusion is that a formal point of uncertainty absorption is needed, as a center where all information can be processed and reconciled: "If anything emerges clearly from a study of this alert, it is the soundness of having a center for evaluating a mass of conflicting signals from specialized or partisan sources" (1962:130). She also discusses the need for an intellectual framework to separate meaningful signals from a background of noise. There are other parallels in the problems confronting policymakers in relating to assessment specialists because "of the poor repute associated with intelligence, inferior rank, and the province of the specialist, or long-hair"

6. Wilensky reaches the same conclusion as I have regarding the tendency of top managers to ignore subordinates' assessments and scan environments directly. He concludes, however, that direct scanning by managers is functional, given the structural barriers to effective intelligence in large organizations. I disagree and prefer organizational solutions to the problem.

7. Secretary's Open Forum, December 1979.

(1962:312). Wohlstetter also points out the constraints imposed on intelligence officers because they lack understanding of, or exposure to, United States foreign policy.

The literature on the United States intelligence community similarly supplies a number of relevant examples. The most salient are barriers to communication between intelligence analysts and policymakers and the resulting difficulty of integrating analysis and policy. Kirkpatrick (1973:113), for example, notes:

> There are those at the policy level who consider themselves experts on given areas and subjects and regard intelligence estimates as superfluous and unworthy of attention. There are also those who favor a particular policy and who are unmoved by intelligence analyses which indicate such a policy unwise. And there are those who wait for a consensus to develop and then get on the bandwagon.

Although a thorough review of the literature and a rigorous comparison with the international firm are not possible here, it is clear even from the two sources quoted and from a scanning of the press that close parallels do exist. The State Department, the Central Intelligence Agency, and the Defense Intelligence Agency differ in function from international firms. Structurally, however, as large hierarchical organizations they are similar and they face similar organizational problems relative to external environments. As Simon (1976a) notes, the scarce resource is not information, but the capacity to process it.

While the subject of political risk assessment may be novel for many American firms, the requisites of more effective performance of this newly emerging function are not. That requires developing strategies to make better use of available resources. Political risk management is a problem of managerial process.

Appendix A
Research Methods
and Sample Characteristics

In this study I utilize a combination of survey and qualitative research techniques. A mail survey of the entire target population was followed by in-depth personal interviews with managers in a subset of firms selected as a stratified quota sample of the respondents to the mailed questionnaire.

The use of multiple research methods, particularly the combination of quantitative and qualitative methods, has distinct advantages. As Jick (1979:604) observes, the concept—which has been called "triangulation"—is based on the assumption that qualitative and quantitative methods are complementary rather than competitive: "Perhaps the most prevalent attempts to use triangulation have been reflected in various efforts to integrate fieldwork and survey methods. The viability and necessity of such linkages have been advocated by various social scientists . . . [who] . . . all argue that quantitative methods can make important contributions to fieldwork, and vice versa."

Survey and qualitative methods are complementary in this research. The survey, designed to elicit a description of current practice, became a guide to the qualitative fieldwork. Although the survey was explanatory and cannot be regarded as definitive, it did furnish an outline of the function and suggested questions for the interviews. As the interviews were held after the survey was conducted, preliminary results of the latter were available when the former began.

The qualitative work made for clearer understanding of the whole problem, as questions raised by the survey could be more fully explored in personal interviews. The interviews also clarified the results of the survey by establishing their limits and putting them in context and, finally, by increasing confidence in their validity. These follow-up interviews, then, flexibly structured as they were, proved to be an excellent medium for achieving the analytical objectives of the study. They allowed for suggesting and exploring possible causal relationships and for generating hypotheses. The survey and the qualitative methods were interactive in that hypotheses suggested by the interviews were further probed through re-analysis of the survey data.

RESEARCH DESIGN

The target population was broadly defined as relatively large, industrial, United States-based international firms. The population does not include firms in the financial sector, such as banks and insurance companies. "Relatively large" firms are those whose 1976 sales were $100 million or more, thus corresponding approximately to the Fortune 1000. "International," as used here, describes firms with at least one substantive operation abroad, that is, with significant productive operations established through foreign direct investment or contract.

Applying those criteria to the Conference Board's *Key Company Directory*, a target population of 455 was drawn from the 5,000 firms listed therein.[1] Questionnaires were mailed to the chief executive officer (CEO) of each firm in the last week of August 1978, each questionnaire accompanied by a letter asking that it be directed to the appropriate international officer. By November 1, 1978, the cutoff date, 193 usable replies (42.4 percent) had been received. Each reply specified the name and position of the respondent. Although the follow-up interviews later revealed that several managers who signed their questionnaires did not actually complete them, in every instance the questionnaires were completed and signed by managers whose responsibilities and experience rendered them fully competent to do so. The degree to which the respondents actually represent the target population is discussed below.

A stratified quota subsample for follow-up interviews was drawn from the respondents to the mailed questionnaire. Quota sampling has obvious limitations, but it is often used for "difficult" populations such as

---

1. Since the usable data on internationalization were somewhat limited, respondents were compared with the target population on the basis of variables such as sales, sector, the number of countries with manufacturing operations, and the maintenance of mining or extractive operations abroad.

business firms (Moser and Kalton, 1972). The decision to select the sample for personal interviewing from respondents to the survey rather than from the target population as a whole was a practical one, since firms that refused to respond to a mail survey would hardly agree to extensive personal interviews. Furthermore, interviews with respondents enabled researchers to utilize, in both selection and analysis, the information supplied by the survey.

Stratified quota sampling requires that the population be structured on the basis of relevant variables. Respondents were grouped into eleven industrial sectors, and a fourth of the firms in each sector were to be selected for the follow-up interviews, with a target sample size of 40. (A minimum of one firm from each sector was selected.) Size provided a second criterion when the number of firms in a given industrial classification was sufficiently large to permit selection of four or more firms for the sample. After these firms had been ranked on the basis of global sales, half were drawn from below the median and half from above it.

At a minimum, interviews were requested with managers responsible for political assessment (if they existed), managers responsible for strategic planning and the financial function, and, most important, with managers at the major decision-making level, the ultimate users of political information. In most instances the request was met, and 113 managers in 37 firms were interviewed. Since three of those firms failed to provide sufficient access, the base for analysis is 110 managers in 34 firms. Structured formats were designed for the interviews, which were conducted between November 1978 and March 1979.[2]

When a selected firm refused to be interviewed, a replacement was drawn from the same stratum. Almost all the firms selected agreed to the interviews, and the satisfying degree of compliance is owing to the high level of interest in a new area of investigation and little fear that proprie-

2. As the number of returns to the survey was larger than expected, the selection of a quarter of the firms would have resulted in an interview subsample of 48 rather than the target of 40. Because of funding and time limitations, the target subsample was maintained at 40 through selective reduction in some of the larger strata. Interviews were conducted by myself and by Stephen Blank and John Basek of the Conference Board. Two procedures were implemented to ensure comparability. First, interview guides were developed and pretested. Second, when possible, interviews were conducted by teams of two of the three investigators, especially in the early stages. Interviews were not taped, but each investigator dictated a report as soon as possible after a visit to a firm. The transcript of the complete set of reports exceeded 700 pages.

tary rights would be infringed. The only sector indifferent or opposed to interviewing was consumer goods. The uncooperativeness of consumer products firms probably reflects the low cost of potential environmental contingencies in that sector (see chap. 5). The policy of replacing a firm that refused interviews with a comparable respondent to the survey ran into a snag in one instance. In a sector having a small number of large firms, the replacement had to be obtained from outside the group of respondents to the mail survey. A firm that returned its questionnaire after the cutoff date agreed to participate.

IMPLEMENTATION

The high rate of response to the mail survey—193 usable questionnaires or 42.4 percent—clearly indicates management interest. Selected characteristics of the respondents to the questionnaire and of the firms interviewed are compared with those of the target population in appendix table 1. Respondents to the survey are representative of the target population on the basis of firm size (global sales), industrial sector, and the existence of mining or extractive operations abroad. Respondents are significantly more likely to operate majority-owned manufacturing subsidiaries in a larger number of countries than the population as a whole (8.1 versus 5.9). It should be noted that mean sales of respondents ($2,573 million) are directionally (i.e., significant at the .10 level) higher than those of the target population ($2,028 million).

Some bias is evident in the subsample of firms interviewed. First, they are clearly larger. Mean sales are double those of the population ($4,181 versus $2,028 million), and the percentage of interviewed firms with sales under $500 million is significantly less (14.7 versus 33.7 percent) and over $5,000 million (23.5 versus 8.2 percent) is significantly higher. Although differences in industrial sector are not statistically significant, considerably more variation (versus the distribution for the target population) is evident than for respondents to the survey.

The firms interviewed may be compared with respondents to the mail survey on two measures of internationalization: the number of countries in which the firm has significant operations and the percentage of sales generated abroad. As expected, the firms interviewed are significantly more widespread internationally than are respondents to the sur-

APPENDIX TABLE 1

COMPARISON OF POPULATION, SURVEY, RESPONDENTS, AND FIRMS
INTERVIEWED
(IN PERCENTAGES)

Variable	Total population (N = 455)	Survey respondents (N = 193)	Firms interviewed (N = 34)
Global sales (in millions of dollars)			
Less than 500	33.7	23.1	14.7
501–1,000	16.7	14.8	5.9
1,001–5,000	41.4	49.0	55.9
5,001–10,000	5.5	9.5	14.7[a]
More than 10,000	2.7	3.7	8.8[a]
(Mean sales)	(2,028)	(2,573)	(4,181)[a]
Number of countries with majority-owned manufacturing facilities			
1–5	60.5	49.7[a]	
6–10	17.2	19.4	
11–20	15.9	20.1	
21 or more	6.5	10.8	
(Mean number of countries)	(5.9)	(8.1[a])	
Mining or extractive operations abroad	17.6	20.4	

vey. Of the former, 68 percent carry on operations in more than twenty countries, versus 38.5 percent of the latter. Corresponding percentages for the proportion of firms reporting more than 25 percent of sales generated abroad are 67.7 and 42.1. (The differences are significant at the .05 level.)

In summary, the respondents to the mail survey are reasonably representative of the target population, and inferences seemingly contain little bias. On the other hand, firms in the subsample interviewed are larger and more widespread internationally (at least versus survey respondents) than the population as a whole.

APPENDIX TABLE 1—*Continued*

Variable	Total population (N = 455)	Survey respondents (N = 193)	Firms interviewed (N = 34)
Sector			
Consumer products, textiles	24.2	22.7	14.7
Extractive industries	11.4	12.6	8.8
Rubber products	6.4	6.8	5.9
Chemicals	9.5	8.9	14.7
Fabricated metals	6.4	6.3	8.8
Machinery	15.0	14.2	11.8
Appliances	7.7	7.4	5.9
Automobiles	3.1	3.2	5.9
Computers, scientific instruments, office equipment	7.3	7.9	2.9
Pharmaceuticals	4.2	5.3	11.8
Miscellaneous	4.8	4.7	8.8

[a]Difference versus population significant at .05 or better.

SAMPLE CHARACTERISTICS

Analyzing the characteristics of the 193 firms that responded to the mail survey serves two purposes. First, because their responses show that they are fairly representative of the population of American international (industrial) firms, knowledge of characteristics of that population can be updated as of the last quarter of 1978. Second, reviewing the characteristics of the sample creates an opportunity to explain in some detail concepts frequently utilized in the analysis.

Appendix table 2 presents characteristics of respondents reflecting size and internationalization. Firms have been categorized as small, medium, or large on the basis of 1976 global sales. As the table shows, the sample divides roughly into thirds: firms that have sales of $750 million or less account for 32.8 percent; those with sales of $751 to $2,500 million, for 36.5 percent; and those with sales of $2,500 million or more, classified as large firms, 30.7 percent. Respondents are widespread internationally. Almost 40 percent generate more than a quarter of their sales

APPENDIX TABLE 2

CHARACTERISTICS OF RESPONDENTS TO MAIL SURVEY

Characteristic	Number of respondents	Percentage of respondents
Global sales	193	
(in millions of dollars)		
Less than 750		32.8
751–2,500		36.5
More than 2,500		30.7
Percentage of sales abroad	183	
0–10		19.7
11–25		35.2
26 or more		39.9
Missing data		5.2
Number of countries	187	
1–4		17.5
5–10		21.8
11–20		20.3
21 or more		37.3
Missing data		3.1
Date of establishment of first subsidiary abroad	183	
Before World War II		36.3
1945–1965		44.5
After 1965		14.0
Missing data		5.2

abroad and/or operate in more than twenty countries. More than three-quarters raise 11 percent or more of their sales abroad, and 57.6 percent operate in eleven or more countries. Establishment of the first subsidiary abroad before 1945 was accomplished by 36.3 percent of the sample firms; during the two decades after World War II, a period of marked expansion of American business abroad, by 44.5 percent. Only a small minority of firms (14 percent) first ventured overseas after 1965.

Respondents also supplied data on organizational structure. As appendix table 3 shows, more than half of the respondents (56.5 percent)

APPENDIX TABLE 3

ORGANIZATIONAL CHARACTERISTICS OF RESPONDENTS

Characteristic	Number of respondents	Percentage of respondents
International division	188	
No		40.9
Yes		56.5
Missing data		2.6
International structure	189	
Product line		31.1
Geographical area		45.6
Matrix form		11.9
Other basis		9.3
Missing data		2.1

International organization	172	Absolute	Adjusted for missing data
Preinternational		23.8	26.7
Int. Div. I		21.8	24.4
Int. Div. II		30.1	33.7
Global		13.5	15.1
Missing data		10.9	—

		Raw percentages			
Organization by structure	169	Product line	Area	Matrix	Other
Preinternational		44.4	33.3	0.0	22.2
Int. Div. I		29.2	55.6	8.3	6.9
Int. Div. II		18.5	74.1	7.4	0.0
Global		38.2	29.4	20.6	11.8

have an international division. However, the questionnaire did not elicit enough information to distinguish between international divisions that have full line responsibility for overseas operations and those that serve a more limited staff function. Furthermore, it is not clear whether firms that lack an international division are in an early stage of internationalization, when such a division has not yet been created, or have evolved through the international division structure and are now organized on a global basis.

Although information on the stage of international organization was not obtained, a proxy was constructed based on the existence of an international division, firm size, and two measures of internationalization. Firms that reported no international division and also less than a fourth of their sales generated abroad, operations in 20 or fewer countries, or global sales of less than $750 million were classified as preinternational. Their limited international operations or their small size suggests that they were indeed in an early stage of internationalization. On the other hand, firms that reported no international division and also 26 percent or more of sales generated abroad or operations in more than 20 countries and worldwide sales of over $750 million were classified as global. Firms reporting an international division were subdivided into two categories based on the extent of internationalization. Those with less than 26 percent of sales generated abroad or with operations in 20 or fewer countries were classified as International Division I. Those with 26 percent or more of sales generated abroad or with operations in more than 20 countries were classified as International Division II.

Although the variable is an approximation, international organization is assumed to represent the continuum of organizational evolution from a preinternational structure, through the international division stage, to globally organized operations. Not all firms, of course, follow this sequence (see chap. 4), but the evidence strongly suggests that it is a common phenomenon. It should be noted that the variable may be regarded as ordinally scaled, given the assumptions underlying its construction.

As seen in appendix table 3, 172 of the 193 respondents may be classified in terms of international organization. Of these, 23.8 percent are categorized as preinternational, 21.8 percent, as International Division I, 30.1 percent, as International Division II, and 13.5 percent, as global. Firms that provided no data and could not be classified amounted to 10.9 percent of the total.

Data obtained on the structure of international operations are also presented in appendix table 3. Nearly half the respondents (45.6 percent) reported international operations structured on a geographical basis, 31.1 percent, on product line, 11.9 percent, on a matrix form of organization, and 9.3 percent, on some other basis. Data are missing for 2.1 percent of the firms. As would be expected, there is a significant relationship be-

APPENDIX TABLE 4
RELATIONSHIPS BETWEEN FACTORS

Factor	Kendall's tau	Significance
Global sales		
Percentage of sales abroad	.224	.0003
Number of countries	.448	.0000
International organization	.475	.0000
Percentage of sales abroad		
Number of countries	.515	.0000

tween organization and structure of international operations (chi-square of 29.8 is significant at better than .001). Sharp differences are evident between firms with an international division and those organized globally. Structure is based on geographical area in 55.6 percent of firms classified as International Division I and in 74.1 percent of those classified as International Division II. Only 29.2 percent of the former and 18.5 percent of the latter structure operations on the basis of product line. On the other hand, 38.2 percent of global firms structure operations on a product-line basis and only 29.2 percent on the basis of area. A more complex matrix organization was reported by 20.6 percent of global firms.

Relationships among measures of size, internationalization, and organization are much as one would expect. There is a fairly strong positive relationship between firm size and the number of countries in which the firm operates and international organization. The relationship between size and percentage of sales generated abroad is weaker but still highly significant. Larger firms tend to be more international and tend to be organized as International Division II or global companies. (See appendix table 4.) The relationship between the two measures of internationalization is also strong and significant—a Kendall's tau of 51.5 percent. Although this finding verifies constructs, it is noteworthy that sales generated abroad and number of countries with operations are not proxies for each other. Whereas both measure degree of internationalization (see chap. 5), they have decidedly different implications as to the impact of the environment on strategy.

Appendix B
Multivariate Logit Analysis
of the Determinants
# of Institutionalization

A number of estimation techniques have been developed to deal with the problems in using ordinary least squares regression analysis to evaluate models containing a discrete dependent variable. Logit analysis, utilizing a maximum likelihood estimate technique, is appropriate for a model containing binary dependent variables and categorical independent variables (Hanushek and Jackson, 1977).[1] There are a number of differences in interpretation of the results of logit analysis and ordinary least squares regression, of which two are immediately relevant. First, the coefficients represent an estimate of the marginal change in the odds (of shifting from one value of the dependent variable to the other) associated with a unit change in the independent variable. (Specifically, the coefficients represent the change in the log of the odds of a shift.) Second, the basic hypothesis tested through statistical inference relates to alternative specifications of the model rather than to individual coefficients. The null hypothesis tested is that the effect of the additional variables is zero (Hanushek and Jackson, 1977). An unconstrained version of the model may be compared with a constrained version (i.e., with only a constant term), or versions with different combinations (of nested) independent variables may be compared with one another. Inference is accomplished through a

---

1. The use of the ordinary least squares model with binary dependent variables may result in biased and inconsistent estimates. Problems stem from the nature of the error terms implicit in each observation and the linear functional form of the model itself. These problems are minimized through the use of a logistic function. See Hanushek and Jackson (1977), esp. chap. 7.

likelihood ratio test with the ratio distributed as chi-square is, with degrees of freedom equal to the number of coefficients being tested.[2]

Logit analysis is first used to inquire further into the relationship of the two measures of internationalization (the percentage of sales generated abroad and the numbers of countries in which a firm operates) to institutionalization and then to explore relationships between the variables analysis has revealed to be the most important determinants of institutionalization. Appendix table 5 shows the results of analyzing INTSALES and COUNTRIES; they are consistent with previous findings. The coefficients reflect the probability that INSTUT will take a value of 1, which represents a noninstitutionalized firm. The expected sign is thus negative in all instances.

Equation (1) reveals a rather weak, only marginally significant relationship between INTSALES and INSTUT. The probability that adding the percentage of sales generated abroad to the constrained equation (containing only a constant term) results in an effect on INSTUT different from zero is .054, and the ratio of the coefficient to its standard error is significant at .06.[3] On the other hand, the relationship between COUNTRIES and INSTUT is clearly significant (equation 2). The results of equation (3) are consistent with the hypothesis. Adding INTSALES to the model containing COUNTRIES does not produce anything approaching a significant additional effect on INSTUT. Furthermore, when both independent variables are added the value of the coefficient of INTSALES is substantially reduced, whereas that of COUNTRIES remains about the same, as compared with equations (2) and (1), respectively. Results of the logit analysis are thus consistent with a hypothesis that the number of countries in which a firm operates—as a measure of heterogeneity of the task environment—is a considerably more important determinant of differentiation and formalization of the political assessment function than is the percentage of sales generated abroad (which is a measure of the importance of international business to the firm).

---

2. The null hypothesis is that the effect of the additional variables or terms in the model is zero. The likelihood ratio is computed as follows:

Lambda = $((-\text{In likelihood}_a) - (-\text{In likelihood}_b))$

with λ distributed as chi^2 with degrees of freedom equal to the number of coefficients being tested. See Hanushek and Jackson (1977); Theil (1971):98–100.

3. It is not clear whether coefficients should be tested using the normal or Students distribution. However, as the number of observations in this instance is quite large, the latter approximates the former.

APPENDIX TABLE 5

LOGIT ANALYSIS ON INSTUT: INTSALES AND COUNTRIES
(RATIO OF COEFFICIENT TO STANDARD ERROR IN PARENTHESES)
(N = 172)

$$INSTUT = 1.38b_1 - .35 \text{ INTSALES} \tag{1}$$
$$(3.00) \quad (-1.90)$$
$$- \text{Ln lkhd} = 110.578 \qquad p = 0.54^a$$

$$INSTUT = 2.89b_1 - .59 \text{ COUNTRIES} \tag{2}$$
$$(4.35) \quad (-3.71)$$
$$- \text{Ln lkhd} = 104.603 \qquad p = .000$$

$$INSTUT = 2.85 b_1 + .07 \text{ INTSALES} - .62 \text{ COUNTRIES} \tag{3}$$
$$(4.20) \quad (.29) \quad (-3.27)$$
$$- \text{Ln lkhd} = 104.558 \qquad p = .000$$

$$- \text{Ln lkhd constrained model} = 112.434$$
$$\text{Lkhd ratio Eq 3 vs. Eq 2} = .09 \text{ d.f.} = 1$$
$$\text{Lkhd ratio Eq 3 vs. Eq 1} = 12.04 \text{ d.f.} = 1$$
$$p = .000$$

[a] Versus constrained model.

The next question of interest is the relative importance of SIZE, COUNTRIES, and INTORG as determinants of INSTUT (see appendix table 6). Adding each of the independent variables separately to a constrained model (equations 1 to 3) results in a highly significant effect on INSTUT in each instance. The coefficients suggest that the effect of SIZE (.92) is considerably more important than that of COUNTRIES (.55) or of INTORG (.69). Equations 4 through 6 permit direct comparison. The model containing SIZE and INTORG (4) produces significant added effects on INSTUT versus models containing SIZE (1) or INTORG (3) alone. Whereas the coefficients of both terms are significant at .05 or better, that of SIZE is larger than that of INTORG and thus the former seems to be more important. Adding COUNTRIES to the model (6) as a third independent variable does not produce a significant incremental effect on INSTUT. The model containing COUNTRIES and INTORG (5) is incrementally significant versus that containing COUN-

APPENDIX TABLE 6

LOGIT ANALYSIS ON INSTUT: SALES, COUNTRIES, AND INTORG

(N = 168)

Equation	Constant	SALES	COUNTRIES	INTORG	−Ln lkhd
1	2.47	−.92			99.430
	(4.98)	(−4.14)			
2	2.75		−.55		102.382
	(4.13)		(−3.41)		
3	2.17			−.69	100.472
	(4.92)			(−3.93)	
4	3.01	−.68		−.45	96.658
	(5.28)	(−2.73)		(−2.32)	
5	2.77		−.26	−.51	99.63
	(4.21)		(−1.29)	(−2.29)	
6	3.18	−.64	−.10	−.40	96.560
	(4.53)	(−2.45)	(−.44)	(−1.71)	

LIKELIHOOD RATIO MATRIX

(PROBABILITY EFFECT OF ADDITIONAL VARIABLES IS ZERO)

	1	2	3	4	5	6
Constrained (−Ln lkhd = 108.894)	.001	.001	.001	.001	.001	.001
4	.02		.01			
5		.02	.10			
6				.50		

NOTE: Ratio of coefficient to standard error: .01 = 2.575; .05 = 1.96; .10 = 1.645.

TRIES alone (2), but not versus that containing only INTORG (3). Furthermore, the coefficient of COUNTRIES is not significantly different from zero. Thus, given the explanatory variables available, a model containing INTORG and SIZE cannot be improved on in terms of explaining the probability that a firm will institutionalize the assessment function.

Equation (5), which contains SIZE and INTORG, correctly predicts institutionalization for 68 percent of the firms.[4] The accuracy of the prediction, however, is asymmetrical with respect to institutionalization. Eighty-four percent of the 109 noninstitutional firms were assigned to the correct category, compared with only 39 percent of the 59 institutionalized firms. The 18 noninstitutionalized firms classified incorrectly are overwhelmingly large, international, and in the latter stages of organizational evolution. Eighty-three percent have sales of more than $2.5 billion; 89 percent operate in 20 or more countries; and 56 percent have a global structure. Misclassification is clearly owing to factors exogenous to the equation.

Industrial sector seems to be relevant. As noted above, industry serves as a proxy for factors such as technology and required asset commitment which affect the perceived impact of political contingencies and thus the differentiation and formalization of the assessment function. A frequency distribution of the industrial sector of the 18 misclassified non-institutionalized firms reveals that 39 percent produce consumer goods such as food, beverages, toiletries, and detergents. Only 16 percent of all respondents are in the consumer goods sector; the difference is significant at .05. As noted above, foreign direct investment decisions of consumer goods firms are usually defensive, motivated by the need to protect market share and to use relatively small amounts of capital. The net result is that the perceived cost of potential environmental contingencies is relatively low and it is therefore difficult to justify the allocation of substantial corporate resources to the institutionalization of the assessment function.

4. The logit algorithm produces an estimate of the probability that the dependent variable is 1 for each observation. Thus all instances can be assigned to one of the two values ($p \geq .5$ or not) and the percentage correctly classified can be computed.

Appendix C
Political Risk
Assessment Methods

In this appendix I discuss political assessment methods that are currently in use.[1] Some have been developed by industrial firms for their own use; others have been devised by consultants for sale as a service. I do not intend to review all the systems actually in use but to illustrate a range of solutions to the assessment problem. The list is far from exhaustive and examples are chosen to represent categories in a typology.

The typology is developed to facilitate comparison. The major distinction is between methods using observational data and those using expert-generated data. The latter are then further classified in terms of structure and systemization.

An objective-subjective dichotomy does not distinguish methods using observational data in "formal" models from those using expert-generated data in a variety of contexts. By observational data I mean those relating to the behavior of individuals or systems which are generally, although not universally, obtained by the analyst from secondary sources. Examples are estimates of gross domestic product, population, and literacy, and data on political events such as coups, revolutions, and regular regime changes. None of the attempts made to forecast political risk in this mode have been entirely successful or are widely used.

Methods using expert-generated data are categorized by their degree of structure and systematization. Structure refers to the presence of an explicit, although not necessarily sophisticated or elegant, conceptual model of process. It denotes the relationship between political events and managerial contingencies. An unstructured method is subjective in that assumptions are not made explicit and the modeling of relationships is

1. This appendix is drawn directly from Kobrin (1981).

intuitive in the sense that it takes place at an unconscious level. It involves mental processes that are difficult to replicate.[2] On the other hand, a structured method is objective in that assumptions and the model of process relating cause and effect are explicit.

The unsystematic/systematic dimension is scaled in terms of the degree of formalization of the forecasting method. Again, the subjective/objective distinction is relevant. A systematic method includes explicit, although not necessarily elegant or sophisticated, assessment and/or forecasting procedures. An intuitive or implicit forecasting method, which relies on the mental process of the forecaster, is difficult to replicate.

OBSERVATIONAL DATA/FORMAL MODELS

The practical application of assessment methods that attempt to use observational data in formal models has been limited by the conceptual and operational problems discussed above. Three approaches, which have been developed by service organizations, are discussed.

Two examples focus on predictions of political instability rather than on potential managerial contingencies. Although Rummel and Heenan (1978) propose an "integrated" approach to risk assessment with four independent dimensions, their published example is limited to a projection of instability. The method is similar to those employed in the quantitative cross-national analysis of political instability and conflict.[3] Indexes measuring two components of instability, turmoil and rebellious conflict, are constructed by using a version of factor analysis applied to time-series political event data. Regression analysis is then used to specify the predictive equations in terms of a number of socioeconomic and political variables. The independent variables are then extrapolated into the future and used to predict values of the components of instability.

The Futures Group (1980) proposes a method for measuring and predicting political stability which it calls Political Stability Prospects. (The procedure is proprietary and can be only generally outlined.) The method is based on observational data and formal models, but the final product takes expert-generated opinion into account. The first step is to

2. For a discussion of implicit and explicit forecasting see Armstrong (1978).
3. For examples of the literature on the quantitative analysis of political conflict, see Gurr (1971), Hibbs (1973), Rummel (1966).

construct a historical index of political stability on the basis of two subindexes: a times series on destabilizing events and one measuring economic deprivation which Gurr (1971) and others regard as an important determinant of the potential for political conflict. The two indexes are combined into a single index of political instability potential expressed in percentiles.

Forecasting entails first extrapolating the political instability potential index, weighting the most recent data most heavily. The extrapolation then serves as a baseline that is "perturbed by a series of events whose probabilities and impacts are generated by country and regional experts." The forecast is then adjusted to take account of a separate forecast of economic deprivation.

A model developed by Howard Johnson (1980) of the Arthur D. Little Company is based on assumptions about political risk which differ from those expressed in this book. First, risks are assumed to be locationally determined, emanating from the macro social-political-economic setting. Second, "despite a widespread belief to the contrary, risk is not specific to an industry, a firm, or a particular project" (1980:6). Johnson, differentiating between risk and hedging tactics against risk, argues that it is the latter and not the former which are case-specific. Risk events are posited to be related to the unevenness of the development process and the strength of the country in terms of national power.

Uneven development is defined in terms of differences in level of political development, social achievement, technical advancement, resource abundance, and domestic peace. An index of each aspect of development is computed by using an appropriate number of social, economic, and political variables. Countries are rank-ordered on each aspect and a raw score is computed by summing the differences between each rank position and each of the other four. The raw uneven development scores are then rank-ordered and the countries are arrayed ordinally. Countries are also rank-ordered in terms of a "composite measure of a country's economic, military and diplomatic power." One can then locate countries in four quadrants determined by two axes measuring degree of power (strong-weak) and unevenness of development. Strong, unevenly developed countries are believed to have the highest potential risk for foreign investors.

The model has been made operational by using expropriation as the dependent variable with aid flows from the United States as a mitigating factor. That is, "strong, unevenly developed countries without proportionate amounts of aid from the United States will have the worst record for taking over companies owned by U.S.–based multinationals" (Johnson, 1980:17).[4] Johnson, noting that this approach does not predict the likelihood of expropriation by any given country, suggests that country-specific forecasts require further analysis of "unevenness of the country in question."

It seems that the use of observational data in formal models is of limited utility at this point. The basic problem is that formal modeling relies on the accumulation of past experience to establish and test relationships and that past experience must be both explicit and subject to quantification. It is no accident that all three such methods reviewed in this paper are concerned with macro risk in terms of political instability/political development. That is the one area of endeavor related to political risk wherein sufficient theory and data exist to allow the formulation and testing of hypotheses and the construction of models. The data simply do not exist to allow formal specification of relationships between a wide range of possible contingencies and organizational and environmental characteristics. As a result, none of the models can assess specific impacts on firms.

Less can be said about the effort of the Futures Group. Still, the approaches of Rummel and Heenan (1978) and Johnson (1980) are already somewhat dated in terms of theoretical constructs and/or analytical method. Rummel and Heenan applied quantitative cross-national techniques developed during the 1960s to facilitate analysis rather than prediction. Although quantitative attempts at forecasting political events are still problematic, considerable methodological sophistication has developed in the past decade. Johnson's concept of expropriation may be more appropriate for the pre-1970 period, when nationalization frequently followed sharp shifts in regime and ideology or was at least a response to social and/or political conflict, than for the more recent past when use of selective expropriation as an instrument of political-economic policy has been more common. It should be noted that we are dealing with the first generation of attempts at quantitative modeling of political risk. Quantitative analysis is of value at present for analytical purposes and should

4. In this situation causality may operate in the reverse direction. It is the act of expropriation that results in a reduction of American aid when prompt, adequate, and effective compensation is not perceived as forthcoming. For example, the United States abstained on a World Bank vote when Guyana expropriated Alcan. See Litvak and Maule (1975) and Einhorn (1974) for further discussion.

be of increasing value in the future as data bases are constructed and, more important, as a better understanding of underlying relationships develops.

METHODS BASED ON EXPERT-GENERATED OPINION

The methods to be reviewed may be positioned on a two-by-two matrix with axes representing the unstructured/structured and unsystematic/systematic dimensions discussed above. As the structured/unsystematic cell is empty, it is reasonable to assume that a relatively explicit model of the process inherently leads to some degree of methodological formalization.

UNSTRUCTURED/UNSYSTEMATIC

Unstructured and unsystematic assessments are characterized by conceptual models and analytical methods that are intuitive and implicit rather than explicit. They represent the most common approach among United States–based international firms (see chap. 9).

Assessments may entail nothing more than a completely intuitive judgment made by line management (e.g., the investment climate looks unfavorable or the country is against free enterprise or foreign investment), but a number of examples illustrate a more considered approach. One of the largest American industrial firms has established a political assessment unit and staffed it with former foreign service officers. Their efforts, in terms of process and output, are analogous to political reporting in the State Department. Asked to prepare a study of Brazil in 1978, for example, the analyst responsible reviewed the available secondary sources and then interviewed a number of individuals, including State Department personnel in Washington and Brazil; other government officials concerned with foreign policy, such as employees of the intelligence community or A.I.D., managers in the firm's Brazilian subsidiary; Brazilian government officials, businessmen, and bankers; United States bankers concerned with Brazil; and a number of academic specialists.

The resulting eight-page report, issued in the fall of 1978, predicted an upsurge of student protests, increased tensions within the military, more militance in the labor force, a new political party structure, and intensified economic nationalism over the next two years. It discussed such issues as liberalization, economic performance and policy, and the role of the military. The last section suggested how labor relations, price controls, technical assistance fees, and economic nationalism would affect the firm.

The report is based on wide knowledge, detailed research, and penetrating analysis of potential impacts on the firm. In the limited and technical sense in which the terms are used in this appendix, however, the approach is unstructured and unsystematic. Neither the underlying conceptual model of the relationship between environment and firm nor the analytical method is explicit.

UNSTRUCTURED/SYSTEMATIC

The least systematic analytical process that can still be characterized as formalized is an outline or a checklist for preparation of a qualitative country study. For example, a manufacturing firm prepares a country study under the direction of the international treasurer whenever a new investment is under consideration. The analyst is guided by a set of instructions including a detailed outline under the headings history, politics (stability, external relations, long-run trends), economics (domestic and international), foreign investment, foreign exchange, financing, taxes, legal matters, and insurance, as well as a summary. The method is unstructured because no explicit conceptual model of the process is evident; it is systematic because an analytical method, albeit a very basic one, is specified. Even this degree of formalization has implications for issues such as comparability and validity.

Two analytical approaches are more formal but still lack structure: (1) the BERI service of BERI, Ltd., and (2) the ESP system of a large chemical company. Of the variety of services provided by BERI, Ltd., to aid in the evaluation of investment environments, only the Business Environmental Risk Index is described here.[5]

BERI is reported for 45 countries on a quarterly basis. It is accompanied by short discussions of each country and by extensive qualitative analysis of two countries each quarter. Panelists rate fifteen factors that affect the business climate on a scale from 0 (unacceptable) to 4 (superior). Examples of factors are political stability (the probability of un-

---

5. Haner (1979) describes the newer Political Risk Index (PRI). See Haner (1975) for a discussion of BERI.

scheduled political change and its possible impact on business), attitude (degree of acceptance of capitalistic principles in combination with the degree to which the political system places the cost of social benefits on private enterprise), balance of payments, bureaucratic delays, professional services and contractors, quality of local management and partners, and long-term credit availability and terms. The fifteen factors are weighted from 1 (e.g., bureaucratic delays) to 3 (e.g., stability) so that the sum of the weighting equals 25 and a perfect environment—each factor scored 4, times its weight—totals 100. (In a 1979 report country scores ranged from 31.0 to 82.6.) Scores are reported for each factor and for the BERI total.

Rankings are supplied by a permanent panel of approximately 105 volunteers from industrial firms, banks, governments, and other institutions. Each panelist rates five to ten countries for a period of six to twelve months in the future. That is, they judgmentally assign a score of 0 to 4 to each of the fifteen factors. An attempt is made to encourage convergence by maintaining a permanent panel—although not all the panelists respond all the time—and by supplying each panelist with his or her previous reply as well as the overall panel average on each factor.

BERI is fairly systematic: although experts' ratings are intuitive, the method is detailed and explicit. It is not structured, however, because the index, except for weighting of the factors, is not based on an explicit model of either the political-economic environment or of its potential impact on the firm.

The advantages and disadvantages of BERI have been discussed extensively in the literature (see esp. Haendel, West, and Meadow, 1975). The service provides a systematic scan of a large number of countries on a regular basis. Given at least minimal consistency in the panel, changes in country scores over time should be useful indicators of the need for more extensive analysis. BERI can serve a "red flag" function. It has, however, a number of important limitations. First, BERI scores do not take industry- and firm-specific factors into account. That failing limits the evaluation to the macro environment and also reduces the scores of factors, such as attitude toward private investment and quality of local management, which often vary by industry, to a common denominator that may have no intrinsic meaning. Second, panelists' rankings are highly subjective. There is no assurance that all respondents define political stability the same way, much less that they agree on the difference between ratings of 1 and 4. Third, despite a reasonable dispersion of professions among panelists, most of them are associated with the private sector and thus view the environment from that vantage point.

The ESP system, developed by a major chemical firm has been used on an ongoing basis in Latin America (Miguel, 1978).[6] After background research is completed, a team composed entirely of company people from the subsidiary, the region, and corporate departments spends three to five days interviewing a variety of groups. The groups, which range from government officials to local entrepreneurs, academics, and the church, are chosen in an effort to get a balanced view of the country. Two questionnaires serve as interview guides, but they are not actually completed during the interviews. One covers business conditions and the other, macroeconomic and sociopolitical factors that may affect business conditions.

After the interviewing is completed, the team fills out the questionnaires, which provide a basis for obtaining a consensus on the key economic, social, and political factors that may affect the business climate. Estimates of variation in the factors are then used to develop four scenarios that cover the next five to six years. The last step is to assign probabilities to each scenario, by secret ballot, so that the sum of the four adds up to 100 percent.

Again, although the procedure is tailored to meet the needs of the firm and although the macroeconomic and sociopolitical factors chosen are those that may have an impact on the business, the process is intuitive and implicit rather than explicit. No a priori explicit model of the relationship between environment and firm exists. Nevertheless, the analytical process is formal and explicit.

STRUCTURED/SYSTEMATIC

Two examples of structured and systematic analytical methods are (1) the World Political Risk Forecasts (WPRF) offered by the Frost and Sullivan Company and (2) the approaches that have evolved from the ASPRO-SPAIR system developed by Shell Oil. The former is based on a deductive model of the political process; the latter incorporates an inductive model of political risk.

World Political Risk Forecasts produces quantitative data on approximately sixty countries and qualitative country reports that are more

---

6. I was given the opportunity to see a second article by Miguel.

detailed. All the data are generated by a panel of experts and are deductive in that a general model of the political process is applied to each country. The forecasts utilize an actor-based model that assumes a pluralistic political process in which policy and political events stem from competition among interested societal groups.[7]

For each issue, such as repatriation restrictions, price controls, or increased taxation, the analyst must first identify individuals or groups within the country—labor, local industrialists, the military—concerned with policy outcomes. The panelist then scores these entities on their position (for, neutral, or against), their ability to influence policymaking, and the importance of the issue to them. The underlying assumption is that issue outcomes reflect the relative power and degree of commitment of interested groups. All else being equal, a group that has a position on an issue—that is, is not neutral, has a strong interest in it, and has enough power to influence policymaking—is most likely to affect the outcome.

For each issue, panelists score each actor's position, power, and salience on a linear scale[8] and also indicate the degree of confidence in his or her estimate. WPRF then combines scores for each actor multiplicatively (i.e., position x power x salience) and sums the issue scores of the actors for the total score. As an actor's position score is negative if that actor is against the issue, the sign and magnitude of the total score are taken as an indication of probable policy outcomes. Raw "probabilities" are calculated by dividing support for an issue (total scores for those actors whose position is positive) by total scores for an issue recalculated ignoring the sign of the position estimate. These probabilities are then combined with subjective estimates to derive final probabilities that issues will occur.

The WPRF summary contains both an eighteen-month and a five-year forecast for sixty countries, but as the former better illustrates the analytical method, I will confine my discussion to it. Issues are standardized: regime change, political turmoil, expropriation, and repatriation restrictions. The summary also contains an eighteen-month political risk indicator for each country, a simple average of the probabilities for the four issues listed above.

The qualitative country reports are generated in the same way. They identify and assess the major actors in the country (the power struc-

7. For a discussion of the basic method see Coplin and O'Leary (1976, 1978).

8. Although the scales vary over time, panelists may, for example, score positions from -3 (strongly against) to +3 (strongly for) and power from 0 to 5.

ture) and then analyze a number of issues relevant to foreign investors. Because panelists are asked to identify issues, those actually discussed vary from country to country. In a recent report on Brazil, for example, WPRF reported on a number of possible governmental actions, such as limitations on wage increases, in addition to making an extended analysis of the four issues covered in its world summary.

The majority of panelists are academics selected on the basis of publications, recommendations, and other indications of expertise. Differences among panelists are reconciled through recontacting individuals or, if necessary, through a judgment made by the staff.

WPRF provides a regular scan of a large number of countries supported by extensive analysis. Despite some concern about the variability of individual responses, the discipline of an explicit model and of a formal assessment method increases confidence in their comparability.

WPRF is not free of problems. These include the selection of country experts and the procedure used to, and indeed the validity of attempting to, achieve convergence. Like other methods, forecasts do not take industry- or firm-specific factors into account. Uncertainty clouds the meaning of the probability of expropriation when it is not known whether the target is an oil firm or a manufacturer of mainframe computers. Other sources of concern are the validity of the probabilities and the applicability of a pluralistic model of policymaking developed in a liberal democratic context to more autocratic and closed societies. (In any event, a completely autocratic and closed society would probably not be a market for foreign direct investment.)

Another method that may be characterized as structured and systematic was developed by the Shell Oil Company. It has been adapted by another oil firm and extended to a broader range of industries by Risk Insights, Inc., of New York. The original model, though modified by other users, is well documented (see Gebelein, Pearson, and Silbergh, 1978) and is used here as the basis for discussion, though only a bare outline of a complex forecasting system is presented. The approach is structured, for it employs an explicit model of the potential impact of the political environment on a project. It is inductive, at least in its original application, because the model was derived by explicitly defining political risk in the context of an oil exploration and production contract and then constructing a causal model composed of independent events that could produce that risk.

Expert-generated data are used to estimate values for the variables in the model. The method is characterized by formal specification of a model of political risk, by explicit attempts to minimize possible errors in human assessments of external events,[9] and by reliance on a statistical algorithm to weigh and combine individual assessments of political-economic factors.

Political risk is defined as the probability of not maintaining a contract for exploration, development, and production of oil, perceived as equitable by both company and host country, over a ten-year period in the face of changing political and economic conditions. Risks spring from two kinds of political actions: (1) those that lead to a unilateral modification of the initial contract so that the return is inadequate; (2) those that constrain the free flow of funds or oil entitlements out of the host country.

These two categories are broken down into nine events—including civil disorder, sudden expropriation, taxation restrictions, restrictions on remittances and on oil export—which have the potentiality of increasing political risk. Specification of the model means developing a complete series of factors for each event—political, social, and economic—which could make the event more likely to happen. For example, evaluating the probability of sudden expropriation depends on such factors as ideological shift, the economic role of foreigners, strength of the economy, and the like. Each factor is presented as a dichotomy: two statements that if true would either support or refute the event in question.

The expert panelist then reviews each factor for each event and renders judgment on the likelihood that the event will occur (the factor is judged either to support or to refute the event) and expresses his or her degree of confidence in the judgment. Judgments may be expressed directly as subjective probabilities or indirectly on a qualitative scale that can be converted to probabilities. In any event, the technique, on the basis of the judgment and the degree of confidence, generates a density function for the probability that the event will occur, given the factor in question. Using Bayes' theorem, the density functions are combined across factors to generate an estimate for each expert on each event and across experts to generate a panel assessment of the probability that the event will occur. Both the expected value of the probability and its variance in terms of 90 percent confidence intervals are reported.

Panelists are recruited from a variety of backgrounds, professions,

9. For biases in human judgment see Armstrong (1978) and Einhorn and Hogarth (1978).

and disciplines. Each is personally interviewed to complete the question-naire. The method is a variant of the delphi approach because panelists are shown the probability estimates resulting from the computational algorithm and are asked for feedback. Although a panel average is presented, the method makes no attempt to reach consensus; instead, it presents results in such a way that estimates made by different types of panelists can be compared.

Important aspects of the ASPRO-SPAIR technique, such as the use of scenarios, modifications made by other users, including the incorporation of cross-impact analysis and the like, have not been discussed. The Shell system and its offshoots are the most sophisticated and most effective approach to political risk assessment reviewed in this paper. It entails development of an explicit model of political risk, which, in most of its incarnations, means specification of potential contingencies for a specific industry, firm, or even project. Experts are carefully selected; their judgments are obtained in the context of a model that is broken down so that experts are estimating a variable rather than the likelihood that an event will occur. The process, though still subjective, reduces individual variability in conception and scaling of phenomena.

Like WPRF, ASPRO-SPAIR has problems. First, each assessment is so costly—each expert is personally interviewed for close to a day—that the method cannot be used frequently. The costs of scanning a large number of countries have proved prohibitive to date. Second, much of the system's value is lost if more general assessments, as for a number of industries, are attempted. This difficulty is another limitation on use of the system. Third, there is concern about the applicability of Bayes' theorem for a number of reasons, including actual degree of independence of the factors.

A significant difference between WPRF and ASPRO-SPAIR lies in the degree of formal structure. Both approaches to political risk assessment are based on explicit models of the underlying process. Both are systematic in using a formal method. The models used, however, are different. WPRF panelists are given a conceptual model and participate in putting it into operation (e.g., identification of actors and sometimes of issues); ASPRO-SPAIR panelists are given a fully specified model and asked to provide subjective estimates of the values of variables, though they may suggest additional factors for any issue.

Bibliography

Adams, J. Stacy (1976). "The Structure and Dynamics of Behavior in Organizational Boundary Roles." In Marvin D. Dunnette, ed., *Handbook of Industrial and Organizational Psychology*, pp. 1175–1199. Chicago: Rand McNally.

Aguilar, Francis Joseph (1967). *Scanning the Business Environment*. New York: Macmillan.

Aharoni, Yair (1966). *The Foreign Investment Decision Process*. Boston: Division of Research, Graduate School of Business Administration, Harvard University.

Ake, Claude (1974). "Modernization and Political Instability: A Theoretical Exploration." *World Politics* (26):271–283.

Aldag, Ramon J., and Ronald G. Storey (1979). "Perceived Environmental Uncertainty: Measures and Correlates." Mimeographed. Madison: University of Wisconsin.

Aldrich, Howard E. (1979). *Organizations and Environments*. Englewood Cliffs, N.J.: Prentice-Hall.

Aldrich, Howard, and Diane Herker (1977). "Boundary Spanning Roles and Organizational Structure." *Academy of Management Review* (2):217–230.

Aliber, Robert Z. (1975). "Exchange Risk, Political Risk, and Investor Demands for External Currency Deposits." *Journal of Money, Credit and Banking* (May): 161–179.

Arendt, Hannah (1977). "Reflections (Thinking—Part 1)." *The New Yorker* (21 November):65–140.

Armstrong, J. Scott (1978). *Long-Range Forecasting*. New York: John Wiley and Sons.

Aronson, Jonathan David, ed. (1979). *Debt and the Less Developed Countries*. Boulder: Westview Press.

Ascher, William (1979). *Forecasting: An Appraisal for Policy Makers and Planners*. Baltimore: Johns Hopkins University Press.

Baglini, Norman A. (1976). *Risk Management in International Corporations*. New York: Risk Studies Foundation.

Baker, James C., and Lawrence J. Beardsley (1975). "Multinational Companies' Use of Risk Evaluation and Profit Measurements for Capital Budgeting Decisions." *Journal of Business Finance* (1):38–43.

Basi, R. S. (1963). *Determinants of United States Private Direct Investment in Foreign Countries*. Kent, OH: Kent State University.

Bauer, Raymond A., Ithiel de Sola Pool, and Lewis A. Dexter (1972). *American Business and Public Policy.* 2d ed. Chicago: Aldine-Atherton.

Bavishi, Vinod B. (1978). "Capital Budgeting for the U.S. Based Multinational Corporations: An Assessment of Theory and Practice." Ph.D. dissertation. Columbus: Ohio State University.

Beckhard, Richard, and Ruben T. Harris (1977). *Organizational Transitions: Managing Complex Change.* Reading, MA: Addison-Wesley.

Behrman, Jack N., J. J. Boddewyn, and Ashok Kapoor (1975). *International Business Government Communications: U.S. Structures, Actors and Issues.* Lexington, MA: Lexington Books.

Bergsten, C. Fred, Thomas Horst, and Theodore H. Moran (1978). *American Multinationals and American Interests.* Washington: Brookings Institution.

Bergsten, C. Fred, Robert O. Keohane, and Joseph S. Nye (1975). "International Politics: A Framework for Analysis." In C. Fred Bergsten and Lawrence B. Krause, eds., *World Politics and International Economics,* pp. 3–36. Washington: Brookings Institution.

Blalock, H. M., Jr. (1972). *Social Statistics.* 2d ed. New York: McGraw-Hill.

Blank, Stephen, with John Basek, Stephen Kobrin, and Joseph La Palombara (1980). *Political Environmental Assessment: An Emerging Corporate Function.* New York: The Conference Board.

Brooke, Michael Z., and H. Lee Remmers (1978). *The Strategy of Multinational Enterprise.* 2d ed. London: Pitman Publishing Co.

Brzezinski, Zbigniew (1970). *Between Two Ages: America in the Technetronic Era.* New York: Viking Press.

Buckley, Peter J., and Mark Casson (1976). *The Future of Multinational Enterprise.* New York: Holmes and Meier.

Carlson, Sunne (1969). *International Financial Decisions.* Uppsala: Institute of Business Studies.

Chandler, Alfred D. (1962). *Strategy and Structure.* Cambridge: MIT Press.

Channon, Derek F., with Michael Jalland (1978). *Multinational Strategic Planning.* New York: AMA Communications Division.

Child, John (1972). "Organizational Structure, Environment and Performance: The Role of Strategic Choice." *Sociology* (6):1–22.

Choucri, Nazli, and Thomas W. Robinson, eds. (1978). *Forecasting in International Relations.* San Francisco: W. Freeman.

Citibank (1976). "The Multinational Corporation: An Environmental Analysis." Investment and Research Department, New York.

Cohen, Michael D., James G. March, and Johan P. Olsen (1972). "A Garbage Can Model of Organizational Choice." *Administrative Science Quarterly* (17):1–25.

Coplin, William D., and Michael O'Leary (1976). *Everyman's Prince: A Guide to Understanding Your Political Problems.* Rev. ed. North Scituate, MA: Duxbury Press.

Coplin, William D., and Michael K. O'Leary (1978). "Policy Profiling: Judgmental Data for Analysis and Improvement of Policy Decision Making." Mimeographed. Syracuse Research Corporation.

Curhan, Joan P., William H. Davidson, and Rajan Suri (1977). *Tracing the Multinationals*. Cambridge: Ballinger Publishing Co.

Cyert, Richard M., and James G. March (1963). *A Behavioral Theory of the Firm*. Englewood Cliffs, N.J.: Prentice-Hall.

Daniels, John D., Ernest W. Ogram, Jr., and Lee Radebaugh (1979). *International Business: Environments and Operations*. 2d ed. Reading, MA: Wesley Publishing Co.

Davis, Stanley M. (1976). "Trends in the Organization of Multinational Corporations." *Columbia Journal of World Business* (XI):59–71.

Dill, William R. (1957). "Environment as an Influence on Managerial Autonomy." *Administrative Science Quarterly* (2):409–443.

———. (1962). "The Impact of Environment on Organizational Development." In Sidney Malick and Edward H. Van Ness, eds., *Concepts and Issues in Administrative Behavior*. Englewood Cliffs, N.J.: Prentice-Hall.

Dill, William R., ed. (1978). *Running the American Corporation*. Englewood Cliffs, N.J.: Prentice-Hall.

Downey, H. Kirk, Don Hellriegel, and W. Slocum, Jr. (1975). "Environmental Uncertainty: The Construct and Its Application." *Administrative Science Quarterly* (20):613–629.

Downey, H. Kirk, and W. Slocum, Jr. (1975). "Uncertainty: Measures, Research and Sources of Variation." *Academy of Management Journal* (18):562–578.

Duncan, Robert B. (1972). "Characteristics of Organizational Environments and Perceived Environmental Uncertainty." *Administrative Science Quarterly* (17): 313–327.

———. (1973). "Multiple Decision-Making Structures in Adapting to Environmental Uncertainty: Impact on Organizational Effectiveness." *Human Relations* (26):273–291.

Easton, David (1968). *The Political System*. New York: Knopf.

Einhorn, Hillel J., and Robin M. Hogarth (1978). "Confidence in Judgement: Persistence of the Illusion of Validity." *Psychological Review* (85):395–416.

Einhorn, Jessica P. (1974). *Expropriation Politics*. Lexington, MA: D.C. Heath.

Eiteman, David K., and Arthur I. Stonehill (1979). *International Business Finance*. 2d ed. Reading, MA: Addison-Wesley.

Emery, F. E. (1967). "The Next Thirty Years." *Human Relations* (20):199–237.

Emery, F. E., and E. L. Trist (1965). "The Causal Texture of Organizational Environments." *Human Relations* (18):21–32.

Emery, Fred (1977). *Futures We Are In*. Leiden: Martinus Nijhoff.

Fahey, Liam, and William R. King (1977). "Environmental Scanning for Corporate Planning." *Business Horizons* (20):61–71.

Fayerweather, John (1978). *International Business Strategy and Administration*. Cambridge: Ballinger Publishing Co.

Festinger, Leon (1954). "A Theory of Social Comparison Processes." *Human Relations* (7):117–140.

Futures Group (1980). "Political Stability Prospects." Mimeographed. Glastonburg, CT.

Galbraith, Jay R., and Daniel A. Nathanson (1978). *Strategy Implementation: The Role of Structure and Process*. St. Paul: West Publishing Company.

Gebelein, C. A., C. E. Pearson, and M. Silbergh (1977). "Assessing Political Risks to Foreign Oil Ventures." Paper presented to the 1977 Society of Petroleum Engineers' Economics and Evaluation Symposium.

———. (1978). "Assessing Political Risk of Oil Investment Ventures." *Journal of Petroleum Technology* (May): 725–730.

Geertz, Clifford (1963). "Primordial Sentiments and Civil Politics in the New States." In Clifford Geertz, ed., *Old Societies and New States*. Chicago: University of Chicago Press.

Gilpin, Robert (1975). *U.S. Power and the Multinational Corporation*. New York: Basic Books.

Gitman, Lawrence J., and John H. Forrester, Jr. (1977). "A Survey of Capital Budgeting Techniques Used by Major U.S. Firms." *Financial Management* (6): 66–71.

Green, Robert T. (1972). *Political Instability as a Determinant of U.S. Foreign Investment*. Austin: Bureau of Business Research, University of Texas at Austin.

Greene, Mark K. (1974). "The Management of Political Risk." *Bests Review*, Property Liability Insurance ed. (July):71–74.

Gurr, Ted Robert (1971). *Why Men Rebel*. Princeton: Princeton University Press.

Gurr, Ted Robert, with Mark Irving Lichback (1978). "A Forecasting Model for Political Conflict within Nations." Mimeographed. Evanston: Northwestern University.

Haendel, Dan H., Gerald T. West, and Robert G. Meadow (1975). *Overseas Investment and Political Risk*. Philadelphia: Foreign Policy Research Institute.

Haner, F. T. (1975). "Business Environment Risk Index." *Bests Review*, Property Liability Insurance ed. (July):79–83.

———. (1979). "Rating Investment Risks Abroad." *Business Horizons* (22): 18–23.

Hanushek, Eric A., and John E. Jackson (1977). *Statistical Methods for Social Scientists*. New York: Academic Press.

Hershbarger, Robert A., and John P. Noerager (1976). "International Risk Management: Some Peculiar Constraints." *Risk Management* (April):23–34.

Hibbs, Douglas, Jr. (1973). *Mass Political Violence: A Cross-National Causal Analysis*. New York: John Wiley and Sons.

Huber, George P., Michael J. O'Connell, and Larry L. Cummings (1975). "Perceived Environmental Uncertainty: Effects of Information and Structure." *Academy of Management Journal* (18):725–740.

Huer, Richard J. (1978). *Quantitative Approaches to Political Intelligence: The CIA Experience.* Boulder: Westview Press.

Huntington, Samuel P. (1968). *Political Order in Changing Societies.* New Haven: Yale University Press.

———. (1973). "Transnational Organizations in World Politics." *World Politics* (XXV):333–368.

Hussey, D. E. (1978). "Portfolio Analysis: Practical Experience with the Directional Policy Matrix." *Long Range Planning* (11):2–8.

Jemison, David B. (1979). "An Empirical Identification of Interorganizational Boundary Spanning Roles." Mimeographed. Bloomington: Indiana University.

———. (1979). "Strategic Decision Making: Influence in Boundary Spanning Roles." *Academy of Management Proceedings*:118–122.

Jick, Todd D. (1979). "Mixing Qualitative and Quantitative Methods: Triangulation in Action." *Administrative Science Quarterly* (24):603–611.

Jodice, David A. (1980). "Sources of Change in Third World Regimes for Foreign Direct Investment, 1968–1976." *International Organization* (34):177–206.

Johanson, Jan, and Jan-Erik Vahine (1977). "The Internationalization Process of the Firm: A Model of Knowledge Development and Increasing Foreign Market Commitments." *Journal of International Business Studies* (8):23–32.

Johnson, Howard (1980). *Risk in Foreign Business Environments: A Framework for Thought and Management.* Cambridge: Arthur D. Little.

Katz, Daniel, and Robert L. Kahn (1978). *The Social Psychology of Organizations.* 2d ed. New York: John Wiley and Sons.

Keegan, Warren S. (1974). "Multinational Scanning: A Study of the Information Sources Utilized by Headquarters Executives in Multinational Companies." *Administrative Science Quarterly* (19):411–421.

Kelly, Margaret (1974). "Evaluating the Risks of Expropriation." *Risk Management* (Jan. 1):23–43.

Keohane, Robert O., and Joseph S. Nye, Jr., eds. (1971). *Transnational Relations and World Politics.* Cambridge: Harvard University Press.

Keohane, Robert O., and Joseph S. Nye, Jr. (1977). *Power and Interdependence.* Boston: Little, Brown.

Khalas, Harvey (1977). "Long Range Planning: An Open Systems View." *Long Range Planning* (10):78–82.

Kindleberger, Charles P. (1969). *American Business Abroad.* New Haven: Yale University Press.

Kirkpatrick, Lyman B., Jr. (1973). *The U.S. Intelligence Community.* New York: Hill and Wang.

Knight, Frank H. (1971). *Risk, Uncertainty and Profit.* Chicago: University of Chicago Press. 1st ed., 1921.

Kobrin, Stephen J. (1976*a*). "Foreign Direct Investment, Industrialization and Social Change." *Journal of Conflict Resolution* (20):497–522.

———. (1976*b*). "The Environmental Determinants of Foreign Direct Manufacturing Investment: An Ex-Post Empirical Analysis." *Journal of International Business Studies* (Fall-Winter):29–42.

———. (1977). *Foreign Direct Investment, Industrialization and Social Change.* Greenwich, CT:JAI Press.

———. (1978). "When Does Political Instability Result in Increased Investment Risk." *Columbia Journal of World Business* (Fall):113–122.

———. (1979). "Political Risk: A Review and Reconsideration." *Journal of International Business Studies* (Spring-Summer):67–80.

———. (1980). "Foreign Enterprise and Forced Divestment in LDCs." *International Organization* (34):65–88.

———. (1981). "Political Assessment by International Firms: Models or Methodologies?" *Journal of Policy Modeling* (Spring).

Kobrin, Stephen J., with John Basek, Stephen Blank, and Joseph La Palombara (1980). "The Assessment and Evaluation of Non-Economic Environments by American Firms: A Preliminary Report." *Journal of International Business Studies* (Spring-Summer):32–48.

Kraar, Louis (1980). "The Multinationals Get Smarter about Political Risks." *Fortune* (March 24):86–200.

Krasner, Stephen D. (1978). *Defending the National Interest.* Princeton: Princeton University Press.

La Palombara, Joseph, and Stephen Blank (1977). *Multinational Corporations in Comparative Perspective.* New York: The Conference Board.

Lasswell, Harold D., and Abraham Kaplan (1950). *Power and Society.* New Haven: Yale University Press.

Lawrence, Paul, and Jay W. Lorsch (1967). *Organization and Environment.* Boston: Division of Research, Graduate School of Business Administration, Harvard University.

———. (1969). *Developing Organizations: Diagnosis and Action.* Reading, MA: Addison-Wesley.

Leifer, Richard, and Andre Delbecq (1978). "Organizational/Environmental Interchange: A Model of Boundary Spanning Activity." *Academy of Management Review* (3):40–50.

Leifer, Richard, and George P. Huber (1977). "Relations among Perceived Environmental Uncertainty, Organizational Structure and Boundary Spanning Behavior." *Administrative Science Quarterly* (22):235–247.

Lindblom, Charles E. (1977). *Politics and Markets.* New York: Basic Books.

Litvak, Isaiah A., and Christopher J. Maule (1975). "Nationalism in the Carribean Bauxite Industry." *International Affairs* (51):43–59.

Lloyd, Bruce (1976). *Political Risk Management.* London: Keith Shipton Developments.

March, James G. (1978). "Bounded Rationality, Ambiguity, and the Engineering of Choice." *Bell Journal of Economics* (Fall):587–608.

March, James G., and Johan P. Olsen (1976). *Ambiguity and Choice in Organizations*. Bergen: Universitetsforlaget.

March, James G., and Herbert A. Simon (1958). *Organizations*. New York: John Wiley and Sons.

Meyer, Marshall W., and Associates (1978). *Environments and Organizations*. San Francisco: Jossey-Bass.

Miguel, Rafael (1978). "The Case for E.S.P. Studies." Paper presented to the Public Affairs Council Seminar, Washington, D.C.

Miles, Matthew B. (1979). "Qualitative Data Analysis as an Attractive Nuisance: The Problem of Analysis." *Administrative Science Quarterly* (24):590–601.

Miles, Raymond E., Charles C. Snow, and Jeffrey Pfeffer (1974). "Organization-Environment: Concepts and Issues." *Industrial Relations* (13):244–269.

Miles, Robert H. (1980). *Macro Organizational Behavior*. Santa Monica: Goodyear Publishing Company.

Montgomery, David B., and Charles B. Weinberg (1979). "Toward Strategic Intelligence Systems." *Journal of Marketing* (43):41–52.

Moran, Theodore H. (1974). *Multinational Corporations and the Politics of Dependence*. Princeton: Princeton University Press.

Moser, C. A., and G. Kalton (1972). *Survey Methods in Social Investigation*. New York: Basic Books.

National Industrial Conference Board (1969). *Obstacles and Incentives to Private Foreign Investment, 1967–68*. Vol. I: *Obstacles*. New York: National Industrial Conference Board.

Nehrt, Charles Lee (1970). *The Political Environment for Foreign Investment*. New York: Praeger.

Neubauer, F. Friedrich, and Norman B. Solomon (1977). "A Managerial Approach to Environmental Assessment." *Long Range Planning* (10):13–20.

Nye, Joseph S., Jr. (1974). "Multinational Corporations in World Politics." *Foreign Affairs* (53):153–175.

Organ, Dennis W. (1971). "Linking Pins between Organization and Environment." *Business Horizons* (14):73–80.

Parvin, Manoucher (1973). "Economic Determinants of Political Unrest." *Journal of Conflict Resolution* (17):271–295.

Perkins, Elizabeth U., ed. (1979). *Results of the Tokyo Round: Proceedings of a Conference on the Multilateral Trade Negotiations*. Washington: Chamber of Commerce of the United States.

Perlmutter, Howard (1969). "The Tortuous Evolution of the Multinational Corporation." *Columbia Journal of World Business* (IV):9–18.

Pfeffer, Jeffrey, Gerald R. Salancik, and Huseyin Leblebici (1976). "The Effect of Uncertainty on the Use of Social Influence in Organizational Decision Making." *Administrative Science Quarterly* (21):227–245.

Piper, James R. (1971). "How U.S. Firms Evaluate Foreign Investment Opportunities." *MSU Business Topics* (Summer):11–20.

Polanyi, Karl (1957). *The Great Transformation*. Boston: Beacon Press.

Preble, John F. (1978). "Corporate Use of Environmental Scanning." *University of Michigan Business Review* (30):12–17.

Richardson, J. David (1971). "Theoretical Considerations in the Analysis of Direct Foreign Investment." *Western Economic Journal* (March):87–98.

Richman, Barry M., and Melvyn R. Copen (1972). *International Management and Economic Development*. New York: McGraw-Hill.

Robinson, Richard D. (1976). *National Control of Foreign Business Entry*. New York: Praeger.

⸻. (1978). *International Business Management*. 2d ed. Hinsdale, IL: Dryden Press.

Robinson, S. J. Q., R. E. Hichens, and D. P. Wade (1978). "The Directional Policy Matrix: Tool for Strategic Planning." *Long Range Planning* (11):8–15.

Robock, Stefan H. (1971). "Political Risk: Identification and Assessment." *Columbia Journal of World Business* (July–Aug.):6–20.

Rodriguez, Rita M., and E. Eugene Carter (1979). *International Financial Management*. 2d ed. Englewood Cliffs, N.J.: Prentice-Hall.

Rogers, Everett M., with Floyd Shoemaker (1971). *Communication of Innovations*. 2d ed. New York: Free Press.

Root, Franklin R. (1968a). "Attitudes of American Executives towards Foreign Governmental Investment Opportunities." *Economics and Business Bulletin*, Temple University (Jan.):14–20.

⸻. (1968b). "U.S. Business Abroad and Political Risks." *MSU Business Topics* (Winter):73–80.

⸻. (1972). "Analyzing Political Risks in International Business." In A. Kapoor and Phillip D. Grub, eds., *The Multinational Enterprise in Transition*, pp. 354–365. Princeton: Darwin Press.

⸻. (1976). "The Management by LDC Governments of the Political Risk Trade-Off in Direct Foreign Investment." Paper presented to the International Studies Association, Toronto.

Root, Franklin R., and Ahmed A. Ahmed (1979). "Empirical Determinants of Manufacturing Direct Foreign Investment in Developing Countries." *Economic Development and Cultural Change* (27):751–767.

Rummel, R. J. (1966). "Dimensions of Conflict Behavior within and between Nations, 1958–1960." *Journal of Conflict Resolution* (X):63–73.

Rummel, R. J., and David A. Heenan (1978). "How Multinationals Analyze Political Risk." *Harvard Business Review* (Jan.-Feb.):67–76.

Schall, Lawrence D., Gary L. Sundem, and William R. Geysbeck, Jr. (1978). "Survey and Analysis of Capital Budgeting Methods." *Journal of Finance* (XXXIII):281–287.

Segev, Eli (1977). "How to Use Environmental Analysis in Strategy Making." *Management Review* (66):4–13.

Shackle, G. L. S. (1969). *Decision, Order and Time in Human Affairs.* 2d ed. Cambridge: Cambridge University Press.

Shapiro, Alan C. (1978). "Capital Budgeting for the Multinational Corporation." *Financial Management* (Spring):7–16.

Simon, Herbert A. (1955). "A Behavioral Model of Rational Choice." *Quarterly Journal of Economics* (89):99:115.

———. (1956). "Rational Choice and the Structure of the Environment." *Psychological Review* (63):120–138.

———. (1976a). *Administrative Behavior.* 3d ed. New York: Free Press.

———. (1976b). "From Substantive to Procedural Rationality." In Spiro J. Latsis, ed., *Method and Appraisal in Economics.* Cambridge: Cambridge University Press.

———. (1978). "Rationality as Process and as Product of Thought." *American Economic Review* (68):1–16.

Smetanka, John Andrew (1977). "International Business and the Dynamics of Global Integration: A Study of Canadian Corporate Executives." Ph.D. dissertation. Cambridge: Harvard University.

Smith, Clifford Neal (1971). "Predicting the Political Environment of International Business." *Long Range Planning* (Sept.):7–14.

Starbuck, William H. (1976). "Organizations and Their Environments." In Marvin D. Dunnette, ed., *Handbook of Industrial and Organizational Psychology*, pp. 1069–1123. Chicago: Rand McNally.

Stobaugh, Robert B., Jr. (1969). "How to Analyze Foreign Investment Climates." *Harvard Business Review* (Sept.-Oct.):100–107.

Stobaugh, Robert, and Daniel Yergin, eds. (1979). *Energy Future.* New York: Random House.

Stonehill, Arthur, and Leonard Nathanson (1968). "Capital Budgeting and the Multinational Corporation." *California Management Review* (Summer): 39–54.

Stopford, John M., and Louis T. Wells, Jr. (1972). *Managing the Multinational Enterprise.* New York: Basic Books.

Swansbrough, Robert H. (1972). "The American Investor's View of Latin American Economic Nationalism." *Inter-American Economic Affairs* (Winter):61–82.

Taylor, Charles Lewis, and Michael D. Hudson (1972). *The World Handbook of Social and Political Indicators.* 2d ed. New Haven: Yale University Press.

Terreberry, Shirley (1968). "The Evolution of Organizational Environments." *Administrative Science Quarterly* (12):591–613.

Theil, Henri (1971). *Principles of Econometrics.* New York: John Wiley and Sons.

Thompson, James D. (1967). *Organizations in Action.* New York: McGraw-Hill.

Thunell, Lars H. (1977). *Political Risks in International Business.* New York: Praeger.

Tocqueville, Alexis de (1956). *Democracy in America,* ed. Richard D. Heffner. New York: Mentor Books.

Van Agtmael, Antoine (1976). "How Business Has Dealt with Political Risk." *Financial Executive* (Jan.) 26–30.

Van Horne, James C. (1971). *Financial Management and Policy.* 2d ed. Englewood Cliffs, N.J.: Prentice-Hall.

Vaupel, James C., and Joan P. Curhan (1969). *The Making of Multinational Enterprise.* Boston: Division of Research, Graduate School of Business Administration, Harvard University.

Vernon, Raymond (1971*a*). "Multinational Business and National Economic Goals." In Robert O. Keohane and Joseph S. Nye, Jr., eds., *Transnational Relations and World Politics,* pp. 343–355. Cambridge: Harvard University Press.

———. (1971*b*). *Sovereignty at Bay.* New York: Basic Books.

———. (1977). *Storm over the Multinationals.* Cambridge: Harvard University Press.

Vogel, Ezra F. (1979). *Japan as Number One.* Cambridge: Harvard University Press.

Walter, Ingo (1980). "International Capital Allocation: Country Risk, Portfolio Decisions and Regulation in International Banking." Mimeographed. Graduate School of Business, New York University.

Weick, Karl E. (1969). *The Social Psychology of Organizing.* Reading, MA: Addison-Wesley.

Wells, Louis T., Jr., ed. (1971). *The Product Life Cycle and International Trade.* Boston: Division of Research, Graduate School of Business Administration, Harvard University.

Weston, V. Fred, and Bart W. Sorge (1972). *International Management Finance.* Homewood, IL: Richard D. Irwin.

Wilensky, Harold (1967). *Organizational Intelligence.* New York: Basic Books.

Wilkins, Mira (1970). *The Emergence of Multinational Enterprise: American Business Abroad from the Colonial Era to 1914.* Cambridge: Harvard University Press.

———. (1974). *The Maturing of Multinational Enterprise: American Business Abroad from 1914 to 1970.* Cambridge: Harvard University Press.

Wohlstetter, Roberta (1962). *Pearl Harbor: Warning and Decision.* Stanford: Stanford University Press.

Yoshino, M. Y. (1976). *Japan's Multinational Enterprises.* Cambridge: Harvard University Press.

Zeeman, E. C. (1976). "Catastrophe Theory." *Scientific American* (234):65–83.

Zink, Dolph Warren (1973). *The Political Risks for Multinational Enterprise in Developing Countries.* New York: Praeger.

Index

Kobrin, Stephen Jay.
   Managing political risk assessment :
strategic response to environmental
change / by Stephen J. Kobrin. --
Berkeley : University of California
Press, c1982.
   xiii, 224 p. : tables ; 24 cm. --
(Studies in international political
economy)

QND

   Bibliography: p. [211]-220.
   Includes index.
   ISBN 0-520-04540-8

(Cont'd on next card)